CONVERSATIONAL REALITIES

INQUIRIES IN SOCIAL CONSTRUCTION

Series editors
Kenneth J. Gergen and John Shotter

This series is designed to facilitate, across discipline and national boundaries, an emergent dialogue within the social sciences which many believe presages a major shift in the western intellectual tradition.

Including among its participants sociologists of science, psychologists, management and communications theorists, cyberneticists, ethnomethodologists, literary theorists, feminists and social historians, it is a dialogue which involves profound challenges to many existing ideas about, for example, the person, selfhood, scientific method and the nature of scientific and everyday knowledge.

It has also given voice to a range of new topics, such as the social construction of personal identities; the role of power in the social making of meanings; rhetoric and narrative in establishing sciences; the centrality of everyday activities; remembering and forgetting as socially constituted activities; reflexivity in method and theorizing. The common thread underlying all these topics is a concern with the processes by which human abilities, experiences, commonsense and scientific knowledge are both *produced in*, and *reproduce*, human communities.

Inquiries in Social Construction affords a vehicle for exploring this new consciousness, the problems raised and the implications for society.

Also in this series

Therapy as Social Construction
edited by Sheila McNamee and Kenneth J. Gergen

Psychology and Postmodernism
edited by Steinar Kvale

Constructing the Social
edited by Theodore Sarbin and John Kitsuse

CONVERSATIONAL REALITIES

Constructing Life through Language

JOHN SHOTTER

SAGE Publications
London • Thousand Oaks • New Delhi

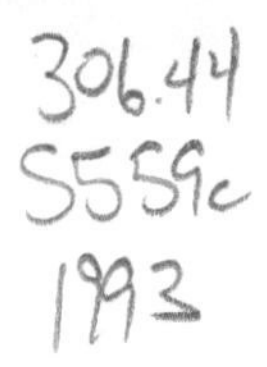

ISBN 0-8039-8932-6 (hbk)
ISBN 0-8039-8933-4 (pbk)

First published 1993
Reprinted 2000, 2002

SAGE Publications Ltd
1 Oliver's Yard, 55 City Road
London EC1Y 1SP

SAGE Publications Inc
2455 Teller Road
Thousand Oaks, California 91320

SAGE Publications India Pvt Ltd
B-42 Panchsheel Enclave
PO Box 4109
New Delhi 110 017

British Library Cataloguing in Publication data
A catalogue record for this book is available from the British Library

Library of Congress Control Number: 93085177

Printed digitally and bound in Great Britain by
Lightning Source UK Ltd., Milton Keynes, Bedfordshire

Contents

Preface and Acknowledgements

Although the aim of this book is to give voice to many topics covered by the other books in this series on social constructionism, it also goes a step further: it attempts to describe crucial features of the conversational world or worlds within which we have our being. For conversation is not just *one* of our many activities in *the* world. On the contrary, we constitute both ourselves and our worlds in our conversational activity. For us they are foundational. They constitute the usually ignored background within which our lives are rooted. But they need not remain so. For, from within our conversational activities themselves, we can draw attention to certain of their crucially important features that would otherwise escape our notice. Thus, we can come to grasp aspects of their nature, *through* our talk itself, even when a vision of it as a whole, in theory, is denied us.

While the introduction and epilogue, and Chapters 1, 2 and 3 were written especially for this volume, other chapters were drawn from the following sources: Chapter 4: Underlabourers for science, or 'toolmakers' for society? *History of the Human Sciences*, 3: 443–57, 1990; Chapter 5: El papel de lo imaginario en la construccion de la vida social. In T. Ibanez (ed.) *El Conocimiento de la Realidad Social.* Barcelona: Sendai Ediciones, 1989; Chapter 6: Speaking practically: Whorf, the formative function of communication, and knowing of the third kind. In R. Rosnow and M. Georgoudi (eds) *Contextualism and Understanding in the Behavioural Sciences.* New York: Praeger, 1986; Chapter 7: Consultant re-authoring: the 'making' and 'finding' of narrative constructions. *Human Systems*, 2: 105–19, 1991; Chapter 8: Paper for the Don Bannister Memorial Conference: Metaphors in Life and Psychotherapy, London, Oct. 1988, Institute of Group Analysis; Chapter 9: The manager as author: a rhetorical–responsive, social constructionist approach to social–organizational problems:. Paper read at Hochlschule St. Gallen conference on *Social-Organizational Theory: From Methodological Individualism to Relational Formulations*, 1990; Chapter 10: Rhetoric and the recovery of civil society. *Economy and Society*, 18: 149–66, 1989. Permission to draw upon these articles from the publishers and editors of them is gratefully acknowledged. Although most of these essays have been worked over and elaborated for this book, repetitions have only been eradicated where sense permitted. Finally, I would like to acknowledge the help and warm friendship of my co-editor on this series, Kenneth J. Gergen.

Introduction: A Rhetorical–Responsive Version of Social Constructionism

> The primary human reality is persons in conversation.
>
> Harré, 1983: 58

> Conversation flows on, the application and interpretation of words, and only in its course do words have their meaning.
>
> Wittgenstein, 1981: no. 135

> Conversation, understood widely enough, is the form of human transactions in general.
>
> MacIntyre, 1981: 197

> If we see knowing not as having an essence, to be described by scientists or philosophers, but rather as a right, by current standards, to believe, then we are well on the way to seeing *conversation* as the ultimate context within which knowledge is to be understood.
>
> Rorty, 1980: 389

Our talk (and our writing) about talk is beginning to take a dialogical or a conversational turn. Instead of taking it for granted that we understand another person's speech simply by grasping the inner ideas they have supposedly put into their words, that picture of how we understand each other is coming to be seen as the exception rather than the rule. Most of the time, we realize, we do not fully understand what another person says. Indeed, in practice, shared understandings occur only occasionally, if they occur at all. And when they do, it is by people testing and checking each other's talk, by them questioning and challenging it, reformulating and elaborating it, and so on. For in practice, shared understandings are developed or negotiated between participants over a period of time, in the course of an ongoing conversation (Garfinkel, 1967). But if people are not simply putting their ideas into words, what are they usually doing in their talk? Primarily, it seems, they are *responding* to each other's utterances in an attempt to link their practical activities in with those of the others around them; and in these attempts at coordinating their activities, people are constructing one or another kind of social relationship (Mills, 1940). It is the character of these conversationally developed and developing relations, and the events occurring within them, that are coming to be seen as of much greater importance than the shared ideas to which they might (or might not) give rise. For it is from within the dynamically sustained context of these actively constructed relations that what is talked about gets its meaning. Thus, instead of focusing immediately upon how individuals come to know the objects and entities in the world around them, we are becoming more interested in how people first develop and sustain certain *ways* of relating themselves to each other in their talk, and then, from within these ways of talking, make sense of their surroundings.

For, although our surroundings may stay materially the same at any one moment in time, how we make sense of them, what we select for attention or to act upon, how we connect those various events, dispersed in time and space, together and attribute significance to them, very much depends upon our use of language. In other words, instead of understanding our thoughts and ideas being presented to us as if *visually*, like we see bounded, material objects, in an instant, we are coming to talk of them as having more the quality of an extended sequence of commands or instructions as to how to act. Indeed, as I shall argue below, it is as if such commands or instructions are presented to us dialogically or conversationally by the *voice* of an other, one who responds to each phase of our action by indicating to us a next feature to which we should attend (see Part I). Thus, instead of in visual and ocular metaphors, we are coming to make sense of our talk in terms of metaphors drawn from the realm of talk itself.

Linguistically constructed relationships and our disciplinary practices

We can perhaps see the importance of such linguistically constructed relationships if we begin by taking an extreme case: what happens at a certain moment in a relationship, when one person says to another, 'I love you.' Quite apart from its function as a statement of fact, such a statement can function (if appropriately responded to by the other) to reconstitute the whole character of the speaker's relation to the person to whom it is addressed. Indeed – and this is especially important – the changed relationship acts back upon the speaker to change the nature of the speaker too. For not only will the speaker now take on new duties (in exchange for new rights) regarding the person of the other, but what he or she will notice and care about in the other will also change: she or he will be changed in their moral sensibility, in their very being, in the kind of person they are. While the speaker was solely responsible for trying to initiate the 'creation' by the couple of a new form of their relationship, and in that sense, made the disclosure out of the blue, in another sense, the speaker will not have acted out of the blue at all. They will have acted at a crucial moment in the changing context of their developing relationship. Usually, he or she will have noticed certain incipient tendencies in their relationship with and to the other: the other might have spent more than a usual time gazing at them, or is disconcerted by their presence, and so on. And they have decided that when in the right situation – when in an appropriate interactive position in relation to the other, at the right interactive moment – to risk making their declaration. For, unless the whole enterprise is bungled, its meaning, its unique meaning for those involved, will be apparent in the flow of activity in which it appears. The words 'I love you' will then draw their power – to change the whole character of the future flow of essentially conversational activity between the partners – very little from the words themselves. They merely function to make a crucial difference at a crucial moment, one that arises as a result of the history of its flow so far; their meaning is mostly in their use at that moment. But to use them thus, takes judgment; hence the speaker's feelings of apprehension and risk.

However, if managed well, the 'declaration of love' works to create a whole new kind of relationship with the other. Where, from within that new kind of relationship, a new kind of 'reality' becomes apparent – for those in love which each other attach a quite different kind of significance to even small tendencies in each other's actions: the lover is enraptured by the loved one, finding them to be a source of 'ceaselessly unforeseen originality' (Barthes, 1983: 34). For being in love is more than just being friends. It is distinctive in that we feel suddenly seized by passions that wrench us out of the mundane flow of everyday life, we are transported into another, special reality, in which things happen in seemingly extraordinary ways. Thus, just as 'the world of the happy man is different from that of the unhappy man' (Wittgenstein, 1961: remark no. 6.43), so the world of those in love is different from those who are not: (i) they are in control of themselves (or not) in different ways; (ii) they expect different things of, notice different things in, and have different motives regarding, each other; (iii) they also use different ways of judging each other's worth. In other words, they are different in their ways of being. And it is against this new background, this new structure of feelings, that certain acts are judged by those involved as fitting or not. Thus, as a result of their declarations of love for each other (assuming the initial declaration to have been reciprocated), they will expect different things of each other in the future. If they take their utterances seriously and are concerned about their (moral) implications, they will not now expect, for instance, often to be left alone, while the other goes off with other friends, and so on. Indeed, speakers not honouring the moral commitments implicit in their avowals can be shamed by being confronted with that fact by those to whom they addressed them.

While not perhaps so emotionally intense, nor quite so exclusive of others, many of our other activities in everyday life take place within the context of such conversationally developed relationships. Some are fleeting, others are more long term. Some are more open and disorderly than others; conversations among friends are less constrained than those in which we have to get some 'business' done; in some contexts – in offices, businesses, bureaucracies, educational establishments, etc. – knowing the order of talk required is a part of one's social competence as an adult. Indeed, so powerful is our talk in affecting our relations to others, that certain ways of talking take on an 'official' or 'sacrosanct' form, and one is sanctioned for talking 'against' them, so to speak. Thus Nietzsche's claim that 'God is dead' is still regarded in many quarters as shocking. And certainly in the United States of America, it is not a taken for granted aspect of the daily world to which one could appeal in opposing some of the social policies being implemented currently by state legislatures under the control of the Christian Right. Within such groups, strong feelings are aroused by talk that undermines the 'basic' ways of talking they use in relating themselves to each other. Talk that undermines the boundaries between our categories of things in the world, undermines 'us', the stability of the kind of beings we take ourselves to be and the shape of the desires, impulses, and urges we have; thus such talk is dangerous (Douglas, 1966). It is not easy to question or to change our 'basic' ways of talking.[1]

In the West, in our everyday, practical talk about ourselves, we take a great number of things for granted. And in our traditional forms of inquiry into ourselves and the nature of our everyday social lives, in psychology and sociology, we have codified these 'basic' ways of talking into a number of explicit assumptions: for instance, we take it that we are self-contained individuals, having minds that contain 'inner mental representations' of possible 'outer' circumstances, set over against other such similar individuals, and against a social and natural background lacking such a cognitive ability (Sampson, 1985, 1988). Indeed, so 'ingrained' is this way of thinking about ourselves, that in our everyday conversations it is difficult for us intelligibly to talk about – and thus to imagine – ourselves in any other way. In fact, we hold each other to these forms of talk; to talk otherwise is considered a bit strange, it is as if one did not quite know what is involved in being a normal person. This is the source of our assumption that to understand something means 'having something like a picture of it in our heads'. And when, prior to the problem of attempting to explain it as a psychological process, we are faced with the problem of saying what understanding 'is', we say to ourselves, that is how it 'must' be – how else could it be? Yet, as the anthropologist Geertz (1975: 49) remarks about this whole conception we have of ourselves, 'however incorrigible it may seem to us, [it is] a rather peculiar idea within the context of the world's cultures'. Other peoples seem to have developed very different ways of accounting for themselves to each other: as Lienhardt (1961: 149) reports for the Dinka, for instance, that they seem to have 'no such interior entity [as a 'mind'] to appear, on reflection, to stand between the experiencing self at any given moment and what is or has been an exterior influence upon the self'. Could it be that our talk of people as having *inner mental states*, and of them as always understanding things in terms of such states, is less universal than we think?

Yet, as we have seen, it is 'basic' for us. It arises out of a whole set of, to an extent interlocking, everyday practices in terms of which we live and make sense of our lives together. Thus, although new ways of talking can be proposed, unless a way of fitting them in with those already existing can be found, difficulties will be raised. In this regard, of particular interest to us as professional academics, are the disciplinary relationships we share with our professional colleagues. Although we have been used in the past to thinking of our disciplines as concerned with dispassionate knowledge, it is clear that this is only so in the centre of the discipline, so to speak. Those who operate there, who have passed their examinations well, who know not only how to draw upon certain already fixed meanings in an order of meanings but how to critically reject all those that do not fit, find an orderly, tranquil world with everything in its expected place. But as Foucault (1972: 223) points out, at the boundaries, as those on the margins of disciplines know to their cost, there are a whole range of *exclusionary practices* working to sustain the limited and orderly nature of its subject matter. 'Within its own limits, every discipline recognizes true and false propositions, but it repulses a whole teratology of learning.' And so it has been in the history of psychology (Danziger, 1990). Each new approach in psychology has had to struggle in from the margins to a place in the centre. For, to those who currently occupy the centre, new approaches can often seem like dangerous monsters on the prowl around outside the discipline, intent, if allowed in, upon destroying any order so far achieved within it. Thus, like friends posed on the brink of being lovers, can we (should we) risk shifting our disciplinary relations onto a new footing? While we might experience what we have never experienced before, we might also lose the basis of all the gains we have made so far. But also like the lovers above, perhaps the risk is not so great as feared. Perhaps we are only required to recognize what it is that we already doing in our relations to and with each other: to recognize and attend to ourselves at work where, before, we thought 'mechanisms' beyond our control must be.

What this book is about

In attempting to do this, to redirect our attention, we shall, as mentioned above, shift from a focus upon how we understand objects to how we understand each other – a shift from an interest in epistemology to one in practical hermeneutics (Shotter, 1984). And in focusing upon people's use of certain ways of talking to construct different kinds of social relationship, this book is concerned with a special dialogical or conversational version of *social constructionism* (Coulter, 1979, 1983, 1989; Gergen, 1982, 1985; Harré, 1983, 1986; Shotter, 1984, 1993b), one that I have called a rhetorical–responsive version. Why I have called it this, is because I want to claim that our ability as individuals to speak representationally – that is, to depict or describe a unique state of affairs (whether real or not), as we please, independently of the influences of our surroundings – arises out of us first and primarily speaking in a way that is *responsive* to the others around us. Indeed, a part of what we must learn in growing up, if we want to be perceived as speaking authoritatively about factual matters, is how to respond to the others around us should they challenge our claims. We must speak with an awareness of the possibility of such challenges, and be able to reply to them by justifying our claims. This is one of the reasons for calling it a *rhetorical* rather than a referential form of language: for more than merely claiming to depict a state of affairs, our ways of talking can 'move' people to action, or change their perceptions. And it can do this – and this is a second reason for calling it rhetorical – because rhetoric makes use of metaphors which can function to help an audience 'make connections' between a speaker's otherwise seemingly unconnected utterances, that is, to give intelligible linguistic form to otherwise merely sensed feelings or tendencies shared between speakers and their audience. This concern – with the social (and ethical) processes involved in the 'making' of such connections – characterizes all the chapters included in this volume. Rather than with language considered in terms of previously existing patterns or systems formed from 'already spoken words', the version of social constructionism explored here focuses upon the formative uses to which 'words in their speaking' are put, and upon the nature of the relational 'situations' thus created between those in communicative contact with each other in their speakings.

Thus, in shifting to a focus upon our conversational talk among ourselves, we direct our attention to a different factors in our human existence. Instead of to events within the inner dynamics of the individual psyche (subjectivism, romanticism, and cognitivism), or to events within the already determined characteristics of the external world (objectivism, modernism, and behaviourism) – the two polarities[2] in terms of which we have thought about ourselves in recent times

(Gergen, 1991; Taylor, 1989; Volosinov, 1973) – in social constructionism, we attend to events within the contingent flow of continuous communicative interaction between human beings. Concern in the past with one or the other of the two polarities above – as well as an Enlightenment urge to produce single, unified *systems* of knowledge – gave rise to an ambition to locate a world beyond the social and historical, and to attempts to discover this world, either in the depths of the supposed organic or psychic nature of the individual, or, perhaps, in larger abstract systems or principles to which the individual was supposedly subject. As a result, until recently, this third sphere of diffuse, sensuous or feelingful[3] activity, this unordered hurly-burly or bustle[4] of everyday social life, has remained in the background, awaiting elucidation in terms of yet to be discovered, ahistorical principles of either mind or world. It is within this flow of responsive and relational activities and practices, I shall claim – a sphere of activity that elsewhere I have called 'joint action' (Shotter, 1984; described further in Chapter 1) – that all the other socially significant dimensions of interpersonal interaction, with their associated modes of subjective or objective being, originate and are formed.[5]

To view our cognitive abilities in this way – as being formed in what we do and say, rather than as being the already existing, well formed sources of our actions and utterances – is, as Harré (1992a) has recently put it, to contribute to a 'second cognitive revolution', one which takes a 'discursive turn' (for example, Edwards and Potter, 1992). While the first was publicly initiated at Harvard in the 1960s by J.S. Bruner and George Miller, and was very much in line (when now we examine it with hindsight) with the instrumental, individualistic, systematic, unitary, ahistorical, representational mainstream thought of the day, this second revolution has been a much more marginal development, taking place not only on the edges of psychology (Berger and Luckman, 1966; Coulter, 1979; Gergen, 1985; Harré, 1983, 1986; Shotter, 1975, 1984), but upon a number of other disciplinary boundaries also, particularly in literary theory and anthropology. It tends to foreground the poetic and rhetorical, the social and historical, the pluralistic, as well as the responsive and sensuous aspects of language use, all the concerns that were left in the background in the first cognitive revolution. But, as we shall see, in taking a dialogical, argumentative view of the growth of knowledge rather than an eliminative, Neo-Darwinian, monological stance, the previous concerns of cognitivism – the instrumental, the systematic, and so on – are not wholly eliminated or backgrounded, they still have a 'voice' in the dialogue. But now, not so loud as to silence the voice of these other concerns.

Until now, these other more responsive, more poetic aspects of language use have been, not so much 'silent', as (in the currently more prominent language of visual metaphors) 'invisible' to us. As modern, self-conscious, autonomous adults (and especially as scholars and academics), we are all very familiar with being able to use our language referentially and representationally to talk (or write) about 'things' and 'states of affairs' as we please – whether the 'things' in question are in the world or in our heads, whether they exist in fact or are merely fictional, whether anyone is there to hear (or read) us or not. As adult individuals, it has seemed to us that this referential–representational function of language is our language's primary function. But, in social constructionism, all of what we might call the *person–world, referential–representational, dimensions of interaction* at the moment available to us as individuals – all the familiar ways we already have of talking about ourselves, about our world(s), and about their possible relationships, which in the past we have taken as in some way primary – we now claim must be seen as secondary and derived, as emerging out of the everyday, conversational background to our lives. Where this dimension of interaction, to contrast with the more familiar representational dimension, may be called the *self–other, rhetorical–responsive, dimension of interaction*. This, then, is what is special to the version of social constructionism discussed in this book: the account of language offered is a communicational, conversational, or dialogical account, in which people's responsive understanding of each other is primary.

Clearly, in acting in this sensuous, responsive way, it might be argued that people are functioning at a lower, psychological level than when they act in ways not seemingly tied to their 'situation'. It could be argued that in adulthood, they leave this situationally responsive form of behaviour behind, and come to act individually and autonomously in terms now of their own inner mental representations. But even as adults acting all alone, people still face the task of making what they do relevant – if not to the immediate conversational situation in which they are placed – then to the social, cultural, historical, and political 'situation' they 'imagine' themselves to be in. And again, their task is responsively (and responsibly) to judge intelligently (and legitimately) how felicitously to fit their responses into the requirements of that situation. Where again, it is the joint activity between them and their socially (and linguistically) constituted situation that 'structures' what they do or say, not wholly they themselves. It *is* just as if we had to conform ourselves to an objective reality existing independently of any of the individuals involved: but we have to conform ourselves to it, not because of its material shape, but because we all require each other *morally* to conform to the 'situations' emerging into existence between us. They exist as third entities, between us and the others around us. Thus, to us as individuals, such situations may seem like one or another kind of 'external' world, as something lying at the other end of the person–world dimension of interaction I mentioned above. However, such situations are not external to 'us' as a social group. As neither 'mine' nor 'yours', they constitute an Otherness that is 'ours', our own peculiar form of Otherness. And it is from within this Otherness[6] that we must distinguish, slowly and gradually, between that which is due to our relations to each other, and that which is not – the task of distinguishing what is dependent upon features of our talk from what is independent of it. This will be a difficult and politically contested task; but it is clear that until now, it is a task that has been ignored.

As some will recognize, to speak in this way of 'others' and of 'Othernesses' is to begin to use some of the vocabulary now appearing – but still in the form of 'theoretical monologues' (Billig et al. 1988: 149) – in postmodern and poststructuralist social theory. This is no accident. My aim, as indeed is the aim of this whole series of books, is to try to release psychology from its 'colonization' by an ahistorical, asocial, instrumental, individualistic 'cognitivism' (Still and Costall, 1991), and to open it up to a more large-scale, participatory or dialogical form of research activity. In such a form of research, instead of it consisting in just the 'theories' and 'systems' formulated by experts, pitted against each other in a Neo-Darwinian struggle for the survival of the fittest, we can begin to see how those within the whole socio-historical background context within which cognitivism itself is embedded – the conversational background which until now has been silent – can begin to take part in the dialogue too. What was an eliminative or exclusionary struggle for the single, systematic, correct 'view' (seeking a 'final solution'), becomes a continuous, non-eliminative, inclusionary, multi-voiced conversation, forming, in Billig's (1987) terms, a 'tradition of argumentation'. Where, at any one time, different argumentative traditions are held together as dynamic unities, not by being conducted within a shared framework, but (as Billig has also pointed out) by originating in, and being directed towards, the dialogical elaboration of certain two or more sided 'dilemmatic themes', 'topics', or 'commonplaces'. And, although no final solutions are ever reached in such traditions, what is important, is that those who win the arguments within them, get an opportunity to try to change the agenda of argumentation. In other words, what matters is not so much the conclusions arrived at as the terms within which arguments are conducted. For to talk in new ways, is to 'construct' new forms of social relation, and, to construct new forms of social relation (of self–other relationships) is to construct new ways of being (of person–world relations) for ourselves.

And this, of course, is precisely what is at stake in this book. Quite explicitly, my purpose is to offer arguments for relocating or 're-grounding' the academic discipline of psychology within the formative social activities at work in the everyday, conversational background of our lives. Or, to put it in other words: to offer arguments for reformulating it in terms appropriate to the study of these activities. For – if the claims I have made so far are correct, and our ways of talking are formative of our social relations – then, new, more ethical and social ways of talking in psychology will work to 'reconstruct' it along more ethical and social lines, thus to establish within it a new 'tradition of argumentation'. Then, rather than the old eliminative and exclusionary struggles, we will be able to provide the opportunities for a whole new set of creative struggles of a quite different, non-eliminative, inclusionary kind to occur, struggles marked out by the tensions, not just, say, between simply mental representations and connectionism in cognitive psychology, but by a whole multitude of other tensions currently without a voice within the discipline. These tensions are present at all those points of uncertainty in our lives where we ourselves are responsible for the 'connections' we make: between ourselves and the others around us, as 'fellows', as 'strangers', as 'foreigners', as 'friends', etc.; between ourselves and 'our past', or 'our future', and 'our death'; 'our environment'; 'the unknown'; the 'transcendental or absolute'; and so on; and it is in our social construction of these connections that we construct our identities, the character of our desires – in short, who we are to ourselves. Psychology – with its insecurities and its struggles to prove itself as worthy of a place among the hard sciences – has incapacitated itself from participating in the crucial debates as to how these connections might be forged. Such debates are a part of that very two-way, socio-historical process of cultural development mentioned at the beginning of this introduction: in which what is at stake is the further articulation and/or transformation of our forms of life. Many have been disappointed in the past at psychology's absence from these debates. The aim of the studies in this book – and the other books in this series – is both to show that in fact we are only a step away from participating in such debates, and to provide some resources for the taking of that step.

The structure of this book

In Part I, I attempt to provide, not a theory of a rhetorical–responsive version of social constructionism, but an *instructive account* of it; that is, a whole tool-box full of 'instructive statements' or 'verbal resources' for use in accounting for, and for making sense of, our everyday conversational activities: joint action; knowing of a third kind ('from within' conversational situations); 'rational-invisibility' and 'illusions of discourse'; rhetorical–responsive vs. referential–representational forms of talk; the emergence of referential forms from, and their 'rootedness' in, responsive forms of talk; the 'sensuous' nature of responsive forms of talk; the ethically negotiated nature of the outcomes of joint, conversational activity; the status of 'mind' and 'identity' as boundary phenomena, and as 'imaginary' entities; the open, incomplete, and negotiated nature of social life; our ways of talking (genres) as formative forms; making and inventing vs. finding and discovering; linguistic prostheses and indicators; and so on. Instead of a single, unified theory, I have gathered together an unsystematic assortment of 'conceptual prosthetics' *through which* to make sense of the background to our lives. As I have outlined in this Introduction, and argue further in Chapter 1, the task of understanding the *background* to our lives cannot be done within the confines of any kind of systematic *theory*. Systematic theories rely upon its taken for granted nature for their possibility and thus leave crucial aspects of it unanalysed; they result in a self-deceptive, externalizing of the ideology of the day (Rorty, 1980; see chapter 1 in this book). Indeed, as mental activities involve dialogical processes of *moral* testing and checking in the context in which they are conducted (Shotter, 1993a), this undermines (Enlightenment inspired) *systematic*, unsituated or decontextualized approaches to the study of 'mind'. Mental activity must be studied in some other way: as situated, practical–moral, joint activity.

But the nature of such activity is puzzling and strange to us; we are unused to speaking of the situations from within which we act as primarily intralinguistic realities; we are unused to accepting that we only make contact with those aspects of the world independent of ourselves, from within such realities, *through* the resources they provide. In an effort to show what their nature might be like *before* we manage to impose upon them an intelligible order, to capture the pluralistic, changeable, incomplete, contested nature of such (background) realities, I attempt in Chapter 2 to situate social constructionism in a world of activities and events (instead of our usual world of things and substances). And I argue that such conversational realities, and the dialogical traditions of argumentation contained within them, must embody a nonsystematic, two-sided form of knowledge – a so-called dilemmatic common sense (*sensus communis*) – that provides those living within them with a flexible, practical resource for use in their sustaining and 'development' of them. In Chapter 3, I explore the dialogical and rhetorical processes productive and reproductive of such a dilemmatic *sensus communis* and the traditions of argumentation it sustains, and go on to show something of what is involved in moving towards conducting psychological research from within such a context, as a dialogical rather than as a monological enterprise. Also, I argue that founding it in a two-sided common sense provides sufficient of a shared basis, without predetermining the outcome of people's arguments, for them to know that they are at least all participating in the same argument – thus avoiding the charge that a social constructionist stance inevitably leads to just an 'anything goes' relativism. If it is situated, or 'rooted', in the conversational background of everyday life, then it is no more relativistic than any of the systematic frameworks formulated in the special sciences; neither their claims, nor those of social constructionists, can transcend the limits on our abilities to make sense, placed upon us by the traditions of argumentation made available to us in our history and culture.

In Part II, I examine realism, the imaginary, and the nature of a world of events. Those who still retain a nondialogical, nonrhetorical view of everyday knowledge, and still think of it as providing a monological, theoretical 'framework' for the interpretation of events, fear the supposed intrinsic relativism of social constructionism. As they see it, it fails to provide any way of making contact with a 'reality' beyond a framework of thought. Thus, many who endorse a social constructionist *theory* of social processes, still wish to endorse a 'realist' *methodology* (Bhaskar, 1989, 1991; Eagleton, 1991; Greenwood, 1989, 1992; Norris, 1990; Parker, 1992). But in all its varieties, realism is born out of an attempt to provide a principled, systematic solution ahead of time to a basic dilemma, the dilemma that arises, on the one hand, from knowing that simply saying cannot make it so, yet, on the other hand, from knowing that nonetheless we can do things with words. As Harré (1990: 304) now claims, the best resolution of this dilemma is a 'policy realism', in which 'we read theories not as sets of true or false statements but as guides to possible scientific acts. Manipulative practices can be successful or unsuccessful.' But politically, this gives rise to a new dilemma, a dilemma that can be rephrased as follows: (i) Does one attempt to resolve such dilemmas as this, ahead of time, by in principle, policy decisions from within a system of thought; if so, *whose* policy (theoretical system) should we accept, and on what 'grounds'? Or: (ii) Do we simply accept the existence of such dilemmas, and agree to resolve them whenever they appear in terms of local, contextual 'grounds', argued for as such by those concerned, and if so, what is the status of the grounds concerned? This, as I see it, is what is at issue in arguments over realism: *whose* 'basic' way of talking – theoreticians or (reflective) practitioners – is to dominate?

I opt for the second choice. As I see it, there are no pre-established orders of things in the world; what orders there are, are humanly constructed and sustained ones. Thus in Chapter 4 – in which I critically examine Bhaskar's influential account of 'scientific or critical realism' – I attempt to bring out some of the political issues involved in such claims as Bhaskar's: that there *are* in fact such pre-existing orders. There I raise questions to do with, for instance: (i) Should philosophers, psychologists, and/or social theorists be 'underlabourers for scientists', or should they be 'toolmakers for society at large'? And (ii) What is involved in elite groups resolving dilemmas theoretically, ahead of time, prior to their more disorderly resolution in more public arenas, in civil society?

In rejecting realism, I reject the idea that there are discoverable, indisputable 'foundations', or 'standards', or 'limits' in term of which claims to truth can be judged. Yet, I do not of course want to go so far as to say that, so long as one can tell a good story in its support, then just 'anything goes'. Again, the key to the resolution of this dilemma is to be found by situating it within a community. It then becomes that of distinguishing, from within the community, between what are 'real' possibilities and what are 'fictitious' possibilities for us, given who we are to ourselves culturally. In chapter 5, I explore this issue in terms of the concept of 'the imaginary'. The concept of the imaginary provides us with the resources we need to talk about those 'political' entities that are not yet wholly in existence, but that are not wholly fictitious either, in terms of which we organize and rhetorically sustain our social relations. Such political entities begin their existence by at first 'subsisting' only in people's talk of them, but – to the extent that new forms of talk tend to 'construct' new forms of social relation – they begin to take on more of a 'real' (morally intransigent) existence as talk 'of' them increases, and they give rise to new social institutions and structures. A process manifested in psychology, for instance, by the change from a behaviourist to a cognitivist psychology that began in the late 1950s and early 1960s; such processes of change are driven, not by new discoveries of the true empirical nature of things, but by people's changed interests. They only begin to go out of existence again as they cease to provide the kind of knowledge required to make sense of important social activities – as the individualistic, scientistic forms of knowledge popular in the deregulated markets of the 1980s seem no longer to work in socially fragmented communities of the 1990s. In an attempt to grasp the nature of a world in which 'events' emerge into and go out of existence in different ways – a world very different from a world of continually existing objects – I examine in Chapter 6 Whorf's writings, and reintroduce his principle of linguistic relativity – and show how, as a victim of itself, it has been read and interpreted as merely a syntactic doctrine. In the reading I offer, it can be seen as offering a rich range of demonstrations useful to social constructionists, as to how ways of talking can work to construct forms of reality, and their interrelated forms of personhood, very different from our own.

Finally, after having provided in Part I a tool-box of rhetorical devices, and in Part II a general account of the contexts in which they might be applied, in Part III I want to study some of the results of their application in different particular spheres. The theme connecting all these studies, is to do with the difficulties arising out of individuals attempting to make sense of people's lives (including their own) from within an orderly framework. For people to pattern their lives according to a single pre-existing order, or for them to have their lives patterned for them in such a way, is to ignore the necessity for people always to respond to the actions of the others around them, in ways 'fitting' their own unique circumstances, according to their own unique use of the resources socially available to them. Whether the prior order is a systematic, mechanical order, or a much richer, nonsystematic narrative order, the case is the same; it is a prior order imposed upon them that does not allow them to sequence their own activities according to their own, unique situation. They feel 'entrapped', prevented from acting according to their needs. In Chapter 7, I examine the case of Ronald Fraser, an oral historian, who writes about his own entrapment in his own past. There, I examine responsive forms of communication at work in his psychoanalysis, in which 'feelings' rather than 'ideas' shape what is said. Fraser begins to escape from his imprisonment when he realizes that rather than a single, fixed story, his past consists in a collection of narrative resources, provided him by the persons around him during his childhood. Making use of them, he realizes that he can become the author of his own childhood, rather than merely the subject of it. The resources are there for him to use as he pleases.

Chapter 8 continues this theme: the possibility of becoming entrapped in stories of our own making. In particular, I discuss there the need that Freud felt in psychoanalysis, to construct coherent, causal narratives, narratives that would satisfy the 'scientific' need for orderly causal explanations. I call the constructions produced in such circumstances 'counterfeit' constructions, for although, like a counterfeit dollar bill or pound note these days, such constructions may convey a perfect 'sense of reality', they nonetheless work to appropriate a communal resource permanently for an individual purpose – that of imposing a pre-established order in favour of psychoanalytic experts. Further, I make it clear in this chapter that the production of an intelligible order in reflection, by the construction of a narrative account, quite often distorts what the character of the situation was in actual practice: it falsely completes what was an open and unfinalized circumstance, whose very openness 'invited' and 'enabled' the action taken within it, as something finalized and complete. This connects also with the problems faced by managers in commerce and industry: they have the problem of clarifying what – in a unique, practical situation – the problem actually 'is'. It is pointless identifying it merely as one of a type, for that is utterly unrevealing of its unique details; yet it requires characterizing in a way which reveals how its details are interconnected, and also connected with its context. Thus in Chapter 9, I explore the character of conversations appropriate for making sense of 'those passing moments and details of things we call "circumstances" ' (Vico). Metaphors are important rhetorical resources available to managers in formulating accounts of the problem circumstances facing them. Their task is one of practical authorship, to 'author' an account of a problem of such a kind, that the others in the company can identify points at which they can play a part in overcoming the company's difficulties.

The trouble with 'natural scientific' approaches is that in claiming to offer general theories, they claim ahead of time to be able to speak in debates, correctly, on behalf of all those they study. But in doing so, they silence them. They deny them their own voice, their opportunity to speak on the nature of their own unique circumstances. They deny them their citizenship in their society. If this is to change, what is required, it would seem, is the fashioning of something which does not currently exist – a new *civil society*, a whole 'social ecology' of interdependent regions and moments of social life within which *possible* ways forward into the future can be explored, discussed, and debated by those actually involved. For, as we have seen, in a social constructionist world, our future is not just a matter of prediction and control, but a matter of how those within it are involved in producing it. This theme is explored in the final chapter, Chapter 10. In particular, it is argued there that if I am to have a sense of belonging in a social reality, then it is not enough for me merely to have a 'place' within it; I must also myself be able to play an unrestrained part in constituting and sustaining it as my own kind of 'social reality', as not 'their' reality, but as of me and my kind, as 'our' reality. If I am unable to play such a part, then I will not sense myself as fully belonging to it; I *will* feel that I am living in a reality not my own, a reality that others have more right to than me. As I argue in Chapter 10, only a society with a proper 'civil society', in which everyone can participate in the constitution of its culture, can provide its citizens with a sense of its culture as being 'their' culture. Thus as a first step toward the construction of such a possibility, it is people's responsibility to sustain a certain 'civility' in their daily conversational lives with each other, a 'civility' that will enable the conversations and debates constitutive of the playful search for such a culture – and this is what politically is at stake in the version of social constructionism offered in this book, for this is a seemingly pointless and unmotivated concern in our current market-individualism.

Notes

1. A good deal of emotion is associated, not so much with the use, as with the maintaining of our 'basic' ways of speaking in existence. It is encountered during those times when an attempt is made to change them in some way. Thus, as Foucault (1972: 216) points out, although speech may not seem to be a very powerful activity in itself 'the prohibitions surrounding it soon reveal its links with power and desirability . . . speech is not merely the medium which manifests – or dissembles – desire; it is also the object of desire. Similarly, historians have constantly impressed upon us that speech is no mere verbalization of conflicts and systems of domination, but that it is the very object of man's conflicts.'

2. To talk like this is, of course, to oversimplify, for these two polarities play into each other and borrow from each other to such an extent that all theories in psychology contain aspects of both tendencies.

3. Here I have in mind Marx's first thesis on Feuerbach, that 'the chief defect of all hitherto existing materialism (that of Feuerbach included) is that the thing, reality, sensuousness, is conceived only in the form of the *object or of contemplation*, but not as *sensuous human activity, practice*, not subjectively' (Marx and Engels, 1977: 121).

4. 'Hurly-burly' and 'bustle' are terms used by Wittgenstein (1980, II: nos. 625, 626, 629) to characterize the indefiniteness of the background that determines our responses to what we experience, and against which we judge events in our everyday life.

5. It is interesting in this respect to note what Toulmin (1982: 64) has to say about the genealogy of the word 'consciousness': 'Etymologically, of course, the term "consciousness" is a knowledge word. This is evidenced by the Latin form, *-sci-*, in the middle of the word. But what are we to make of the prefix *con-* that precedes it? Look at the usage of the term in Roman Law, and the answer will be easy enough. Two or more agents who act jointly – having formed a common intention, framed a plan, and concerted their actions – are as a result *conscientes*. They act as they do knowing one another's plans: they act *jointly knowing*.'

6. As both Harré (1990) and I (Shotter, 1984) have remarked, following Uexkull (1957), we could talk here of the human *Umwelt*.

PART I

A RHETORICAL–RESPONSIVE VERSION OF SOCIAL CONSTRUCTIONISM

1
The Conversational Background of Social Life: Beyond Representationalism

> The human sciences, when dealing with what is representation (in either conscious or unconscious form), find themselves treating as their object what is in fact their condition of possibility . . . They proceed from that which is given to representation to that which renders representation possible, but which is still representation . . . On the horizon of any human science, there is the project of bringing man's consciousness back to its real conditions, of restoring it to the contents and forms that brought it into being, and elude us within in it . . .
>
> Foucault, 1970: 364

One of the aims of formulating a rhetorical–responsive version of social constructionism corresponds with that mentioned above by Foucault: it can confront us with the 'real' socio-historical and socio-cultural conditions of our lives, those making the current nature of our consciousnesses possible – where, of course, in the view taken in this book, it is a part of what it is for these to be the 'real' conditions of our lives that all attempts to characterize them are, by their very nature, contested. If this is the case, we must cease thinking of the 'reality' within which we live as homogeneous, as everywhere the same for everyone. Different people in different positions at different moments will live in different realities. Thus we must begin to rethink it as being differentiated, as heterogeneous, as consisting in a set of different regions and moments, all with different properties to them. We can begin to think of social reality at large as a turbulent flow of continuous social activity, containing within it two basic kinds of activity: (i) a set of relatively stable centres of well ordered, self-reproducing activity, sustained by those within them being accountable to each other for their actions (Mills, 1940; Shotter, 1984) – but with the forms of justification used being themselves open to contest (Billig, 1987; MacIntyre, 1981); (ii) with these diverse regions or moments of institutionalized order being separated from each other by zones of much more disorderly, unaccountable, chaotic activity. It is in these unaccountable, marginal regions – on the edge of chaos, away from the orderly centres of social life – that the events of interest to us occur.

In fact, as we move from a modern towards a postmodern world to confront the times in which we live, we begin to realize that our reality is often a much more disorderly, fragmented, and heterogeneous affair than we had previously thought.[1] Thus, (i) if uncertainty, vagueness, and ambiguity are *real* features of much of the world in which we live; *and* (ii) how we 'construct' or 'specify' these features further influences the nature of our own future lives together, then their contested nature comes as no surprise: for what is at stake, is which of a possible plurality of future next steps should we take for the best? Whose version points towards a best future for us?

Knowing of the third kind: Knowing 'from-within'

As I have already mentioned, it is a part of the rhetorical–responsive version of social constructionism canvassed here to argue that the importance of these contests inheres, not simply in their outcomes, but in the forms of talk in which they are conducted. For they are constitutive of different centres of institutionalized social life. Thus, an important change occurs, not simply when one or another side in an institution wins an argument, but when such an opportunity is used to change the style of future argumentation – that is, the permitted forms of talk within that institution. For instance, the move begun in the seventeenth century during the Enlightenment – to talk less about our lives in religious and more in secular terms, less in terms of 'souls' and the 'human spirit' and more in terms of 'brains' and 'minds', less in terms of God's will and more in terms of natural mechanisms – was, and still is, just as important for the new ways of talking and the new forms of social relationship (and new forms of contest) it introduced, as for any of the particular conclusions so far reached. Indeed, within the sphere of our socio-psychological interests here, these new forms of talk are of prime importance to us. But not so much for what they have privileged as central, as for what they have attempted to prohibit, to exclude, or marginalize (Foucault, 1972). Thus in pursuing the project of restoring to consciousness an understanding of the conditions of its own possibility, I want to argue that present in the conversational background to our lives are many other forms of talk, with their own peculiar properties, currently without a 'voice' in the contests within this sphere. If they were to gain a voice, it could change our lives.

Indeed, it is one of the claims explored in this book that an important, special third kind of knowledge, embodied in the conversational background to our lives, has been 'unvoiced' in our socio-psychological debates so far: a special kind of knowledge – to do with how *to be* a person of this or that particular kind according to the culture into which one develops as a child – that does not have to be finalized or formalized in a set of proven theoretical statements before it can be applied. It is not theoretical knowledge (a 'knowing-that' in Ryle's (1949) terminology) for it is knowledge-in-practice, nor is it merely knowledge or a craft or skill ('knowing-how'), for it is joint knowledge, knowledge-held-in-common with others. It is a third kind of knowledge, *sui generis*, that cannot be reduced to either of the other two, the kind of knowledge one has *from within* a situation, a group, social institution, or society; it is what we might call a 'knowing-from'.[2] Bernstein (1983) has called it 'practical–moral knowledge'.

Elsewhere, I have discussed the nature of this special third kind of knowledge extensively (Shotter, 1984, 1993b). This volume explores various of its implications in certain different spheres of psychology further, as well as other, more general implications of its nature. Specifically, these studies address the question of how it is that we come to experience ourselves, our world, and our language, in the particular ways that at the moment we do, and how we might come to talk about ourselves differently. Why, for instance, do we currently simply take it for granted that we each have minds within our heads, and that they work in terms of inner mental representations which resemble in some way the structure of the external world? Why do we feel that we live our social lives within certain independently existing social structures, and act within them as if according to rules? Why do we think that the best way to make sense of our lives and to act for the best is in terms of theoretical formulations provided us by experts (rather than in terms of more practical, everyday forms of knowledge)? And also, why do we feel that our language works primarily by us using it accurately to represent and to refer to things and states of affairs in the circumstances surrounding us, rather than by us using it to influence each other's and our own behaviour? In other words, why do we feel *impelled* or *compelled* to talk about ourselves as we do? What is it in the conversational background to our lives that shapes our passions, and leads us to talk about ourselves and our world as we do – thus to 'construct' all our social relations along individualistic and instrumental dimensions, and our psychology in terms only of mental representations – while preventing us from noticing the consequences of so doing?

Externalizing the ideology of the day

In this connection, Rorty (1980: 11) has argued that 'the attempt (which has defined traditional philosophy) to explicate "rationality" and "objectivity" in terms of conditions of accurate representation is a self-deceptive effort to externalize the normal discourse[3] of the day, and that, since the Greeks, philosophy's self-image has been dominated by this attempt' – where the normal discourse of the day represents, as we shall see, an ideology in the sense of being a way of talking that benefits a certain social group, or groups, over others. Thus, in calling the version of social constructionism displayed in the studies below a rhetorical–responsive version, I want to call attention to the fact that central to it is an attitude towards the nature of language which contrasts markedly with the 'normal discourse of the day' in this regard: the taken-for-granted nature of language as a referential–representational system or code of meaningful signs. That stance, it can be argued (Harris, 1980, 1981; Volosinov, 1973) – in which language is treated as a systematic object of thought, structured as if according to rules, or, as a system of differences – arose out the study of *already spoken words*, after all contest over their speaking has ceased.

By contrast, the studies in this book, display an interest in the contested activity of *words in their speaking*; that is, in the practicalities of their use as means or as 'tools' in effecting everyday communicative processes, and in particular, in their formative or 'shaping' function, and the 'resistances' they meet, in such processes.[4] Thus the stance I take in all the following chapters, is that in an everyday process involving a myriad of spontaneous, responsive, practical, unselfconscious, but contested interactions, we unknowingly 'shape' or 'construct' between ourselves as already mentioned, not only a sense of our own identities, but also a sense of our own 'social worlds'. Or, to put it another way, that plane upon which we talk about what we think of as the orderly, accountable, self-evidently knowable and controllable characteristics of both ourselves (as autonomous individual persons) and our world, is constructed upon another, lower plane, in a set of unacknowledged and unintended, disorderly, conversational forms of interaction involving struggles between ourselves and others.

Historically, it is upon the more orderly, accountable plane – conducted in terms of certain 'basic' ways of talking – that we have attempted to construct and establish yet more orderly, or institutionalized ways of talking: that is, disciplinary discourses, supposedly 'rational' bodies of speech or writing. Where, in Foucault's terms, such discourses are 'practices that systematically form the objects of which they speak' (1972: 49); that is, form them as objects of rational contemplation and debate, thus to establish the modern academic departments. While the modern academic disciplines – especially, the 'human sciences' (Foucault, 1970) – were founded *as disciplines* – that is, established and institutionalized as professions – in the optimism of the nineteenth century, the conditions making this possible were a product of the Enlightenment of the seventeenth century, and it will be useful here just to list what some of these conditions were. The very notion of being enlightened – simply stated as the attempt to live one's life in the light of reason – was that of people being self-determined by reason in the conduct of their own lives, rather than having their lives determined by others in authority over them.

Indeed, it was a movement in which a certain middle to upper class group – known as the *philosophes*, the first secular (and semi-professional) group of intellectuals powerful enough to challenge the clergy – questioned the legitimacy of the clergy's right to decree society's 'basic' ways of talking. New, secular ways of warranting claims to truth were fashioned (Gergen, 1989), ways that subverted the traditional authority of the priests. Central to these new ways were the following features: (i) the elaboration of a special 'analytic' way of 'seeing', based in observation, which, it was claimed, worked to reveal the hidden, systematic order of things underlying mere appearances; (ii) the idea of language as being a shared *code* closely linking words to things; (iii) the idea that the knowledge gained through this special form of observation could be symbolically formulated in terms of representations (which resembled in their form of order the order of that hidden reality); (iv) the idea of the world as already a mechanism, or an orderly system, whose principles of operation it was our task to discover; (v) the idea of individuals as containing wholly within themselves the resources required for the making of such discoveries; where (vi) the new forms of knowledge could be formed without drawing upon previous, historical or traditional forms of knowledge – thus we had, besides a lack of interest in history, the denigration of traditional knowledge, practical knowledge, and rhetoric as 'mere' rhetoric. They also held (as we now realize) a wholly inadequate view of society, as a mere, homogeneous aggregate of individuals – a view which made it possible for them to dream that if only we could arrive at an appropriate form of enlightened self-knowledge, then society itself could be controlled, through the prediction and control of the behaviour of individuals, and thus 'improved'.

It is against this background that, as Foucault (1970) points out, the 'human sciences' of sociology, psychology, and those disciplines concerned with the analysis of literature and mythology, emerged. For within these special disciplines, 'man' is not just

> that living being with a peculiar form (a somewhat special physiology and an almost unique autonomy); he is that living being who, from within the life to which he entirely belongs and by which he is traversed in his whole being, constitutes representations by means of which he lives, and on the basis of which he possesses that strange capacity of being able to represent to himself precisely that life. (1970: 352).

Thus the subject matter of the human sciences is – as has finally become obvious from the emergence of *cognitive science*, with its concern with mental representations, as the central arena of current debate from out of the more heterogeneous arena of the *behavioural sciences* – not language itself as such, but a certain form of human being: that which is formed within a certain set of established discourses. Where the discourses in question, let it be said, are of an ideological nature, in that they were first formulated by the *philosophes* (as a group) according to *their* interests, interests that they hoped would be shared by everyone, but in the first instance, *their* interests nonetheless, an interest in the overthrow of history and traditions.

It is my purpose in the chapters below, of course, to question the norms that sustain these discourses in existence, to attempt to reveal their more disorderly, conversational origins, and to show how – in the transition from everyday conversation to the forming of discourse – ideological processes working to benefit certain groups over others were, and still are, at play.

Psychology as a moral not a natural science

Turning now to professional, academic psychology, we can begin by remarking that, in our 'official doctrines' (Ryle, 1949) it is thought 'natural', so to speak, to think of ourselves as possessing within ourselves something we call our 'mind' – an internal, secular organ of thought which mediates between us and the external reality surrounding us. And furthermore, it is also 'natural' to think that as such, our minds have their own discoverable, natural *principles of operation* which owe nothing either to history or to society for their nature. Thus, it is the task of a natural scientific psychology, of course, to discover what these principles are. Thus, within the ideology of the day, there is no necessity for professional psychologists to justify their projects or programmes of research; they appear to be 'obviously' of the correct form.

This conception of 'mind' is, however, I think, a myth: our talk *of* our minds leads us to experience ourselves as talking *about* our minds – that is, to talking amongst ourselves as if our 'minds' exist as the real things underlying our behaviour. But, I claim, there is no such 'underlying reality' to be found, and the belief that there is has led psychology into a number of dangerous mistakes. And in this introduction, I want to explore just one of them, the one which I think is the most central and the most dangerous: the failure to take account of the fact that in our everyday social life together, we do not find it easy to relate ourselves to each other in ways which are *both* intelligible (and legitimate), *and* which also are appropriate to '*our*' (unique) circumstances; and the fact that on occasions at least, we nonetheless do succeed in doing so. Attention to the actual, empirical details of such transactions reveals a complex but uncertain process of testing and checking, of negotiating the form of the relationship in terms of a whole great range of, essentially, *ethical* issues – issues to do with judgments about matters of care, concern, and respect, about justice, entitlements, etc. For in our social lives together, the fact is, we all have a part to play in *a major corporate responsibility*: that of both maintaining in existence the communicative 'currency', so to speak, in terms of which we conduct all our social transactions, and, that of developing and updating it to cope with changes in our surroundings as they occur. This is what is involved in us maintaining a civility in our social lives together. For our ways and means of 'making sense' to (and with) one another have not been given us as a 'natural' endowment, nor do they simply of themselves endure; what is possible between us is what we (or our predecessors) have 'made' possible. It is this responsibility that modern psychology has ignored, and which has led it, mistakenly, to give professional support to the view 'that "I" can still be "me" without "you" ' – a view which, as I shall show in the next chapter, renders most of our actual social life 'rationally-invisible'; that is, beyond rational discussion and debate.

Thus, against the claim that psychology is 'naturally' a biological science, requiring for its conduct the methods of the morally neutral natural sciences, I wish to differ, and to claim (see also Shotter, 1975, 1984, 1993b) that it is not a *natural* but a *moral* science, and that this gives it an entirely new character. The major change introduced is this: the abandoning of the attempt simply to *discover* our supposed 'natural' natures, and a turning to the study of how we actually do *treat* each other as being in everyday life, communicative activities – a change which leads us on to a concern with 'making', with processes of 'social construction' (Harré, 1979, 1983; Gergen, 1982, 1985; Shotter 1975, 1984, 1993b; Shotter and Gergen, 1989). What I want to do in the rest of this introduction, then, is to discuss two issues: (1) to explore why we are so attached to (in fact, 'entrapped' by) this myth of a 'naturally principled' mind, and other such similar myths to do with its supposed 'contents', such as 'ideas', 'intentions', 'desires', etc.; and (2) to explore the nature of an alternative assumption in terms of which to orient psychological investigations, an alternative which gives just as much a place to our 'makings' as to our 'findings'.

Textual realities and the myths of mind

Why do we seem so 'fixated', so to speak, upon the idea that there *must* be, somewhere in everyone, a 'mind', working upon some already existing or 'natural' *systematic principles* that, with the appropriate methods, can be discovered? Similarly, why are we so passionately convinced that there must be a single, well-ordered 'reality' to be discovered underlying appearances, as well as an 'objective' viewpoint, in terms of which it can be characterized? There are, I think, at least two main reasons, both to do with our concern with *systems* inherited from the Enlightenment, already broached above. Let me discuss these reasons in turn.

Firstly: as I have already partially mentioned but must now elaborate, ever since the ancient Greeks, people in the West have believed that 'reality' is to be 'found behind appearances'. Thus, it has long been thought that a very special power resides in the nature of reflective or theoretical thought: it can penetrate through the surface forms of things and activities to grasp the nature of a deeper 'form of order', an underlying order from which all human thought and activity *must* in fact spring. Thus, society at large has accepted it as a legitimate task of a certain special group of people – called priests, then scholars, and now philosophers, scientists, or just intellectuals – to attempt to articulate the nature of this deeper order. But the problems they face are: Where is this special underlying order to be found? And, how is it to be made visible?

In the West, we first looked for this deeper order unsuccessfully in religious and metaphysical *systems*. But then, during the Enlightenment, having lost faith in 'the spirit of systems', we adopted in our investigations, says Cassirer (1951: vii), 'the systematizing spirit'. And this, I think, is still the project implicit in modern psychology that we have inherited from the Enlightenment: the task of 'discovering' a supposedly neutral set of underlying 'mental' principles upon which the rest of life *should*, rationally, be based. Few of us now, however, possess the intellectual or the moral confidence (passion) still to accept this brief in good faith. Yet, although we cannot entirely give up the belief that there must be *some* worth in the effort to think seriously about life's choices, we find it very difficult to devise alternatives: we keep finding ourselves as if 'entrapped' within an invisible maze, from which there is no escape – this is because, within our professional academic practices as they are currently conducted, as systematic enterprises conducted within logical frameworks, there isn't!

This brings me to the second of my two reasons why we find it so difficult to formulate intelligible, alternative accounts of ourselves: in fulfilling our responsibilities as competent and professional academics, we must write *systematic texts*; we run the risk of being accounted incompetent if we do not. Until recently, we have taken such texts for granted as a neutral means to use how we please. This, I now want to claim, is a mistake, and now we must study their influence. But why should a concern with the nature of the literary and rhetorical devices constituting the structure of a *systematic, decontextualized text* now be of such concern to scientific psychologists?

Because theorists, in attempting to represent the open, vague, and temporally changing nature of the world as closed, well-defined and orderly, make use of certain textual and rhetorical strategies to construct within their text *a closed set of intralinguistic references*. They have not, however, appreciated the nature of the social processes involved in this achievement. But the fact is, in moving from an ordinary conversational use of language to the construction of a systematic textual discourse, there is transition from a reliance on particular, practical and unique meanings, negotiated 'on the spot' with reference to the immediate context, to a reliance upon links with a certain body of *already determined* meanings – a body of special, interpretative resources into which the properly trained professional reader has been 'educated' in making sense of such texts.[5] Being able to make reference to already determined meanings in such texts allows a decrease of reference within them to what 'is', and a consequent increase of reference to what 'might be'. But to be able to talk in this way, as a professional participant in a disciplinary discourse, one must develop *methods* for *warranting* in the course of one's talk, one's claims about what 'might be' *as being* what 'is'. It is by the use of such rhetorical devices – as reference to 'special methods of investigation', 'objective evidence', 'special methods of proof', 'independent witnesses', etc. – that those with competence in such procedures can construct their statements as 'factual statements', and claim authority for them as revealing a special 'true' reality behind appearances, without any reference to the everyday context of their claims (see Dreyfus and Rabinow, 1982: 48).

But this process can produce, and for us in the social sciences *does* produce, what Ossorio (1981) has called '*ex post facto* fact' fallacies: the fallacious retrospective claim that, for present events to be as they are, their causes *must* have been of a certain kind. Someone who has already studied the general nature of this fallacy in relation to scientific affairs is Fleck (1979). He comments upon its general nature as follows:

> once a statement is published it constitutes part of the social forces which form concepts and create habits of thought. Together with all other

> statements it determines 'what cannot be thought of in any other way' . . . There emerges a closed, harmonious system within which the logical origin of individual elements can no longer be traced. (Fleck, 1979: 37)

In attempting retrospectively to understand the origins and development (and the current movement) of our thought, we describe their nature within our, to an extent, now finished and systematic schematisms. But in doing so 'we can no longer express the previously incomplete thoughts with these now finished concepts' (Fleck, 1979: 80).

But the trouble is, once 'inside' such systems, it is extremely difficult to escape from them. We can, as Stolzenberg (1978) puts it, become 'entrapped' in the following sense: that 'an objective demonstration that certain of the beliefs are incorrect' can exist, but 'certain of the attitudes and habits of thought prevent this from being recognized' (Stolzenberg, 1978: 224). This, I think, is the trap within which we have ensnared ourselves in our systematic academic thought about ourselves and our psychology. But it means that our scientifically acquired knowledge of the world and ourselves is not determined by ours or the world's 'natures' to anything like the degree we have believed (and hoped) in the past; but instead, our knowledge is influenced by the 'ways', the literary and textual means, we have used in formulating our concerns. To go further: it means that we have spent our time researching into myths of our own making – the myths of 'mind', 'an already ordered reality', and 'objectivity' being cases in point. How can we escape from this entrapment? By studying how it is that we come to entrap ourselves in the first place, we must study the parts played rhetorically by such terms in our talk. For, far from talk of 'mind', 'an ordered reality', and 'objectivity' being in contrast to rhetoric, in my view, they are a part of it. This is why I think that it is important to study the actual, empirical nature of our ordinary, everyday, nonprofessional, nontextual, conversational ways and means of making sense together; for we are 'talked into' our supposed 'realities' by its means.

Events within conversational realities

As I have already mentioned above, the essence of textual communication is its so-called *intertextuality*: the fact that it draws upon people's knowledge of a certain body of *already formulated* meanings in the making of its meanings – this is why texts can be understood without contexts, that is, independently of immediate and local contexts. And it is also why, I think, experts can become trapped within systems of thought of their own making. But, as Garfinkel (1967) points out, in ordinary conversation people refuse to permit each other to understand what they are talking about in this way. A meaning unique and appropriate to the situation and to the people in it is developed. But that is not easy to negotiate. Thus, what precisely is 'being talked about' in a conversation, as we all in fact know from our own experience, is often at many points in the conversation necessarily unclear; we *must* offer each other opportunities to contribute to the making of agreed meanings.

In such a process, only gradually does 'the matter talked about' develop. Indeed, as Garfinkel (1967: 40) puts it, it is a 'developed and developing event' within the course of action that produces it. Thus as such, it is only 'known by both parties [involved in its production] *from within* this development . . . ' I cannot emphasize too strongly the deep and revolutionary or strange nature of what Garfinkel is claiming here: the nature of the 'reality' occupied by conversational events is at least as strange as any of the 'realities' discussed in modern physics. 'Making sense' of such an event from within a conversational reality, constructing a grasp of what is being 'talked about' from what is 'said', is not, according to Garfinkel, a simple 'one-pass' matter of an individual saying a sentence and a listener 'understanding' it. The events talked about are 'specifically vague'; that is, 'not only do they not frame a clearly restricted set of possible determinations but the depicted events include as their essentially intended and sanctioned features an accompanying "fringe" of determinations that are open with respect to internal relationships, relationships to other events, and relationships to retrospective and prospective possibilities' (Garfinkel, 1967: 40–1). Specifying or determining them sufficiently for the relevant practical purposes involves a complex back-and-forth process of negotiation both between speaker and hearer, and between what has already been said and what currently is being said, the making use of tests and assumptions, the use of both the present context and the waiting for something said later to make clear what was meant earlier, and the use of many other 'seen but unnoticed' (Garfinkel, 1967: 36) background features of everyday scenes.[6]

These strange temporal and spatial properties of conversational events, are in fact, Garfinkel claims, the properties of ordinary conversational talk. And as he says (1967: 41–2):

> People require these properties of discourse as conditions under which they are themselves entitled and entitle others to claim that they know what they are talking about, and that what they are saying is understandable and ought to be understood. In short, their seen but unnoticed presence is used to entitle persons to conduct their common conversational affairs without interference. Departures from such usages call forth immediate attempts to restore a right state of affairs.

We can thus begin to see why, when Garfinkel had his students try to talk to others as if single words should have already clear and determined meanings,[7] it provoked a morally motivated anger in the student's victims. People felt that in some way their rights had been transgressed – and as Garfinkel shows, they had! In having other people's pre-established meanings imposed upon them, they had been deprived of their right to participate in the making of meanings relevant just to the situation they were in, to negotiate a properly *shared* outcome; they were unable to make a unique meaning appropriate to their own unique circumstances. Moral sanctions follow such transgressions, people feel aggrieved and attempt to sanction or 'punish' those who perpetrate them.

But if we take this view – that what is 'talked about' by *us* is developed from what is 'said' by *each* – what should we say about the nature of words and their meanings, if we are not to see them as having already determined meanings? Rather than *already* having a meaning, we perhaps should see the *use* of a word as a *means* (but only as *one* means among many others) in the social making of a meaning. To claim that they *must* already have a meaning of some kind, is yet again to ignore that special but unrecognized, third kind of knowledge to do with how we grasp 'what is being talked about' in a conversation in the course of all our talk 'about' it. Ignoring it leads us to ignore the unique and very special 'developmental' nature of such conversational situations or events *and* the rights of the people within them. Indeed, to insist words have pre-determined meanings is to attempt to rob people of their rights, both to participate in developing a conversational topic with others, and to their own individual way of making that contribution. But even more than this is involved: it is to deprive one's culture of those conversational occasions or events in which people's individuality is constituted and reproduced. It is also to substitute the authority of professional texts in warranting claims to truth (on the basis as we now see of the unwarranted claim that they give us access to an independent, extralinguistic reality), for the *good reasons* we ordinarily give one another in our more informal conversations and debates. But, if we cannot find the foundations we require for an academic psychology in the writings of philosophers, or the researches of our scientists, where can we find them?

The foundations of psychology: In principles of mind, or in everyday, conversational realities?

The move from a referential–representational view of language to a rhetorical–responsive view, entails also the move from a decontextualized concern with a theoretical-explanatory 'psychology of mind', to a 'situated' concern with a practical-descriptive 'psychology of socio-moral relations' I mentioned earlier. For 'mind', as such, ceases to be something to be explained, and becomes instead a rhetorical device, something we talk of at various different times for various different purposes. And what we require are ways of critically describing those purposes – where, a *critical* description is one alive to ideological biases inherent in the normal discourse of the day; that is, alive to the fact that we are not always correct in our theories as to why it is that we talk about ourselves as we do. Such a change, however, a change to a critical practical-descriptive approach, entails a change in what we take the *foundations* of our discipline to be.

As we know, our Cartesian tradition has it that our investigations must, if they are to be accounted intellectually respectable, possess foundations in explicitly stated, self-evidently true, propositional statements. And to deny this (as indeed Rorty (1980) has done) seems to open the door to an 'anything goes' chaos. It seems as if there is nothing at all in terms of which claims to knowledge can be judged. This, however, is simply not the case. For let me state again what seems to me to be the undeniable empirical fact which a natural scientific psychology has consistently ignored: the fact that our daily lives are not rooted in written texts or in contemplative reflection, but in oral encounter and reciprocal speech. In other words, we live our daily social lives within an ambience of conversation, discussion, argumentation, negotiation, criticism and justification; much of it to do with problems of intelligibility and the legitimation of claims to truth. Anybody wanting to deny it will immediately confront us with an empirical example of its truth. And it is this 'rooting' of all our activities in our involvements with those around us, which prevents an 'anything goes' chaos. But only if we possess a certain kind of *common sense*, a special kind of ethical sensibility acquired in the course of our growth from childhood to adulthood to do with sensing or feeling what they are trying to do in their actions, do we qualify for such an involvement. Lacking it, our right to act freely, our autonomous status, is denied us. This sense, these *feelings* (which are not properly called emotions) work as the 'standards' against which our more explicit formulations are judged for their adequacy and appropriateness. In fact, I want to claim along with Wittgenstein (1980, II: nos. 624–9) that:

> We judge an action according to its background within human life . . . The background is the bustle of life. And our concept points to something within this bustle . . . Not what *one* man is doing now, but the whole hurly-burly, is the background against which we see an action, and it determines our judgment, our concepts, and our reactions.

Although, I hasten to add, that it does not determine them in an instant, nor is all the *possible* background bustle and hurly-burly of life present 'in' an instant either. The foundations of our lives never cease being contested.

But it is this claim – that the roots or foundations of our actions are to be found generally within ordinary people's everyday activities (including the uncompleted 'tendencies' to action they contain), and not within certain, already ordered principles of mind – that we professional academics have found, and still do find, difficult to stomach. For it means that anything we propose depends for its acceptance just as much (if not more) upon the common, collective, but 'disorderly', *embodied* sensibility of people in society at large, as upon the refined, systematic, and self-consciously formulated notions of academics and intellectuals. But what this means, is that in the growth of a noncognitive, non-Cartesian, rhetorical, social constructionist approach to psychology as a *moral science*, an obvious next step is a growing interest, not in the mind or the brain, but in the living body – or more correctly, in the unreflective bodily activities of the whole person. For paradoxical though it may be to say it, it is in sensuous bodily activities, I think, that ideas start, not in 'the mind'; such sensuous or feelingful activities are both the *terminus a quo* and *terminus ad quem* of all our social constructions (Shotter, 1993b).

The rhetorical–responsive social constructionist stance I shall take, then, marks a radical departure from the 'analytic' aims of the Enlightenment: the dream of discovering the 'real', already existing, orderly principles underlying our behaviour, either in the 'minds' of individuals, or, in the 'rules' regulating a systematic, social order. In fact, the 'realist' rhetoric legitimating that project seems to authorize a way of talking 'about' certain 'entities', or 'structures' – such as 'the mind', or 'society', and other supposedly 'objectively real things' – when no such orderly 'things' or 'structures' as such may actually exist. Indeed, it makes no distinction between a people's 'social reality' – understood, currently, in terms of who and what they are to themselves, as the inhabitants of a Western, liberal, individualistic, scientistic culture – and the forms of 'reality' with which they might make contact, from within such social realities. Such a rhetoric makes it appear as if one's task is merely that of describing as accurately as possible how one has 'observed' the social world, or a person's mentality, to be. But this form of 'analysis' as such is only of use here if we all already know perfectly well what the orderly 'it' *is*, that is being analyzed. But in our talk about such contested concepts as 'minds' or 'subjectivities', or 'cultures', 'histories' or 'societies', etc., this is not the case. These are 'political or contested objects' whose function, very largely, is in the constitution of different forms of social relations. Thus, it is not surprising that different people have different 'views' as to what their supposed orderly nature *should* be, and express their views in the different 'images' they employ (Shotter, 1975). In the social constructionist view I am proposing here, such 'political objects' as these exist only to the extent that they play a part within a conversation. That is, a 'tradition of argumentation' structured in their terms works to bring a certain form of human being into existence – where 'to imagine a language is to imagine a form of life' (Wittgenstein, 1953: no. 19). In other words, *accounting* for ourselves by talk of such 'inner entities' as 'thoughts', 'motives', 'memories', and such like, allows us to structure and manage our *individualistic* forms of life, and to create certain forms of social institutions, not available to those lacking such a 'language of mind' (see Whorf on the native-American Hopi, in Chapter 6 below). This, indeed, *is* the nature of *our* 'social reality'; we sustain and manage it through such forms of talk.

But when we academics treat ordinary people's everyday talk *of* their 'thoughts', 'memories', 'perceptions', 'motives', 'needs', and 'desires', and such, uncritically, as ordinary people themselves treat it – in short, as talk *about* their 'minds' – then we fail to take into account 'the contents and forms that brought it [such talk] into being' (Foucault, 1970: 364). In such talk, in a social constructionist view, people are not making a *reference* to the nature of their already existing minds, but are taking part in a contested (or at least contestable) process, a tradition of argumentation, in which they are still struggling over the constitution of their own mental make-up. At a personal level, the whole lexicon of 'mind' and 'mental activity' terms provides a set of rhetorical resources or devices for use by them to serve their own personal interests in that struggle; while at a social level, it is a way of talking that serves to sustain, and perhaps develop further, our own Western form of social life and personhood. If we want to change it, we must engage in argument, where, as Billig et al. (1988: 149) suggest, 'one of the goals of social action or of social reform is to win a present argument, in order to change the agenda of argumentation' – and this is the task in which, in contest with cognitivists, social constructionists are now engaged.

Notes

1. A fact, perhaps, reflected in the number of books about 'chaos theory' and similar matters (e.g., Bohm, 1985; Gleik, 1987; Peat, 1990; Prigogine and Stengers, 1984).

2. It is the kind of knowledge one has, not only *from within a social situation*, a group, or an institution, and which thus takes into account (and is accountable within) the social situation within which it is known. It is also knowledge that one has *from within oneself as a human being and as a socially competent member of a culture* – hence I know 'from the inside', so to speak, what it is like to be involved in conversation (see my chapter 2, epigraph quote from Garfinkel, 1967: 40). So, although I may not able to reflectively contemplate the nature of that knowledge as an inner, mental representation, according to the questions asked, I can nonetheless call upon it as a practical resource in framing appropriate answers.

3. Below, what Rorty calls a 'normal discourse', i.e., a discourse which *dominates* our talk in the sense of providing the basic or the final unquestioned terms in which we make sense of things, I shall call a 'basic' way of talking.

4. The '*word is a two-sided act.* It is determined equally by *whose* word it is and *for whom* it is meant . . . it is precisely *the product of the reciprocal relationship between speaker and listener, addresser and addressee.* Each and every word expresses the "one" in relation to the "other". I give myself verbal shape from another's point of view, ultimately, from the point of view of the community to which I belong' (Volosinov, 1973: 86).

5. As Foucault (1972: 255) points out, a disciplinary discourse lays down ritual that those participating in it must observe: 'it lays down gestures to be made . . . it lays down the supposed, or imposed significance of the words used, their effect upon those to whom they are addressed, the limitations of their supposed validity.'

6. 'Demonstrably he [a speaker] is responsive to this background [in terms of various expectancies], while at the same time he is at a loss to tell us specifically of what the expectancies consist. When we ask him about them he has little or nothing to say' (Garfinkel, 1967: 36–7). As Garfinkel suggests, some of these expectancies will depend upon *prior* agreements and will be according to agreed practices or 'methods', but others, I claim, due to the intrinsic properties of joint action, will emerge out of the immediate and local practical circumstances of the conversation in question.

7. The idea that language works in terms of a set of pre-established, basic meanings, a code, has long been a commonplace of academic linguistics. Witness Jakobson's (1956: 71) claim that 'the speaker and the listener have at their disposal more or less the same "filing cabinet of prefabricated representations": the addresser of a verbal message preselects one of these "preconceived possibilities" and the addressee is supposed to make an identical choice from the same assembly . . . Thus the efficiency of a speech event demands the use of a common code by its participants.'

2
Situating Social Constructionism: Knowing 'from Within'

> 'the matter talked about' as a developing and developed event over the course of the action that produced it, as both the process and the product [is] known *from within* this development by both parties, each for himself as well as on behalf of the other.
>
> Garfinkel, 1967: 40

In this chapter I want to explore further the consequences of situating social constructionist studies in a conversational background or context. That is, I want to question what is involved in conducting our studies from within a continually ongoing flow of differentiated, turbulent but formative, social activity – where our concerns are to do with 'something within this bustle' (to repeat Wittgenstein's phrase quoted in the previous chapter). Classically, once we have perceptually foregrounded an entity for study, we are also used to treating it as having its own isolated existence, and ignoring its background; we are unused to treating it as existing only in virtue of its continued interaction with its background surroundings. But, as the 'I love you' example in the introduction illustrated, words uttered in such contexts draw their power from how they function to make a crucial difference at a crucial moment in that background flow of activity.[1] A possible difference arose as a result of the history of the flow of activity between the people involved, and the words uttered served to realize that possibility: they had their meaning mostly in their use at that moment. Thus, in many such situations as this, what is being talked about (to refer to the Garfinkel quote above), is a developing and developed event, an event that is only properly known from within this development by those who are producing it. Crucial in such events are those points in a conversation when a 'gap' must be bridged: when either a change in speaking subject occurs, or when, to put it another way, what one person says or does must be accounted for, made sense of, or responded to in some way, by an other (or by the person themselves).

In situating the kind of social constructionism I want to outline in this way, I want to emphasize its concern with a special set of problems to do with investigating and linguistically articulating the nature of our everyday, background common sense, its structured and changing nature as we live our lives.[2] Where it is that background (i) from out of which all our activities emerge; (ii) towards aspects of which (however mistakenly) they are all directed; (iii) as well as against which they are all judged as to their fittingness; and (iv) upon which they act back historically to modify. Thus the rhetorical–responsive version of social constructionism proposed here is not only directed towards an understanding of how we constitute (make) and reconstitute (remake) that common sense, or ethos, but also towards how we make and remake ourselves in the process. It is this dialectical emphasis upon *both* our making of, *and* being made by, our own social realities, that is, I think, common to social constructionism in all its versions.

However, having situated our social constructionist studies within the bustle or hurly-burly of everyday social life, and having accepted that all the words we utter – if they are effective at all – function to make crucial differences at crucial moments – how should we report the results of our investigations? For we can no longer claim to be presenting neutral 'pictures' of fixed, already existing states of affairs, awaiting our judgment as to their truth or falsity. The answer would seem to hinge upon the kind of activity in which we see ourselves as engaged. As I mentioned in the previous chapter, in a social constructionist psychology, psychologists are not Olympian scientists looking down upon the society they are studying with no part to play within it themselves; they are engaged in a tradition of argumentation. They are taking part in a contested (or at least contestable) process, a struggle to do with the constitution of our own mental make-up. And crucial in that struggle is the 'basic' language ('vocabulary of motives' – Mills, 1940) in terms of which we *account* for ourselves, the terms in which we justify our actions to others when challenged by them to do so. Thus in what follows, in response to the question above as to how we might report the results of our investigations, instead of theories, I shall offer a number of *instructive statements*: they provide an *account* of a number of what I feel are crucial aspects in the nature of conversational exchanges. Their function is not to represent a state of affairs, but to direct people's attention to crucial features of the context, features that 'show' connections between things that otherwise would go unnoticed. They have the form: '*attend to X* if you want to grasp the crucial feature that gives you insight into the issue in question here'. They have point only in a context; they are important at just those points in the flow of everyday interaction when the people involved sense that a change in the character of that form of life is at issue – hence their argumentative force. And that is how I intend my accounts to be read here: as suggesting a change in language in terms of which we currently conduct our debates in psychology about our own psychological nature.

In terming such accounts 'instructive', I want to call upon aspects of Vygotsky's (1978, 1986) important account of words as 'psychological tools or instruments'. Words function in this instrumental fashion when, for instance, others make use of various forms of talk, to draw our attention to features of our circumstances that otherwise would escape our notice, or, how to conduct ourselves in certain circumstances; they can instruct us in how to manage or organize our ways of perceiving and acting. As Vygotsky (1978: 32) comments, in learning to coordinate their actions linguistically with the actions of those around them, 'the child begins to perceive the world not only through his eyes but also through his speech'. And he goes on to show how the ways in which others can at first verbally instruct us can later become our own; as they verbally instructed us, so we can come to verbally instruct ourselves. What the nature of these forms of talk is, and how they exert their function, will become clear to us as we proceed. But what I hope is already clear, this 'instructive' use of language is very different from its referential–representational function. And we shall find it crucial in elucidating the nature of a rhetorical–responsive, social constructionist psychology, and how such a psychology can function from within the everyday conversational background within which it is situated.

The creation, in self–other relations, of person–world relations

Above, I have mentioned a number of times the importance of our 'basic' ways of talking about ourselves and our world. What in particular I want to explore in this chapter is how it is that, within the everyday, disorderly, practical, self–other relationships constituting the usually unnoticed background to our lives, we unknowingly construct between ourselves those orderly forms of (intralinguistic) relations I earlier called person–world relations. Where, what is special in such relations, to repeat, is that the orderly ways of talking constituting them form our ways of accounting for and making sense of ourselves and our world, ways that are 'basic' in the sense that they form a lexicon of justificatory ultimates, so to speak (Mills, 1940): a whole taken-for-granted vocabulary of things and processes we talk of being the 'basic' nature of both ourselves and the world in which we live.

Although I shall argue here that the character or style of our 'basic' person–world relations is both 'produced by' and 'contained in' our self–other relations, in our self-conscious experience (and in other cultures too), clearly, it is *as if* they are 'given' us by an 'external' agency. We have no awareness of our own involvement in their construction. It is as if our person–world relations are independent of, or 'orthogonal' to, our self–other relationships. Like the movements of

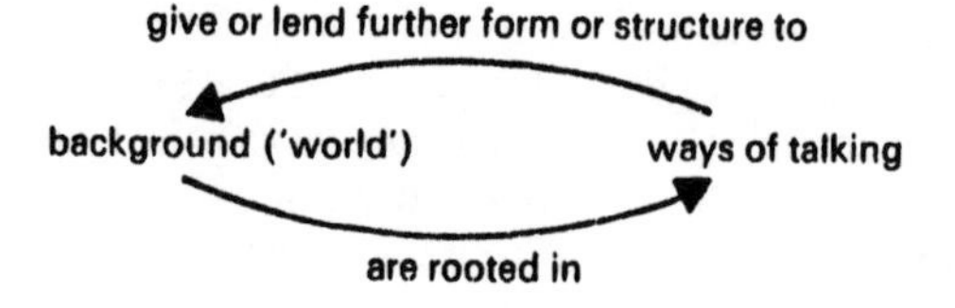

Figure 1

the wineglass upon the *ouija* board, people (and peoples) seem to lack any individual sense of responsibility for such socially produced outcomes – a fact that will concern us in a moment when we turn to a discussion of 'joint action' below. Yet, nonetheless, it is from within this rhetorical–responsive, two-way flow of relational, sensuously channelled, self–other activities and practices, I suggest, that all the other dimensions of the person–world polarity that are significant for us originate and are formed.

The two-way process involved may be diagrammed as in Figure 1, as a process in which people, rooted in a background and making use of the linguistic resources it provides, act back upon those background circumstances (their 'world') to give or to lend them further form or structure. In such a two-way process, we can see our self–other, background activities as, on the one hand, formative of the routine, everyday, person–world ways of talking we as ordinary persons use in *normatively*[3] *accounting* for ourselves and our world to others in the 'social realities' we occupy. On the other hand, to the extent that our accountable forms emerge out of them, those forms can also be seen as 'rooted' in them; that is, as providing a shared 'structure of feeling' as a basis in terms of which accountable formulations may be judged as appropriate or not (see note 1). It is because our accountable forms of talk still remain functionally embedded in the conversational background from out of which they have perceptually emerged, that our accounting does come to an end – an ultimate justification is agreed to in terms of what is 'felt' to right by all.

In terms of exactly the same two-way process again – but now with our everyday, accountable activities as their basis – we can also see how our special, disciplinary forms of life may be developed, along with what is 'felt' to be right within them. Where we are 'schooled' in such feelings from our reading of (and being examined in) the appropriate disciplinary texts. With one such *feeling* in the social and behavioural sciences being, at the moment, the feeling that it is crucial to attempt to *explain* our 'external' worlds only in terms of particular kinds of objectively and theoretically identifiable entities – an account is called 'merely' descriptive and sensed as inadequate. For until recently, in thinking that if only we could stand upon the shoulders of giants, we could see to the far reaches of our forms of life, we have felt it reasonable to argue that certain of our special modes of being – such as actor, playwright, novelist, painter, journalist, poet, businessman, designer, academic, and especially the scientist – give us the opportunity of 'seeing' the whole. Reformulating the issue in terms of a basis in a structure of feeling, situated within a context, suggests that it is impossible to articulate the nature of the whole from the point of view of just a specialized part of it. More than a 'view' is required. Thus, it is from within our status as ordinary persons, as we move about over the whole differentiated, background landscape of our lives, crossing from one institutional centre to another, experiencing the crossing of boundaries, the differences between the centre from the margins, and the margins from the centre, and so on, that we must attempt our account of it.[4]

Turning, then, to the issue of how people account to the others around them, both for themselves and for the general character of their surroundings: As we have already seen, in the earlier discussion of Geertz's (1975) and Lienhardt's (1961) respective accounts of Western and Dinka forms of consciousness, people within different socio-historical groups seem to account for themselves, and their world, in very different ways. As we saw earlier, much of what *we* experience as a part of *ourselves*, as an aspect of our agency under our own control, the Dinka experience as a presence in their surroundings, acting upon them from without. One feels that talk of an *ethos*, of finding ourselves embedded in a structure of feeling, would be more immediately intelligible to them than it is to us. To reinforce the point, we might also compare how we experience the problematic relation of ourselves to our world, with how Whorf (1956: 150) claims the seeming nature of that relation to be for the native American Hopi: while 'we are dimly aware that we carry about with us a whole imaginary space, full of mental surrogates . . . The Hopi thought-world has no such imaginary space . . . [A Hopi 'naturally'] suppose[s] that his thought (or he himself) traffics with the [thing] that he is thinking about'. Thus, where we 'plan' for the future, by drawing up a theoretical schematism, placing representations of things in their proper relation to each other ahead of time, thus to get it right when we apply the plan in practice, the Hopi 'prepare' for the future in quite a different way. For them, the present moment, in carrying forward the 'impress' of past activities, makes the carrying forward of yet further 'impresses' possible. Thus, for them, repetitions, the cumulative outcomes of innumerable small contributory (often ritual) acts, are not lost, but are stored up as a power in their surroundings, a power that will hold over into later events. Something that we in the West try to do, perhaps, when, by chanting at football matches, we try to build up a 'charge' to carry our team through to greater efforts; though we possess much less vocabulary than they for justifying and explaining the efficacy of such practices to those who might challenge them. But as for the Hopi, so for the Dinka: in the ordinary run of affairs, their world would seem to be a much more spiritually charged and chargeable place than ours.

How the Dinka and the Hopi experience their world is, perhaps, to an extent how things might appear to us if we were solely engaged in *practical* affairs, and faced the task of formulating the nature of such affairs exclusively from within their conduct – without ever being able to 'view' them, or talk of them, retrospectively or from an 'external' third-person point of view, thus to 'explain' them from within a theoretical context. In other words, their (the Dinka and the Hopi) ways of 'being ordinary', embodied as they are in their ways of speaking, in their social institutions and ways of doing things, in their tools and implements, along with their ways of judging the rightness of things, provide a background ethos that determines, not only what counts as real for them, but also a whole range of other things and categories they find strange or extra-ordinary. In the same way, our background ethos also determines for us, not only (i) our own ways of being ordinary, but also, in particular, what we think of as (ii) the imaginary, the nonexistent, the impossible, the extraordinary, as well as (iii) a whole range of things we do not even notice that we do not even notice[5] – things, events and situations which, to invert a phrase of Garfinkel's (1967: vii), are rendered 'rationally-*in*visible' to us; that is, things which our ways of perceiving, acting, talking, and evaluating *fail* to make visibly-rational to us, and thus amenable to rational discourse and debate. In our case, it is precisely the third sphere of activity I mentioned above – the unordered, diffuse, back-and-forth flow of practical, sensuous activity – that has remained 'rationally-invisible' to us.

'Joint action' and conversational realities

Turning to that third sphere or category of events, it is clear that the activity of interest to us occurs in a zone of indeterminacy, a zone of uncertainty somewhere between the other two polarities mentioned above upon which we have focused our attention in the past. It occurs in a zone between (i) *actions* (what I as an individual 'do'), and (ii) *events* (what merely 'happens' to, in, or around me, outside of my agency as an individual to control), and as such, does not seem amenable to characterization at all. Yet this, however, is not entirely the case. Indeed, it is its very lack of specificity, its lack of any pre-determined order, and thus its openness to being specified or determined by those involved in it, that is its central defining feature.[6] (iii) I shall call activity in this third sphere, in this zone of uncertainty, 'joint action' (Shotter, 1984). It has two major features:

1 As people coordinate their activity in with the activities of others, and 'respond' to them in what they do, what they as individuals desire and what actually results in their exchanges are often two very different things. In short, joint action produces *unintended* and unpredictable outcomes. These generate a 'situation', or an 'organized practical-moral setting' existing between all the participants. As its organization cannot be traced back to the intentions of any particular individuals, it is *as if* it has a 'given', a 'natural', or an 'externally caused' nature; though, to those within it, it is 'their/our' situation.
2 Although such a setting is unintended by any of the individuals within it, it nonetheless has an *intentional* quality to it: it seems both to have a 'content', as well as to 'indicate' or to be 'related to something other than or beyond itself';[7] that is, participants find themselves both immersed 'in' an already *given* situation, but one with a *horizon* to it, that makes it 'open' to their actions. Indeed, its 'organization' is such that the practical-moral constraints (and enablements) it makes available to them influence, that is, 'invite' and 'motivate', their next possible actions.

And as Giddens (1984: 8) describes it, such socially constructed but 'unintended consequences may systematically feedback to be the unacknowledged conditions of further acts'. The notion of joint action is, I claim, just the kind of notion we need, *through* which to see[8] the workings of processes of social construction.

By its use, we can see that in the ordinary two-way flow of activity between them, people create, without a conscious realization of the fact, a changing sea[9] of *moral* enablements and constraints, of privileges and entitlements, and obligations and sanctions – in short, an ethos. And the changing settings created are *practical-moral settings* because the different 'places' or 'positions' they make available have to do, not so much with people's 'rights' and 'duties' (for we might formulate its ethical nature in different ways, at different times), as with the nurturance or injury to the basic being of a person. For individual members of a people can have a *sense* of 'belonging' in that people's 'reality', only if the others around them are prepared to respond to what they do and say *seriously*; that is if they are treated as a proper participant in that people's 'authoring' of their reality, and not excluded from it in some way. For only then will they feel that the reality in which they live is as much theirs as anyone else's. In other words, to the extent that we all participate in our own different ways, 'we' can be the authors not only of our 'realities' but also of our own 'selves'. This does not mean that we will unthinkingly feel a sense of total harmony with those around us. But it does mean not having a sense of being an intrusive alien, of being able to realize one's 'true self' in the world around one (rather than only in one's dreams).

This view – of what it is to belong to a social group, to feel that one is not excluded from the social activities involved in that group's construction of its own reality – is very closely connected, I feel, with Harré's (1983, 1990) claim that the primary human reality is conversation. Although many may disagree and feel that many other (more nonverbal) spheres of human interaction are more basic,[10] here I shall take it as primary in the following (judgmental) sense: as human realities do not endure through the physical rigidity of their structures (indeed, it makes no sense even to talk of them in this way), to repeat the by now familiar theme, they must be sustained in existence by being continually remade in people's everyday social activities. In such processes, however, people mutually judge and correct both each other and themselves as to the 'fittingness' of their actions to what they take their reality to be. As Wittgenstein (1953: no. 242) insists, 'if language is to be a means of communication there must be agreement not only in definitions but also (queer as this may sound) in judgments'. Utterances are judged, then, not solely or primarily in terms of their grammatical form, but are evaluated in terms of the 'countless' (Wittgenstein, 1953: no. 23) uses they can have in relation to the social reality in which they occur. And conversation is the ultimate sphere in which all such judging and evaluating takes place, and in which such assessments are negotiated and shared agreements are reached. But this judging and evaluating is done against a certain background, an ethos, a common sense, and it is to the nature of that background, that 'structure of feeling' (Williams, 1977) that I now want to turn – though it will be some time before we are in a position to grasp its nature.

Knowing of the third kind and sensuous ways of talking

In discussing the nature of conversational realities[11] and our 'basic' ways of talking, I want to argue for the importance within them of the third, extraordinary form of nonrepresentational, embodied or sensuous, practical–moral knowledge I introduced in Chapter 1. As I have said before, it is a separate, special kind of knowledge, *sui generis*, which is prior to both theoretical and merely technical knowledge, for, in being linked to people's social and personal identities, it determines the available forms of these other two kinds of knowledge. It is an embodied form of practical–moral knowledge in terms of which people are able to influence each other in their being, rather than just in their intellects; that is, to actually 'move' them rather than just 'giving them ideas'. Given our current 'basic' ways of talking, however, we cannot easily grasp the nature of such knowledge. Indeed, to the extent that we cannot 'command a clear view' (Wittgenstein, 1953: no. 122) of its overall nature, we cannot rationally imagine it. Further, because it cannot be represented (or formed) as an object of knowledge within a normative or disciplined form of talk – that is, within a discourse – its nature, for us, is *extraordinary*. Yet, I want to claim, there are nonetheless ways (see below) in which we can elucidate its nature.

It is at this point, I want to turn in some detail to Vygotsky's work. His project was to show how 'all the higher functions originate as actual relations between human individuals', he says (1978: 57). We develop from creatures functioning under the control of our surrounding (social) circumstances to functioning under our own control. We come to be able to plan, direct, control, and to organize our own 'higher mental functions or processes' as we come to incorporate within ourselves the forms of talk that others use in controlling, directing, and organizing our behaviour for us. Thus, at the centre of his whole approach is the fact that besides (and prior to) their referential–representational function, words also work in a noncognitive, formative way to 'shape' our unreflective, embodied or sensuous ways of looking and acting – in short, to 'move' us. Indeed, without the sensory, sensuous or affective function of words, to 'move' people to perceive and act in different ways, his whole project falls to the ground. Thus, in attempting at the outset to clarify the nature of the problem as he sees it, we find him saying that 'when we approach the problems of the interrelation between thought and language . . . the first question that arises is that of intellect and affect' (Vygotsky, 1986: 10). If they are separated, then, he says, 'the door is closed on the issue of the causation and origin of our thoughts . . .' (ibid.), for we are unable to understand 'the motive forces that direct thought into this or that channel' (ibid.). Hence, the approach he adopts 'shows that every idea contains a transmuted affective attitude toward the bit of reality to which it refers' (ibid.). In other words, the affective attitude which provides the thoughts and ideas of an individual with their dynamic – that is, with their particular motives and valencies[12] thus linking them to each other and their surroundings in a particular way – is a transmuted version of a social relationship. But of what kind?

Well, quite literally, of an 'instructional' kind; we come to 'instruct' ourselves as others instruct us: they 'point things out to us' ('Look at this!'); 'change our perspective' ('Look at it like this'); 'order' our actions ('Look at the model first, then at the puzzle pieces'); 'shape' our actions ('Turn it over, then it will fit'); 'remind' us ('Think what you did last time', 'What do you already know that's relevant?'); 'encourage' us

('Try again'); 'restrain' us ('Don't be too hasty'); 'evaluate' for us ('That's not right', 'Don't do that, that's greedy'); 'set our goals' ('Try to put these pieces together to match that [pointing at a model]'); 'count' ('How many will it take?'); make 'measurements' ('Will that fit properly?' 'Just compare'); make us 'check' our descriptions ('Is that right?' 'Who else says so?' 'What's the reason for your belief?'); and so on, and so on, for no doubt a countless number of functions. Indeed, we can form such instructions into sequences, to construct step-by-step programmes of perception and action. First: 'survey', then 'choose', then 'act', then 'survey again', and so on. These are the *means* Vygotsky has in mind when he says (Vygotsky, 1986: 102, my emphasis) that 'the main question about the process of concept formation – or, about any goal-directed activity – is the question of the *means* by which the operation is accomplished . . . To explain the higher forms of human behavior, we must uncover the *means* by which man learns to organize and direct his behavior.' And, 'our experimental study proved that it was the functional use of the word, or any other sign, as *means* of focusing one's attention, selecting distinctive features and analyzing and synthesizing them, that plays a central role in concept formation' (1986: 106). 'Learning to direct one's own mental processes with the aid of words or signs is an integral part of the process of concept formation' (1986: 108).

Wertsch (1991: 27) quotes a useful illustrative example from Tharp and Gallimore (1988: 14):

> A 6-year-old child has lost a toy and asks her father for help. The father asks where she last saw the toy; and the child says 'I can't remember'. He asks a series of questions – did you have it in your room? Outside? Next door? To each question the child answers 'no'. When he says 'in the car?', she says 'I think so' and goes to retrieve the toy.

In such a case, as Wertsch points out, we cannot answer the question 'who did the remembering?' by pointing to one person or the other. It is a joint accomplishment, and what the child now does with the father's help, she later comes to do for herself; that is 'manage' the relations between her knowledge, thought, and action herself, in terms of similar such 'instructions'. And at a more advanced level, this is what one learns to do in thinking conceptually. In Vygotsky's terms, one learns not to compare the configuration of a supposed mental representation with the configuration of a state of affairs in reality, but something else much more complicated: one has grasped how to organize and assemble in a socially intelligible way, that is, a way which makes sense to the others around one, bits and pieces of information dispersed in space and time in accordance with 'instructions' they (the others around one) at first provided, and which now a supposed 'concept' provides.

A rhetorically and ethically negotiated 'inner life'

In this view, what it is to have formed a concept is to have formed for ourselves, from the words of others, a 'psychological instrument' *through* which we can both perceive and act; that is, an instrumental aid in terms of which we can both 'instruct' ourselves in a programme for gathering and organizing perceptual data, as well as for ordering and sequencing a plan of action. Thus, rather than a self-contained, simply subjective activity within an individual – dealing with merely inner, cognitive 'pictures' which may, or may not, be accurate representations of an outer reality – thinking conceptually (according to the 'instructions' of others) becomes a special kind of social practice. And furthermore, it becomes a social practice in which speech, thought and feeling are, at least at first and for the most part, interlinked with their surrounding circumstances in 'a dynamic system of meaning' (Vygotsky, 1986: 10–11). Only gradually, and probably as a result of the effects of becoming literate – in which, 'in learning to write, the child must disengage himself from the sensory aspect of speech and replace words by images[13] of words' (Vygotsky, 1986: 181) – can we learn to think like self-contained academics, and develop modes of formal, decontextualized rationality; that is, to think in wholly representational[14] terms. Influenced by this 'picture' of what thinking is, traditional methods fail 'to take into account the perception and the mental elaboration of the sensory material that gave birth to the concept. The sensory material and the word are both indispensable parts of concept formation' (Vygotsky, 1986: 96–7).

But, if this is so, what kind of account of the act of speaking do we need to describe the relation between words and their sense, to elucidate the relation of form to feeling? As Vygotsky (1986) sees it, rather than issuing mechanically, from already well-formed and orderly cognitions at the centre of our being, the expression[15] of a thought or an intention, such as the saying of a sentence or the doing of a deed, first originates in a person's vague and unordered *sense* of the situation they are in. Its appropriate *orderly* realization or formation is then 'developed' in a complex set of temporally conducted, interwoven negotiations, connecting themselves (or, their 'selves'), their feelings, their utterances, and those to whom they must address their utterances. In other words, speakers are sensitive in their very acts of speaking, to the kind of 'links' – between themselves, their listeners and their circumstances – that they must construct as they speak. Thus:

> the relation of thought to word is not a thing but a process, a continual movement backward and forth from thought to word and from word to thought. In that process, the relation of thought to word undergoes changes that themselves may be regarded as developmental in the functional sense. Thought is not merely expressed in words; it comes into existence through

> them. Every thought tends to connect something with something else, to establish a relation between things. Every thought moves, grows and develops, fulfils a function, solves a problem. (1986: 218)

And, at a later point in the text he adds that 'the structure of speech does not simply mirror the structure of thought; that is why words cannot be put on by thought like a ready-made garment' (1986: 219). 'Precisely because thought does not have its automatic counterpart in words,[16] the transition of thought to word leads through meaning. In our speech, there is always the hidden thought, the subtext' (1986: 251). The unique *sense* of our words in the context of their use is 'shown', not in the form or pattern of the words we have said, but in our saying of them, in our intoning[17] of them. In our actual speaking, we 'show' more than we are ever able to 'say' (Wittgenstein); what we 'show' is there in the 'movement' of our words.

Thus there is a 'subtext' to our speech, as every utterance constitutes only *an attempt* (which is hardly ever completely satisfactory) to 'develop' a sensed thought-seed into a voiced utterance-flower. What we try to say, and what we are understood as meaning, are often at odds with each other. Hence the necessity for the realization of a thought to be 'successively developed' (and checked) in a back-and-forth process, in which the transition of thought to word is through meaning. Unformulated in words, a thought-seed remains vague and provides only the possibility of having a meaning: 'The relation between thought and word is a living process; thought is born through words. A word devoid of thought is a dead thing . . . But thought that fails to realize itself in words remains a "Stygian shadow" [O. Mandelstam] . . . The connection between thought and word, however, is neither preformed nor constant. It emerges in the course of development, and itself evolves' (1986: 255). The voiced utterance-flower, which can move us and guide us in our actions, emerges in the course of a dialogic process of what Vygotsky calls 'inner speech,' a process which can vary in its character according to the 'others' involved in the thought's 'development' – those with whom, about whom, and to whom, in one's inner speech one speaks.

In other words, even when all alone, the 'inner' process in which one's vague thoughts are formulated into clear programmes for sequencing and guiding socially intelligible and legitimate action, involves events similar to the 'outer' transactions between people. Thus, people's attempts to realize their thoughts – to formulate their thoughts to themselves in ways which make those thoughts socially *usable*, so to speak – must be *negotiated* in an inner back-and-forth process, in which they must attempt to understand and challenge their own proposed formulations as the others around them might. For one's task in developing into a morally autonomous adult in one's own society is not just that of learning to direct one's own mental processes with the aid of words or signs, but of doing so in a way that makes sense and is considered legitimate by others. In this view, then, our 'inner' lives are structured by us living 'into' and 'through', so to speak, the opportunities or enablements offered us by the 'others' and 'otherness' both around us and within us. Thus our mental life is never wholly our own. We live in a way which is both responsive, and in response to, what is both 'within us' in some way, but which is also 'other than' ourselves.

Conclusions

In this *communicational* view of ourselves, then, the current view we have of persons, as all equal, self-enclosed (essentially indistinguishable) atomic individuals, possessing an inner sovereignty, each living their separate lives, all in isolation from each other – the supposed experience of the modern self – is an illusion, maintained by the institution between us of certain special forms of communication, certain 'basic' ways of talking, as I have called them above. It is an illusion which, besides misleading us about our own nature as human beings, also misleads us about the nature of thought and of language – we have come to think about both as if they are like the closed, unitary systems of signs in mathematics rather than as a heterogeneous set of means or devices for us to link ourselves to our surroundings.[18] This is precisely the assumption Vygotsky (1986: 1–2) challenges at the very outset of his work:

> The unity of consciousness and the interrelation of all psychological functions were, it is true, accepted by all; the single functions were assumed to operate inseparably, in an uninterrupted connection with one another. But this unity of consciousness was usually taken as a postulate, rather than a subject of study . . . It was taken for granted that the relation between two given functions never varied; that perception, for example, was always connected in an ideal way with attention, memory with perceptions, thought with memory.

Yet, as he goes on to say, 'all that is known about psychic development indicates that its very essence lies in the change of the interfunctional nature of consciousness' (1986: 2).

In other words, Vygotsky opened up 'gaps' between all the different psychological functions, 'responsive gaps' that we can bridge in different ways, at different times, in different circumstances, by the use of various, socially fashioned 'mediatory devices'. The bridging of the 'gap' – between, say, a first speaker's question and a second speaker's answer – by the second speaker responding 'into' the context fashioned by the first's asking of a question, *is* the making of the link. And there are not just a few 'principled' or 'rule-governed' ways of making links, but countless, creative ways in which such links might be made. And it is in treating the 'links' between thoughts and words as having a 'developmental', 'formative', or 'creative' character, rather than being related in a merely systematic, mechanical, or logical manner, that leads to the introduction of an *ethical* and *rhetorical* (justificatory) note into accounts of how people organize and 'manage' their own mental activities – as well as, of course, to a much less systematic and less unified view of language itself.

What then in this view is the nature of our supposed 'inner' lives? It would seem that people's 'inner' lives are neither so private, nor so inner, nor so merely orderly or logical, as has been assumed. Instead, the 'movement of the mind' reflects essentially the same ethical and rhetorical considerations as those influencing the transactions between people, out in the world.[19] This is because, as Vygotsky claims, it is only through the semiotic mediation of signs that 'the mind' as such comes into existence at all. Thus our thoughts, our self-consciously known thoughts, are not first organized at the inner centre of our being (in a nonmaterial 'soul', or a physiological 'lingua mentis'), thus later to be given outer orderly expression or not in words. They only become organized, in a moment-by-moment, back-and-forth, formative or developmental process at the boundaries of our being, involving similar 'linguistically mediated ethical negotiations' as those we conduct in our everyday dialogues with others. As Vygotsky (1966: 41) noted, 'reflection is the transfer of argumentation within'.

In this view, then, the process of *internalization* occurring in a person's development, their supposed 'acquisition' of their culture, is not the transferral of something (some already existing 'thing') from an external to an inner plane of activity, but the actual linguistic *constitution* of a distinctly socio-ethical mode of psychological being. In learning how *to be* a responsible member of certain social groups, one must learn how *to do* certain things in the right kind of way: how to perceive, think, talk, act, and to experience one's surroundings in ways that make sense to the others around one. Thus, on this view, what one has in common with other members of one's social group is not so much a set of shared beliefs or values as such, but a set of shared semiotic procedures or ethnomethods (Garfinkel), ways of making sense – and a certain set of *ordered* forms of communication, or speech genres (Bakhtin, 1986). Thus internalization is not a special geographical movement inwards, from a realm of bodily activity into a nonmaterial realm of 'the mind', but a socio-practical-ethical movement, in which 'children grow into the intellectual life of those around them' (Vygotsky, 1978: 88). And the child not only learns how 'to practice with respect to himself the same forms of behavior that others formerly practiced with respect to him', but also learns the socio-practical means to bring other people (and *their* mental resources) within his or her own personal agency to control. Hence, in becoming an autonomous adult within a group, one learns a grasp of what might be called the 'ethical logistics' involved in the management of personal transactions within that group, the means to coordinate the different responsibilities involved in negotiating the social construction of meanings (Shotter, 1993b).

But yet more than this is involved in learning how properly to 'position' oneself within particular speech genres than the ways of sense-making they entail, for speech genres can be characterized by the 'topics' they embody, the sources in terms of which utterances belonging to the genre are formulated. If this is so, then the character of our 'inwardness' – the way we appear (or feel we should appear) to ourselves – will depend upon the speech genres within which we account for ourselves (Gergen, 1989). Where, as Billig (1987; Billig et al. 1988) argues, many of the 'topics' within a genre are dilemmatic; that is,they are two-sided. Hence, even within a genre, quite different argumentative positions may be intelligibly formulated. If this is so, then our 'basic' ways of talking about ourselves are neither so closed nor so limited as to wholly exclude alternatives. Thus, our account of internalization as an ethico-rhetorical phenomenon clearly has a number of further strands to it worth investigating. I shall study Billig's (1987, 1991; Billig et al. 1988), Bakhtin's (1981, 1984, 1986), and Vico's (1965, 1968, 1988) contributions in more detail in the next chapter, and attempt there to make more prominent some of the alternatives till now ignored in our current 'basic' ways of talking. Where it is important to understand our own part in their construction, for, as I have said before, it is only from within the contested social realities they sustain, that we can reach out to attempt to make contact with that which is other than ourselves.

Notes

1. 'The outwardly actualized utterance is an island rising from the boundless sea of inner speech . . . ' (Volosinov, 1973: 96).

2. Raymond Williams (1977: 132) uses the term 'structures of feeling' to characterize meanings and values as they are actively lived and felt; while Vico (1968: paras. 141–2) calls it the 'sensus communis' of a class; it is 'judgment without reflection.'

3. I am hesitant about the word 'normative' here. I do not want to suggest that there are, in general, any pre-established normative conventions ruling conversational moves or responses; the forming of a felicitous response is a matter of 'fitting' it into the momentarily available conversational context at the time. Its 'fittingness' is a matter, not of it according with prior norms, but of it as a 'sensible' response to a previous speaker's utterance, in the developing development of the conversation.

4. Where, as Wittgenstein (1953) noted, it is seemingly impossible to 'weld' such investigations into 'a natural order without breaks', i.e., to form a coherent 'picture' of the terrain as such: 'And this was, of course, connected with the very nature of the investigation. For this compels us to travel over a wide field of thought criss-cross in every direction.—The philosophical remarks in this book are, as it were, a number of sketches of landscapes which were made in the course of these long and involved journeyings' (1953: ix).

5. 'The real foundations of his enquiry do not strike a man at all. Unless *that* fact has at some time struck him' (Wittgenstein, 1953: 129).

6. Wittgenstein (1953: 227) formulated the difficulty here as follows: it is 'to put all indefiniteness, correctly and unfalsified, into words'. This is why there is a 'difficulty of renouncing all theory: One has to regard what appears so obviously incomplete, as something complete' (1980, I: no. 723).

7. 'Ahead of what I can see and perceive, there is, it is true, nothing more actually visible, but my world is carried forward by lines of intentionality which trace out in advance at least the style of what is to come' (Merleau-Ponty, 1962: 416).

8. If, that is, this way of talking in terms of 'seeing' is the right way to talk about the matter at all. In another vocabulary altogether, a speech communicational one, we might simply say instead that the account of joint action I provide, furnishes us with a vocabulary that enables rational discussion of the process of social construction to take place – without any mention of any mysterious, inner processes of conceptual 'seeing'.

9. Some here may want to speak of 'landscapes with their horizons', but this seems to me to be too static a metaphor. Drawing upon my own experiences of sailing, I prefer talk of 'seascapes'.

10. Basic in a political-moral (and methodological) sense if not the ontological sense: that is, I want to argue that, even if there is no already fixed *basis* in terms of which to 'root' or to 'ground' our claims, we can still nonetheless identify the 'place' or 'sphere of activity' within which the *judging* of people's claims can be located. The 'grounds' for settling arguments are to be found within arguments themselves, not outside them, and hence the moment when politics is at its most intense is to be found there too. A lack of 'foundations' is not a lack of bases for judgment. This is not to say, however, that it is in the sphere of verbal interaction that, ontologically, we should seek the developmental *origins* of all our verbal formulations.

11. Although I have not the space available to discuss the matter at length here, conversational realities should be sharply distinguished from disciplinary (academic) discourses (Foucault, 1972). In open conversation, one switches from metaphor to metaphor as one pleases, according to the requirements of the conversation. In a disciplinary discourse, certain metaphors are literalized into 'pictures' or 'models', and talk within them is disciplined by the 'order' required to sustain such a 'picture' within one's talk (Shotter, 1991b, 1993b). A 'basic' way of talking is sustained (at least at first), not so much by a 'picture' as by certain institutionalized practices.

12. Here we might also talk of *formative or architectonic tendencies* . . . a bit of extra vocabulary is always useful.

13. That is, the complex affective and communicational intentionalities in actual acts of speaking, intentionalities which change and 'temporally develop' as an utterance is executed, must be replaced by something merely imaginable: an already completed, spatialized image.

14. In this view, the emergence of 'representation' is due to the fact that, as linguistic competency increases, one becomes more adept in constructing a network of *intralinguistic* references to function as a context into which to direct one's utterances. In other words, there is a move away from a reliance upon the sense of one's speech, i.e. a

reliance upon a referent in the immediate, shared context, and a move toward a reliance upon meaning and syntax, i.e. upon links within what has already been, or with what might be, said. In essence, this is a decrease of reference to what 'is' with a consequent increase of reference to what 'might be', an increased reference to an hermeneutically constructed imaginary (or theoretical) world.

As a result, what is said requires less and less grounding in an extralinguistic context – for it can find its supports almost wholly within a new, intralinguistically constructed context. Thus one can tell people about (represent to them or give them an account of) situations not actually at the moment present. Such a consequence requires, however, the development of methods for *warranting* in the course of one's talk (i.e. giving support to) one's claims about what 'might be' as being in fact what 'is' – one must learn to say, for instance, when making a claim about a state of affairs, that others saw it that way too, and so on. By the use of such methods and procedures, adults can construct their statements as factual statements, and adult forms of speech can thus come to function with a large degree of independence from their immediate context.

15. This, as we shall discover, is the wrong term, if 'express' is taken to mean representing in an order of words the supposed order of one's thoughts (the 'picture theory'). 'Experience teaches us that thought does not express itself in words, but rather realizes itself in them' (Vygotsky, 1986: 251).

16. Vygotsky (1986) distinguishes between words as in a dictionary (which have a *meaning*) and words in use in a context (which have a *sense*). 'A word acquires its sense from the context in which it appears; in different contexts, it changes its sense. Meaning remains stable throughout the changes of sense. The dictionary meaning of a word is no more than a stone in the edifice of sense, no more than a potentiality that finds diversified realization in speech' (1986: 245).

17. Vygotsky (1986: 240–2) illustrates this with an anecdote from Dostoevsky's *The Diary of a Writer*, in which Dostoevsky relates a conversation between six drunks, who traverse an intricate landscape of positions and evaluations in their utterances, in turn, of the same unprintable word with six different intonations.

18. 'The idea of the *conventionality, the arbitrariness of language*, is a typical one for rationalism as a whole, and no less typical is the *comparison of language to the system of mathematical signs*. What interests the mathematically minded rationalist is not the relationship of the sign to the actual reality it reflects nor to the individual who is its originator, but the *relationship of sign to sign within a closed system* already accepted and authorized. In other words, they are interested only in the *inner logic of the system of signs itself*, taken, as in algebra, completely independently of the ideological meanings that give the signs their content' (Volosinov, 1973: 57–8). See also Wittgenstein (1953: no. 81).

19. 'It is misleading . . . to talk of thinking as a "mental activity". We may say that thinking is essentially the activity of operating with signs' (Wittgenstein, 1965: 6).

3
Dialogue and Rhetoric in the Construction of Social Relations

> The actual reality of language-speech is not the abstract system of linguistic forms, not the isolated monologic utterance, and not the psychophysiological act of its implementation, but the social event of verbal interaction implemented in an utterance or utterances. Thus, verbal interaction is the basic reality of language.
>
> Volosinov, 1973: 94

In moving on further towards a grasp of our 'basic' ways of talking, it will be useful to turn both to Volosinov's, Bahktin's and to Wittgenstein's accounts of the dialogic nature of speech communication, and to explore what might be called the primary rhetorical–responsive function of *utterances* – in these accounts (as in Vygotsky's), the referential–representational function of speech becomes a secondary and derived function. In particular, we shall be interested in the *method of comparisons* Wittgenstein introduced in his *Philosophical Investigations* (1953) for bringing many important features of our language and our ways of talking to our attention. Although we may not be able to accurately and correctly represent the nature of our everyday ways of talking theoretically, that does not prevent us from introducing other special ways of talking *through* which to perceive certain of their features, special ways of talking that work to draw our attention to certain characteristics that we would otherwise ignore. Certain metaphors play a central part in these special ways of talking, not only the *metaphor* of 'language-games' in all their different varieties, but many others: of words as being *like* 'tools' or 'instruments'; of them as being *like* the other items in a 'tool box' too, such as the glue and nails; of our knowledge of language being *like* our knowledge of an 'ancient city'; of words as being *like* the 'handles in the cab of a steam locomotive'; and so on. These all function as aids in making various points both about the nature of language and of our knowledge of it, by drawing our attention to differences between such models and our actual linguistic activities and practices.

Like Volosinov and Bakhtin, Wittgenstein is also concerned to combat the misleading comparison of language with a system of mathematical signs operating according to strict rules, a calculus. As he saw it, the temptation to identify the use of words with games and calculi, and to say someone who is using language *must* be playing such a game, is to be resisted – you must even resist saying that it is *nearly* like it. For, 'if you say that our languages only *approximate* to such calculi you are standing upon the brink of a misunderstanding. For then it may look as if we are talking about an *ideal* language', (Wittgenstein, 1953: no. 81) when none such exists (at least, so he would claim). Our use of language is not as if it is *ideally* according to rules, but in practice falls short – like bodies falling under gravity are prevented by air resistance from achieving their ideal velocity; the context or conditions to which it is sensitive in its use are of a different kind entirely. Yet the comparison is useful nonetheless for the differences it reveals. Rather than rationality-as-representation, we have here a rationality-achieved-through-contrasts (Edwards, 1982). Bakhtin and Volosinov also are concerned to combat the notion of language-as-a-system. They take utterances, or words in their speaking, rather than sentences, or patterns of already spoken words, as the basic unit of dialogic speech communication, and it is to their account of the utterance as the basic analytic unit of speech communication that we now turn.

Utterances

Bakhtin feels that the claim, made by such linguists as Saussure (followed, of course, by Chomsky) that the single sentence, with all its individuality and monologic creativity, can be regarded as a completely free combination of forms of language, is not true of utterances. Actual utterances in a dialogue must take into account the (already linguistically shaped) context to which they are a response, and into which they are directed. Thus for Bakhtin (1986: 91):

> Any concrete utterance is a link in the chain of speech communication of a particular sphere. The very boundaries of the utterance are determined by a change of speech subjects. Utterances are not indifferent to one another, and are not self-sufficient; they are aware of and mutually reflect one another . . . Every utterance must be regarded as primarily a *response* to preceding utterances of the given sphere (we understand the word 'response' here in the broadest sense). Each utterance refutes, affirms, supplements, and relies upon the others, presupposes them to be known, and somehow takes them into account . . . Therefore, each kind of utterance is filled with various kinds of responsive reactions to other utterances of the given sphere of speech communication.

Listening too must be responsive, in that listeners must be preparing themselves to respond to what they are hearing. Indeed,

> when the listener perceives and understands the meaning (the language meaning) of speech, he simultaneously takes an active, responsive attitude

> toward it. He either agrees or disagrees with it (completely or partially), augments it, applies it, prepares for its execution, and so on. And the listener adopts this responsive attitude for the entire duration of the process of listening and understanding, from the very beginning – sometimes literally from the speaker's first word. (1986: 68)

And the speaker too, instead of a passive understanding that 'only duplicates his [or her] own idea in someone else's mind' (Bahktin, 1986: 69), also talks with an active expectation of a response, an agreement, sympathy, challenge, criticism, objection, obedience, and so on. In other words, the rhetorical–responsive form of understanding at work in the practical conduct of a dialogue, is very different in kind from the representational–referential form of understanding required of a reader of a text, concerned with what the text is 'about': speakers, unlike readers, must be almost continuously sensitive to the intervention of another 'voice'. Indeed, with this in mind, I want to add another component to this 'responsive' or 'bodily reactive' account of an utterance's meaning: the idea – following Billig's (1987; Billig et al. 1988) work upon the rhetorical, and ideological, nature of speech communication – that our utterances are not, of course, always acceptable to, or accepted by others. They respond to what we say or do with criticisms, with challenges to justify ourselves, and we must show how our actions 'fit in with' theirs (Mills, 1940). Acceptable responses must be negotiated within a context of argumentation. Hence my designation of this account of language use as not just *responsive*, but as *rhetorical–responsive*.[1] When a person utters a word, whose word is it? For 'a word is territory shared by both addresser and addressee, by speaker and his interlocutor . . . The immediate social situation and the broader social milieu wholly determine – and determine *from within*, so to speak – the structure of an utterance' (Volosinov, 1973: 86). Where here, of course, its structure does not inhere in the formal pattern of syntax it can be seen as matching (or approximating), but in its responsive voicing, the temporal unfolding of its intoning: as angry, indignant, confident, arrogant, apologetic, indifferent, as inviting or repulsing reply, and so on.

Further, it is important to add that Volosinov and Bakhtin do not see the contexts of our speech as ever being an isolated, ahistorical kind. The claim that any concrete utterance is a link in the stream or chain of speech communication of a particular sphere, means, as they see it, that in being responsive, our utterances always strike into an ongoing flow of conversation of one kind or another. And it is this, the historical nature of the ways of talking in question, not the fact of our language belonging to a system, that influences the acceptability of our forms of talk to those to whom it is addressed, where the ease of its acceptance is a question of whether we are speaking in one or another of the more institutionalized centres of social life, or on the more disorganized peripheries. As they see it:

> Social psychology is first and foremost an atmosphere made up of multifarious speech performances that engulf and wash over all persistent forms and kinds of ideological creativity: unofficial discussions, exchanges of opinion at the theatre or concert or at various kinds of social gatherings, purely chance exchanges of words, one's manner of verbal reaction to happenings in one's life and daily existence, one's inner-world manner of identifying oneself and identifying one's position in society, and so on. Social psychology exists primarily in a wide variety of forms of the 'utterance', of little *speech genres* of internal and external kinds – things left completely unstudied to the present day . . . All these forms of speech interchange operate in extremely close connection with the conditions of the social situation in which they occur and exhibit extraordinary sensitivity to the fluctuations in the social atmosphere. (Volosinov, 1973: 19–20).

In the more institutionalized centres of social life, with a competence in the more orderly genres in place there, we will be able to speak with sensitivity to the fluctuations in social atmosphere, and expect (mostly) to be routinely understood – such a sensitivity is a part of what it is for us to be competent in these spheres. However, on the more disorderly margins of social life, we cannot expect such routine understanding; a more negotiated, back-and-forth process is to be expected. But even here, on the margins – as is only too predictable – life is not without its historically foreseeable characteristics.

To sum up: the importance of this account of utterances lies in the way in which it opens it up to study, those *dialogical or interactive moments* when and where there is a 'gap' in the stream of communication between two (or more) speaking subjects. And no matter how *systematic* the speech of each may be while speaking,[2] when one has finished speaking and the other can respond, the bridging of that 'gap' is an opportunity for a completely unique, unrepeatable response, one that is 'crafted' or 'tailored' to fit the unique circumstances of its utterance. Indeed, it is on the boundary between two consciousnesses, two subjects, that the *life* – whatever it is that is 'living' in the communicative act – is manifested (Bakhtin, 1986: 106). Thus we can appreciate, as Volosinov (1973: 68) says, that:

> What the speaker values is not that aspect of the form which is invariably identical in all instances of its usage, despite the nature of those instances, but that aspect of the linguistic form because of which it can figure in the given, concrete context, because of which it becomes a sign adequate to the conditions of the given, concrete situation. We can express it this way: *what is important for the speaker about the linguistic form is not that it is a stable and always self-equivalent signal, but that it is an always changeable and adaptable sign.*

Further, the account emphasizes how supportive, so to speak, the speech context is, to the life of linguistic signs. Thus, just as the effect produced by poking a stick into a stream of water depends upon the whole character of the flow of water at the time – with different effects depending upon the power (or lack of it) already in the stream's flow – so for us, the effect of our words depends upon where in the stream of communication they occur. It is in their 'rooting' in the stream of communication, in their responsive connection to the other voices in that stream, that our words have their 'life' – by their use, we continually live out our connections to the others around us. Indeed, in both Billig's and Bakhtin's views, even within the speech of a single individual or the writing of a single author, as an event in the stream, in a living text or utterance many 'voices' can be at work, and as such, 'gaps' can be found in what they say or write that prompt us to affectively react to what they have to say, to a responsive understanding of it.[3] With Vygotsky's notion of 'instructional' forms of speech in mind, along with the Bakhtin/Billig, rhetorical–responsive account of speech communication, it will be useful to return to the problem of our 'basic', embodied forms of talk to examine their nature further. For, if the 'gaps' in our forms of talk are not bridged systematically and automatically, how are they bridged in our everyday talk? Here we shall find Vico's account of a culture's common sense, and the working of rhetorical forms of communication important.

The importance of the *sensus communis*, rhetoric and metaphor

Elsewhere (Shotter, 1984, 1986, 1991a, 1993b), I have discussed Vico's account of the origins of a culture's 'common sense' (*sensus communis*). Briefly here: the social processes involved, he claims, are based not upon anything pre-established either in people or their surroundings, but in socially shared *identities of feeling* they themselves create in the flow of activity between them. These, he calls 'sensory topics' – 'topics' (Gr. *topos* = 'place') because they give rise to 'commonplaces', that is, to shared moments in a flow of social activity which afford common reference, and 'sensory' because they are moments in which shared *feelings* for already shared circumstances are created. A paradigm situation here is everyone running to take shelter from thunder; everyone's responsive reaction to the fear expressed in the character of people's bodily activities gives a shared *sense* to an *already shared* circumstance. It is at this point that he introduced the idea of an 'imaginative universal': in the case of thunder, this is Jove, the image of a giant being speaking giant words, but one can easily imagine other such shared circumstances in which shared feeling, expressed in the same responsive, bodily reactions, might occur – the birth of a child, the death of a group member, and so on. Thus these first anchor points are to do, not with 'seeing' in common, but with 'feeling' in common, with the 'giving' or 'lending' of a shared *significance* to shared *feelings* in an *already shared* circumstance. In other words, the first mute language is the immediate responsive-representation in gesture of a moment or place of common reference, where the gesture functions *metaphorically*, not to refer to something already known about, but to indicate an 'is', to *establish* a 'something' with common significance.

What Vico outlines above, then, is a poetic image, a metaphor, in terms of which one might understand the *mute*, extraordinary, common-sense basis for an articulate language – where such a basis constitutes the unsystematized, primordial contents of the human mind, its basic paradigms or prototypes. These are the feelings or intuitions – the sensory topics or commonplaces that make up the basis of a community's *sensus communis* – in terms of which our first words can have their sense, and against which, much later, the adequacy of our concepts may be judged.

Vico was particularly interested in what might be called 'civic rhetoric' and the problem of what constituted good government (Mooney, 1985; Schaeffer, 1990), but he developed his views against a background within which the tradition of rhetoric was under attack by the new 'geometric method' of reasoning promoted by the Cartesians. And to an extent, his arguments constitute a counter-attack upon it, for he saw it as completely inimical to his concerns. In his *On the Study Methods of Our Time* (first published in 1709), he defends rhetoric on many grounds, but particularly upon the necessity for eloquence in one's speech: for, says Vico, quoting Cardinal Ludvico Madruzzi, 'Rulers should see to it not only that their actions are true and in conformity with justice, but that they *seem* to be so [to everyone]' (Vico, 1965: 36). In other words, those who are satisfied with abstract truth alone, and do not bother to find out whether their opinion is shared by the generality of people, cause political calamities. Thus, not only should politicians judge human actions as they actually *are*, rather than in terms of what they think they *ought* to be, they should also – in terms of the *sensus communis* – be able eloquently to persuade the people of their judgment's correctness. But how might such persuading be done? What is involved in us accepting (if not the absolute truth) the truth of a claim relative to our current circumstances?

Here we are back again at our original problem – the understanding of that speech which, rather than simply influencing us in our intellects, 'moves' us to accept its claims in our very being – but we are now in a somewhat stronger position to confront its nature. The problem arises when we give *reasons* for any claims we may make; for why should these reasons be accepted as a *proof* of the claim?

They are accepted, suggests Vico, not because we as speakers supply a demonstrable proof, a full syllogistic structure which our listeners are passively compelled (logically) to accept. But because in their incomplete, enthymemic structure, we offer initially unconnected premises that (most of) our audience will be able to connect up for us – and feel that it is they who have 'seen' the point! They themselves make the connection by drawing upon the (perhaps in themselves inarticulable) *topoi* in the *sensus communis* already existing between them and us as speakers. Hence, for Vico, the importance in rhetoric, of what he calls the 'art of topics' [*ars topica*]. Where 'argument' in this art

> is not 'the arrangement of a proof', as commonly assumed, what in Latin is known as *argumentatio*; rather, it is that third idea which is found to tie together the two in the issue being debated – what in the Schools is called the 'middle term' – such that topics is the art of finding the middle term. But I claim more: Topics is the art of apprehending the true, for it is the art of seeing all the aspects or *loci* of a thing that enable us to distinguish it well and gain an adequate concept of it. For judgments turn out to be false when their concepts are either greater or lesser than the things they propose to signify . . . ' (Vico, 1988: 178, though I have preferred Mooney's (1985: 134) translation here)

So, the special nature of the speech that we use here works to create the 'space' in which a 'proof' can come into existence as such. Grassi (1980: 20), a Vico scholar, characterizes this kind of speech as

> immediately a 'showing' – and for this reason 'figurative' or 'imaginative', and thus in the original sense 'theoretical' [*theorein* – i.e. to see]. It is metaphorical, i.e. it shows something which has a sense, and this means that to the figure, to that which is shown, the speech transfers [*metapherein*] a signification;[4] in this way the speech which realizes this showing 'leads before the eyes' [*phainesthai*] a significance.

This, says Grassi, is *true rhetorical speech*; it is nonconceptual, moving and indicative; it does not just function persuasively, but practically: the metaphor is central to it. In transferring[5] significance from the *sensus communis* to what is said, a metaphor makes 'visible', or 'shows', listeners a common quality that is not rationally deducible. As such, it cannot be 'explained' in any way (either from within an academic discourse, or in any other way); indeed, it is the speech which is the basis of all rational thought. Thus, it is with such a way of talking that we must begin all our investigations.[6]

After theory: A critical descriptive approach

Until recently (until these so-called 'Postmodern' times), we in the West, in our attempts to make sense of our social lives, seem to have been entrapped in what might be called a modernist 'way of theory'[7] – a procedure that has worked very effectively in aiding our 'mastery' of the 'natural' world, but which gives us nothing but trouble when applied to our social lives. As with the natural world, so with our social lives, we have felt motivated by a desire to be able, contemplatively, as an external observer of it, to survey a whole *order*. Indeed, associated with the modern way of theory is a strong (in fact) embodied compulsion to search for such a form of knowledge, for without it, without an inner mental picture, an orderly, mentally surveyable image of a 'subject matter's' structure, we feel that our knowledge is of a quite inadequate kind. Without such a compulsion, much of our present academic activity would make little sense to us. Thus, in our studies we have attempted to treat sets of essentially historical, often still temporally developing events, retrospectively and reflectively – as if they are a set of 'already made' events in which we are not involved – with the overarching aim of bringing them all under a unitary, orderly, conceptual scheme. Thus, in following the way of theory, the project of individual researchers becomes that of formulating, monologically, a single framework to function as a 'structured container' for all such events, thus to create a stable, coherent and intelligible order amongst them, one that can be intellectually grasped in a detached, uninvolved way, by individual readers of the theoretical (textual) formulations they write.

In discussing the source of this compulsion, we could argue, of course, that such a project manifests a dream that has come down to us, through the Enlightenment, from the ancient Greeks. Indeed, we might articulate the dream thus: if there is an already determined but 'hidden' inner *order* to be discerned in things, then it might be possible to 'see' into their inner workings and interconnections so well (as if with a God's-eye view) as to be able to 'play' through possibly important sequences of events, ahead of time, thus to be ready for them in some way when they occur. And thus, we could *rationally* justify it as such. But that would be to misdescribe its character entirely. For, as Wittgenstein (1969: no. 151) points out, this is not a form of knowledge amenable to doubt or justification; it is 'an absolutely solid part of our *method* of doubt and enquiry'; our enquiries must come to an end somewhere, 'but the end is not an ungrounded presupposition: it is an ungrounded way of acting' (1969: no. 109). In other words, just as for the Dinka or the Hopi – who literally do not know how to doubt that, for them, the influences we speak of as in our heads, are in their surroundings – so for us. We find the idea that our thought goes on in our heads, and that it consists in inner representations of outer states of affairs, so basic to our way of being in the world, that we (almost) do not know how to doubt it. It is *basically* what we 'are' to ourselves, and what our world 'is' for us. Yet doubt it we must, if we want to grasp the nature of our third, sensuous, involved kind of knowing. But how might we provoke such a doubt within ourselves, let alone the task of giving it intelligible expression?

Here we must turn to Wittgenstein's (1953, 1969, 1980) account of our language use. First, we must note (as is well known) that the meaning of our words shows up, he claims, in their use. In other words, if we think of words as being reflexively like the tools of the carpenter, in that they can be used both (i) for the doing of many things to do with shaping and joining, and making a difference to things, but also (ii) as reminders for the general kinds of functions they can serve, then we can perhaps appreciate one of his most basic claims: that 'grammar tells us what kind of object anything is' (1953: no. 373). For it is a person's choice of words as they shape and formulate their utterances – sensing the adequacy of what they are saying to what they feel is the subject matter of their talk – that reveals the *essence* (for them) of what they are talking about. Thus, for Wittgenstein, a wrong description of a usage is *not* one 'that does not accord with established usage', but 'one which does not accord with the practice of the person giving the description' (1980, I: no. 548).

In other words, the crucial event to focus upon is not speaking in general, but upon this or that particular act of speaking; and the task is to describe (critically) the influences at work in its shaping; that is, not to say theoretically what *must* be the case in general, in principle, on the basis of evidence, etc., but to be able to say in particular, according to an utterance's particular circumstances, what the influences are at work in it – '*in spite of* an urge to misunderstand them [those workings]' (1953: no. 109). This is why the kind of description we need is a *critical description*: for we must overcome the compulsions and urges we feel as to what a supposed proper understanding here is like (that is, those I have identified as belonging to the way of theory), and we must search for a new kind of understanding. But how can we investigate the nature of something that lacks specificity, whose very openness to being specified or determined by those involved in it is its central defining feature?

This is where Wittgenstein's notion of 'perspicuous representations' play their part (Edwards, 1982). In breaking away from the way of theory, he set up the metaphor of language-games, not to serve as an idealization (as a usual first move, prior to the production of a rigorous theory), but for another reason altogether:

> Our clear and simple language-games are not preparatory studies for a future regularization of language – as it were approximations, ignoring friction and air resistance. The language-games are rather set up as *objects of comparison* which are meant to throw light on the facts of our language by way not only of similarities, but also of dissimilarities. (1953: no. 130).[8]

We must not begin with a preconceived idea to which the reality of our language *must* correspond (if our idea of it is to be correct); what we want is something with which to contrast it, some measuring rod or instrument which, by its very existence, serves to create a dimension (or dimensions) of comparison, a way of talking about the character of what it is we want to study, where each 'instrument' reveals interconnections between aspects and characteristics otherwise unnoticed. Thus all the metaphors used by Wittgenstein (many of them already mentioned above), bring to our attention aspects of language, and of our knowledge of language, that were previously rationally-invisible to us, such as its 'rule-like' features, the characteristics of its 'boundaries', its 'archeology', and so on. They serve the function of creating

> an order in our knowledge of the use of language: an order with a particular end in view; one out of many possible orders; not *the* order. To this end we shall constantly be giving prominence to distinctions which our ordinary forms of language easily make us overlook . . .' (1953: no. 132).

Such metaphors cannot *represent* any already fixed orders in our use of language, for by their very nature in being open to determination in the context of their occurrence, they do not belong to any such orders. But what they do do for us, in artificially creating an order where none before existed, is to make an aspect of our use of language 'pictureable'; that is, to both (1) make that aspect of our language use 'rationally-visible' (in Garfinkel's terms) and thus publicly discussable and debatable; and also, (2) make it into a 'psychological instrument' (in Vygotsky's terms) and thus into something, a practical resource, with which and through which we can think, act and perceive.

Practical-theory or analytic 'tools'

In this view, then, the task of characterizing the nature of conversational realities is not, if Wittgenstein is correct, the theoretical one, of trying in the face of countless previous failures to present a now claimed correct 'view' of the true nature of our human being as linguistic creatures; no 'view' as such is possible. The task is of a more partial and particular kind: it is that of providing, in the articulation of certain aspects of its nature, a number of perspicuous representations, or psychological instruments, appropriate to their understanding – where, the kind of understanding provided is in the 'seeing of connections' between otherwise seemingly unconnected aspects of our lives. To this end, among others, I have introduced the following notions: besides those of perspicuous representations and psychological instruments themselves, those of 'joint action'; Bakhtin's notions of the 'utterance' and of 'responsive understanding'; Billig's extension of responsive understanding into a 'rhetorical' context;

Vico's notions of 'sensory topics', 'imaginative universals', and his concern with *ars topica*, that is, with the rhetorical enthymeme in which an argumentative structure, unavailable to an individual speaker, is completed by the speaker's audience as an aspect of joint action.

In previous chapters, I have introduced the concept of knowing 'from within', 'rational-invisibility', 'traditions of argumentation', the 'negotiated nature of social phenomena', and other such notions. All these are examples of what elsewhere (Shotter, 1984: 40), I have called practical-theory: these ways of speaking, terms of art, metaphors, or images, all function as probes or prostheses, as 'objects of comparison', as 'measuring-rods', *through* which like blind person's sticks, or, like telescopes or microscopes in other sciences, we can 'see' influences at work which would remain otherwise rationally-invisible to us. They are 'tools' of use to us in accounting for our claims as what is actually occurring in the disorderly zones of uncertainty in which we conduct the politically negotiable aspects of our everyday social lives. For too long in our social sciences, we have hidden these political struggles from publicly debatable investigation by the assumption that social life is a 'natural' phenomenon just like all others, which, as an already orderly and coherent process (the systems view), merely awaits our discovery of its 'laws'. Thus, rather than as still developing socio-historical constructions constitutive of our own being, as social scientists, we have treated our social orders as if already made entities in our 'external' world, as seemingly separate 'containers' for us as already psychologically self-contained, individual beings. We have not realized that what we ourselves experience as our own *being*, and what we experience as the *being*[9] of our world, are both determined by us and for us in all the self–other relationships in which we are involved as we develop into adults and are inducted into current social scientific traditions of investigation and debate. We have not realized that these self–other relationships are constitutive for us of what I have called the dimension of our person–world relations. Thus, all those seemingly minor moments we each experience, in which we find ourselves 'put in our place', when all taken together, result in the positioning of each of us in our place in the overall political scheme of things. By making these disorderly moments rationally-visible, by critically describing them from within the event itself, we can bring into view the character of the social negotiations, conflicts and struggles involved in the production, reproduction and transformation of our current social orders.

For us in the West, enthralled by the power of theory, it has long seemed as if we can *individually* investigate the character of the 'world' around us. We now must begin to face the fact that such an activity is only possible if what we study is already ordered. In the movement to a postmodern science of mental life, the assumption that we all live within the same social order cannot be sustained; we have to accept that there is no single, already made meaningful order to be found in our social lives. But if that is the case, if there is no *a priori* social order, if our practical, everyday activities take place in, and deal with, a pluralistic, only fragmentarily known, and only partially shared social world, then we must turn away from the project of attempting to understand our social lives through the imposition of monologic, theoretical systems of order, and turn to a study of the more dialogic forms of practical-moral knowledge in terms of which they are lived. For the task now is to invent appropriate practical-theoretical devices – that is, the apposite perspicuous representations – that work to render rationally-visible the influences at work upon us, thus to fashion them as topics of public discussion and debate.

Conclusions: Dialogical versus monological practices

Let me now try to draw upon the resources arrayed above to form some conclusions about our future practices in this kind of social constructionist research. We can first note that thinking of our own intellectual traditions as 'living', dialogical traditions, or as multi-voiced 'traditions of argumentation', gives us a very different view of what intellectual progress is. Traditionally, in the mainstream, as I have already mentioned, we have seen progress as arising out of different hierarchically structured, monological systems of knowledge being pitted against each other in a Neo-Darwinian struggle for supremacy. Billig and Bakhtin, however, allow us to see the whole process in quite a different light: as a multi-voiced activity, with both centre (or centres) and margins, forming a tradition of argumentation that affords a set of positions to a whole plurality of consciousnesses, each with their own world. Where, instead of being oriented to the usual scientific tasks of prediction and control, or mastery and possession, the new task would be simply that of understanding: 'that understanding which consists in "seeing connections" ' (Wittgenstein, 1953: no. 122), and, I will add, also in 'making' connections.

This, as I have already said, is a form of rationality-achieved-through-contrasts, rather than rationality-as-representation. In it, we bring out the nature of what *we* do, *our* practices by comparison with what others (actual and invented) do, or don't do. We make use of the notion of language-games, not to explain our use of language, but simply to note what in a certain context of language use we seem to be doing; and often that is sufficient. For some things we just do understand in practice without the need of any analysis or explanation. If we always had to understand a person's reply to our questions by use, say, of a logical or scientific analysis to *explain* them, the ordinary play of questions and answers in everyday life (as well as the understanding of the logical or scientific analysis) would be impossible. But clearly, this form of understanding – that consists in seeing connections – depends upon the use of that special form of true rhetorical speech that, as Vico and Grassi suggest, relies upon its dialogical and metaphorical nature. It is not a form of reasoning that can be conducted by individuals alone, nor can it be mechanized. Thus, in the current atmosphere, in which such forms are valued, we cannot expect the transition to such dialogical and metaphorical ways of reasoning to be to an easy one. We can expect a struggle: with current monological forms of reasoning at the centre attempting to repel or expel dialogical forms out onto the margins. For, 'monologism, at its extreme, denies the existence outside itself of another consciousness with equal rights and equal responsibilities, another *I* with equal rights (thou). With a monologic approach (in its extreme or pure form) *another person* remains wholly and merely an *object* of consciousness. Monologue is finalized and deaf to the other's response, does not expect it and does not acknowledge in it any *decisive* force' (Bakhtin 1984: 292–3).

And this is, of course, the traditional scientific view of things: we treat what we are studying as an object of thought in order to form theories to guide our further, deliberate actions in relation to it. Our representations of things suggest to us ways in which they can be manipulated and which give us power over them. Lacking such 'inner' pictures, we feel an uncertainty, a lack of confidence in an our knowledge; we don't quite know were we stand.

But this urge for certainty cannot be satisfied in dialogue. For traditions of argumentation, the multi-voiced polyphony of a world in dialogic discussion with itself cannot be 'pictured'. However, instead of certainty (as accuracy of representation), we can concern ourselves with adequacy, with doing justice to the being of what we are studying (Shotter, 1991b, 1993b). Where, according to Bakhtin, 'the single adequate form for *verbally expressing* authentic human life is the *open-ended* dialogue. Life by its very nature is dialogic. To live means to participate in dialogue: to ask questions, to heed, to respond, to agree, and so forth. In this dialogue a person participates wholly and throughout his whole life: with his eyes, lips, hands, soul, spirit, with his whole body and deeds' (Bakhtin, 1984: 293). Those denied this possibility can, to say the least, be expected to feel humiliated and angered.

Thus, within a research tradition organized around dialogical, rather than monological practices, instead of the simple Darwinian struggle for the survival of the supposedly fittest theory (representing an already existing order), we can expect to see a whole host of other and new kinds of struggle. Especially, we can expect struggles to do with claims of an ethical kind, to do with what is involved in treating others (and otherness) with due respect – to replace the struggles we have had in the past over how they (and it) might best be manipulated. Thus, we can expect a concern with fashioning new orders of relationship (out of chaos). Consequently, we can expect contests between different perspicuous representations; that is, between different metaphorical accounts which 'give form' to our circumstances in ways which have not been 'seen' before, providing novel understandings 'making new connections'.[10] We can also expect to see such representations, and claims for their worth, issuing from many different 'positions' in the tradition other than from within the mainstream (centre). Further, such claims will not just be critical of the mainstream, but of each other also. There will be struggles too between different genres of writing, and the form-producing ideologies, that is, the 'imaginary worlds', they embody. Indeed, the study of writers' practices, rather than their content, can be expected to extend to a study of the *tone* in which they write, for the different dialogical opportunities for relationship (and being) offered to readers by authors will become important.[11] Finally, there will be political struggles over which representations of a 'worldview' should be 'literalized' into an 'world-order'. For, in what is now becoming an almost world-wide phenomenon, those who are concerned with finding a 'history' or a 'tradition' of their own, have begun to object to the monological, ahistorical systems of 'central-planning and administration' which exclude them.

Indeed, as we move out of a political world of supposed equals, of people existing as indistinguishable atoms, psychologically, all in competition with one another for *power*, and move into a political world of people possessing psychological characteristics according to their 'positions' in relation to each other, we begin to see a whole different dynamic at work. Instead of a 'politics of power', a new 'politics of identity' is beginning, a politics of access to or exclusion from a political economy of ontological opportunities for different ways of being. If one is to participate in this political economy with equal opportunity, then 'membership' of the community of struggle, the tradition of argumentation, cannot be conditional: one must feel one has a right, unconditionally, to 'belong'. And these claims to 'belong' are now being posed by a whole host of groups previously marginalized by professional academics: not only women, black and other ethnic movements, ecologists, and so on, but also many others without 'expert' or 'professional' credentials. We are moving into a new world of problems posed by a genuine recognition of the importance of differences rather than similarities, and the importance of that world in influencing the character of the questions we now feel it crucial to pursue.

Notes

1. 'There is no reason for saying that meaning belongs to a word as such. In essence, meaning belongs to a word in its position between speakers; that is, meaning is realized only in the process of active, responsive understanding . . . meaning is the effect of interaction between speaker and listener produced via the material of a particular sound complex' (Volosinov, 1973: 102–3).

2. Although, here too, Bakhtin points out that other 'voices' are at work: 'The word cannot be assigned to a single speaker. The author (speaker) has his own inalienable right to the word, but the listener has his rights, and those whose voices are heard in the word before the author comes upon it also have their rights (after all, there are no words that belong to no one)' (Bakhtin, 1986: 121–2).

3. Indeed, the talk of a single person may exhibit what Bakhtin calls 'hidden dialogicality', that is, 'although only one person is speaking . . . [each] uttered word responds and reacts with its every fiber to [an] invisible speaker, points to something outside itself, beyond its own limits, to the unspoken words of another person' (Bahktin, 1984: 197).

4. Rorty (1989: 19) approves of 'the Davidson claim that metaphors do not have meanings . . .', and takes it as implying that we cannot therefore *argue* for new ways of talking, for meanings as such, he claims, can only come 'from the interior of a language game' (ibid.: 47). Thus all we can do is to try to make vocabularies we don't like 'look bad' (ibid.: 44). If Vico and Grassi are right, this is nonsense; the presentation of a new metaphor *is* an argument.

5. Grassi notes that the term 'metaphor' is itself a metaphor, as it is derived from the verb *metapherein* 'to transfer' which originally described a concrete activity.

6. As C.W. Mills (1940: 439) said now more than 50 years ago, 'the differing reasons men give for their actions are not themselves without reasons . . . What we want is analysis of the integrating, controlling, and specifying functions a certain type of speech fulfills in socially situated actions'.

7. The view that *proper* theory should provide a foolproof method, a mathematical formula, leading to the prediction and control of behaviour, is a product of modern philosophy. As Grassi (1980: 20) makes clear – see quote in text – this is not the original sense of what is involved in speaking theoretically.

8. See also Wittgenstein (1953: nos. 131, 132 and 133).

9. Or better, the 'becoming' of both ourselves and our social worlds.

10. Others, no doubt, contesting my version of joint action, will be a case in point.

11. Most current texts in psychology place the reader in the position of the Saussurian, passive recipient of the author's ideas – quite literally, we cannot find ourselves in such texts (Shotter, 1991b).

PART II

REALISM, THE IMAGINARY, AND A WORLD OF EVENTS

4
The Limits of Realism

One of social constructionism's most immediate contenders is realism, and one its major exponents is Bhaskar. His recent *Reclaiming Reality: A Critical Introduction to Contemporary Philosophy* (Bhaskar, 1989), is one of his most important books. And it is important to discuss it here, as many see in Bhaskar's critical realism, with his transformational model of social activity (TMSA) – to be discussed below – a clear alternative to social constructionism. For although many now espouse social constructionist *theories* of social action – Bhaskar included – few are prepared to endorse a thoroughgoing social constructionist *methodology* (of the nontheoretical kind, say, outlined in the previous three chapters). They claim that it is irredeemably committed to an 'anything goes' relativism, a fate that Bhaskar's realism – with its separate accounts of ontology and epistemology – seems clearly to avoid. Thus in the chapter that follows, I review this book in an attempt to pinpoint precisely where difficulties arise for social constructionists in Bhaskar's account of realism: they arise, as we shall see, in realist's claims to be able to identify ahead of time the structures of social life that constructionists would maintain are, in reality, still contested.

Turning now to the book, we can begin by noting that in it he brings together in a manageable and accessible form the broad sweep of much of his recent work. In a series of interlinked essays (most of which have been published before, but which he has carefully arranged into a 'narrative' structure), he develops yet further his realist theory of science, and applies it to the discussion of a number of pressing philosophical and political problems. In particular, in 'reclaiming' reality, he not only wants to reclaim it from poststructuralist idealists and so-called 'new-realists' – both of whom he sees as undermining the confidence of those who believe in the possibility of emancipatory human sciences and a socialist society – but also and most importantly, he wants to reclaim reality 'for itself'; that is, to let it be a genuine 'otherness', a de-anthropomorphized reality able to surprise us, not a predetermined world characterized in (human) terms already familiar to us. Hence, central to his whole account is (i) the formulation of a separate and explicit ontological dimension, irreducibly distinct from epistemological realms; and (ii) the 'non-human', 'de-divinized'[1] nature of this ontology.

The 'epistemic fallacy' and human emancipation

As Bhaskar sees it, all previous philosophies of science, and many current ones, fall victim to what he calls the 'epistemic fallacy' – the definition of being in terms of our knowledge of it. In other words, they fail to make a clear distinction between epistemology and ontology. Thus, on the one hand, they are ontologically too *restrictive* – for in drawing their (hidden) ontologies from an anthropomorphic epistemology, in which people are conceived individualistically as passive responders to atomistic events, they presume a world of closed systems and atomistic events – and thus rule out, as epistemologically untenable, adequate formulations of the socio-historical nature of embodied human agency. And on the other hand, they are epistemologically too *permissive* (for they allow, especially in psychology, quite incredible theories of human nature to become institutionally entrenched). It is his fashioning of two separate dimensions within which to talk about science – an 'intransitive', ontological dimension existing independently of scientists and their activity, and a 'transitive', epistemological or historical sociological dimension – which he sees as crucial in overcoming these (and other) difficulties. While our knowledge of the world is a social product, produced by transformational social activity from previously existing knowledge, the being of the world must be conceived of (at least at the moment of its scientific investigation) as existing independently of our thoughts about it. For only if this is so can we discover our theories of its nature to be wrong, thus making a scientific investigation of its *reality* a genuine possibility.

This is the 'hard core', so to speak, of Bhaskar's philosophical research programme (indeed, he says so explicity – 1989: 183), but what is its point? Right from the start Bhaskar makes his overall aim perfectly clear. If the point of philosophy is to *change* the world, then the transformation of society towards socialism depends upon a knowledge of its real underlying structures. 'The world cannot be changed unless it is adequately interpreted' (1989: 5). Thus for him, the point of all the essays collected together in that volume is that they 'all seek to *underlabour* – at different levels and in different ways – for the sciences, and especially the human sciences, in so far as they might illuminate and empower the project of human self-emancipation' (1989: vii) – and to the extent that my review here will be selective, it will deal with the extent to which his work can contribute to this project. Indeed, I shall want to question whether the kind of (Lockean) philosophical underlabouring he proposes – to do *prior* ground clearing – is necessarily a way-station on the route to human self-emancipation, or whether other forms of underlabouring might not be more suitable – as tool-makers, say, *during* actual processes of construction, or as rhetoricians, say, *afterwards*, either to persuade others of a construction's worth, or to dissuade its critics. For straightaway, it must be said that Bhaskar's version of philosophical realism is not, in itself, aimed at providing either a set of substantive analyses or a set of practical policies; neither is it a substitute for empirically controlled investigations into 'the structures generating social phenomena'; rather its aim is 'to guide' them, in the sense of setting out 'the conditions of the possibility of emancipatory practices in general' (1989: 113).

Above, then, is his aim in this book; his strategy is next to rehearse his transcendental realist account of causal laws in the natural sciences. He then makes use of it in criticizing current philosophies of science, in order in the middle of the book to introduce his own, naturalistic approach to emancipatory, social scientific knowledge. This is then related both to theoretical issues in Marxist thought, and also to a critique of Rorty (as a seeming important opponent of realism). The book ends with a chapter tracing how the programme of transcendental realism has developed a critical dimension, concerned with explaining the causes of a false consciousness of nature. I will not in my review here make any major comments upon these latter chapters, as my main interest is in what he calls his *transformational model of social activity* (TMSA), as well as in his account of (embodied) human agency. To turn now to his account of realism in the natural sciences; this plays a pivotal part in all his subsequent arguments.

Epistemology and ideology

Central to this account are the ontological claims (first worked out in his earlier 1975 book) – and it is important to note, as already mentioned, that the scientific experiment is for him a paradigm of rational social action 'at work', so to speak, and he clearly uses it as the site upon which he first 'tests' further developments in his thought. Influenced by the accounts, both of scientific activity and of 'causal powers' provided by Harré (1970a and b), Bhaskar (1975) argued for the existence of an 'ontological gap' between observed patterns of events and causal laws. As he now puts it, in an experiment:

> What distinguishes the phenomena the scientists *actually* produce out of the totality of phenomena they *could* produce is that, when the experiment is successful, it is an index of what they do *not* produce. A *real* distinction between the objects of experimental investigation, such as causal laws, and patterns of events is thus a condition of intelligibility of experimental activity. (1975: 15)

Hence, his claim, already mentioned above, of the necessity for, and nonidentity of, both an ontological and an epistemological dimension in any adequate account of scientific activity.

Having argued for its necessity, he next turns to the critical discussion of currently influential philosophical positions to reveal certain ideological biases hidden in them. In chapter 3 he discusses those inaugurated by Popper and Bachelard, while in chapter 4 he discusses positivism. His central point in both these chapters is that the persistent attempt to reduce ontology to epistemology results in an ontology which is denied while being presupposed – for it must be assumed that the world is such that it could be the object of certain human cognitive operations; if it lacks that nature it cannot be known. Hence we have Feyerabend (who trades both upon Popper's failure to provide anything other than a humanly made basis for science – his demarcation criterion – and the failure of Lakatos's *methodology of scientific research programmes* to predict the future development of a science), concluding that scientific change must be irrational, and advocating an 'anything goes' *theoretical dadaism*. For Feyerabend, science has no greater authority than any other form of life, thus it has no business restricting the lives of members of a free society. But, as Bhaskar asks, is being free to choose what you want to do when you want to do it (which seems to be Feyerabend's concept of freedom), of any use at all unless one possesses reliable knowledge? Feyerabend fails to grasp the necessity for the enablements that emerge from a science with *ontological depth*.

Bhaskar finds Bachelard interesting for the distinction he draws between science and *reverie* – the dreamlike character of everyday experience that forms the stuff of art and poetry. But although Bachelard opposes two seemingly ontologically distinct realms in his philosophy, neither in Bhaskar's terms is an intransitive realm of real objects. So, for Bachelard, the struggle of a subject to form a scientific mind 'splits him and demands of him, often to the point of him being existentially torn, that he make a *break* with the "spontaneous" interests of everyday life' (Bachelard, 1927: 15) – where the break required is not to do with making contact with an unfamiliar 'otherness', with 'magical forces immanent in reality', but with 'a rational force immanent in the mind' already fashioned by a world of a science. A science 'instructs itself by what it constructs', says Bachelard (1934: 12). Thus its claims are sustained as scientific claims, not by the nature of its contact with reality, but by the social character of its institutions, the cohesion and effectivity of what Bachelard calls 'the scientific city'. But as Bhaskar points out, such a science, which only allows the study of rationally constructed objects, excludes imagination, and the exclusion of imagination precludes the possibility of any genuine growth.

These difficulties are only minor, however, compared with those he raises with the 'house philosophy' of our times, positivism. Positivism is a theory of *knowledge* which, because it lacks its own distinct ontological dimension (to repeat the by now familiar refrain), presupposes one. To the extent that it talks of knowledge in particular, as being made up of events sensed in perception, and general knowledge as consisting in patterns of such events, it presupposes an ontology of atomistic events and closed systems. Furthermore, in its account of science, it presupposes a *sociology* also: an inter-individualistic sociology of human beings who act as passive sensors of given facts, and who record their constant conjunctions. It can thus neither sustain the idea of an independent reality, nor the idea of socially produced scientific knowledge. Thus, in positivism, we have a philosophy which is either (i) consistent with its own epistemology, but is of no use to science, as Bhaskar (1975) shows; or (ii) useful to science (in that its sense-data do yield knowledge of material objects), but is inconsistent with its own epistemology. It is in the inconsistent system – or perhaps more strictly, lack of system – so resulting that positivism's tremendous versatility and resilience as an ideology lies.

Indeed, as Billig et al. (1988) have shown, lived ideologies gain their power to motivate interminable argument just because they do *not* consist in *systems* of thought, but in 'themes' with mutually contrary sub-themes to them, such as freedom *and* necessity; individual *and* society; subjectivity *and* objectivity; etc. Thus a philosophy which provides cognitive resources for mutually contradictory argumentation is a fertile site for the working of ideological influences; this emphatically seems to be the case with positivism. Indeed, as Bhaskar puts it, 'practically, it is in the contradictions yielded by the necessity to hold two incompatible positions, as conditions of each other, that the most fertile ground of ideology lies' (1989: 57) – and, I must add, for other forms of creativity too (because later I shall propose that the answer to tensions between two incompatible positions which are conditions of each other, is not always to attempt a theoretical resolution ahead of time, but to explore these tensions practically and politically).

Bhaskar explores the ideological effects of positivism at work in both the transitive and the intransitive dimensions. The concept most pregnant with ideological connotations in the transitive dimension is that of a fact. In the philosophy of positivism, and its associated spontaneous scientific consciousness, we tend to see the world *as if* it were itself constituted of facts. Facts, however, are not the cause of our perceptual processes, but their result. The mystification achieved is the transformation of the qualities which belong to them as *socio-historical products* into qualities belonging to them as *natural things*. In other words, something which is essentially *made* is transformed into something apparently *found*. Similarly, in the intransitive dimension, a similar concealing of *social processes* takes place. Reality becomes unstructured, uniform and unchanging. This results, in the social sciences, in a social world in which 'mankind is much the same in all times and in all places' (Hume). In other words, society is conceived of as being constituted of human beings who are 'naturally', indistinguishable, atomic individuals; who are motivated by given desires; who reason how best their desires may be satisfied; and who are conjoined, if at all, by contract. Thus, both a differentiated social reality of unequally distributed opportunities and resources for action, as well as a socially produced unique individuality, become unthinkable within a positivistic social science. In positivism we have, therefore, an ideology both *for* and *of* science: the former rationalizing the scientific status quo (Kuhn's 'normal science'); and the latter constituting beliefs about the nature of society and of knowledge within it. An 'atomized' individualism, that is nonsocial, nonhistorical individualism, both in theory and practice, is an ideological consequence (and condition) of positivism – the consequence of deriving a social ontology from an empiricist epistemology.

Vygotsky's socio-historical ontology

The next step in Bhaskar's project is thus to ask whether the ontology he has developed for the natural world – an ontology of things possessing causal powers to generate patterns of events, whose causal laws must be analysed as tendencies, manifested as empirical invariances only under specially contrived closed conditions – can also be of use in the social sciences. In other words, can society be studied in the same way as nature? Or, to put the question another way: What is the character of the society–nature relation? But before turning to Bhaskar's answer to these questions, I would like to refer to Vygotsky's (1962, 1966, 1986) work in psychology, to consider Bhaskar's formulations in their light. For (in post-revolutionary Russia) he also worried about essentially the same questions as Bhaskar.

For Vygotsky (1966: 11–12):

> Traditional views of the development of the higher mental functions are erroneous and onesided primarily and mainly because they are unable to see facts as facts of historical development, regard them as natural processes and formations, confuse them and fail to differentiate the organic from the cultural, the natural from the historical, the biological from the social in the child's mental development . . .

It is all too easy, Vygotsky feels, to divide psychology metaphysically into two quite distinct approaches, into a lower and a higher form:

> into two separate and independent sciences: physiologic, natural-science, explanatory or causal psychology, on the one hand, and conceptual, descriptive, or teleological psychology of the spirit, as the basis of all the humanities, on the other hand. (1966: 15)

The main weakness in the traditional approach, as Vygotsky saw it, is a onesidedness which meant, in experimental investigations, focusing only upon changing people's conditions of existence and studying the outcome. But such an approach, he said, 'forgets that "man also reacts on nature, changing it and creating new conditions of existence for himself" ' (Vygotsky, 1966: 21, quoting from Engels's *Dialectics of Nature*). And what is novel, and central to Vygotsky's whole approach, is his analysis of the *means*, the 'psychological instruments' we invent in creating new conditions for ourselves.

To give an example, he discusses (Vygotsky, 1966: 24–7) what people might do in finding themselves in the position of Buridan's ass – apparently unable to decide which of two equally attractive foods to eat. Unlike the ass, they solve the problem by the use of an artificial device, by casting lots: the person's behaviour is now determined 'not by the stimuli on hand, but by a new or invariably man-made psychological situation' (Vygotsky, 1966: 27). And later, having grasped what is involved in casting lots or tossing coins, people may 'internalize' the process, making use of imaginary, embodied equivalents to form 'psychological instruments' for themselves. Also, it is by acting *through* such 'instruments' – that is, out towards the world – that people can reveal aspects of its nature otherwise unavailable to them – such as the blind person's stick as a sensory prosthetic. It is this use of such means which sets people apart from animals. Here again, Vygotsky was influenced by Engels: 'the animal merely *uses* external nature', said Engels (quoted in Vygotsky, 1966: 22), 'man, by his changes, makes it serves his ends, *masters* it', and in mastering it, Vygotsky adds, learns how to master himself. The most important of all the psychological instruments invented by human beings is, of course, language.

As Vygotsky sees it, in linguistic communication, words are first a *means* (a 'tool') for use in influencing another person's behaviour

(Vygotsky, 1962: 56), a means for use in the negotiation of *meanings*. Only later, do they – in learning written forms of communication – come to take on (to a degree) pre-determined meanings. Learning to write produces (see Vygotsky, 1962: 98–101) a radical and irreversible difference in what a language 'is' for members of a literate society – to such an extent that it is next to impossible for us, as members of such a community, to imagine what speech is for those in an oral culture. But as Vygotsky (1962: 98) points out: '*Writing* is speech in thought and image only, lacking the musical, expressive, intonational qualities of oral speech. In learning to write, the child must disengage himself from the sensory aspect of speech and replace words by images of words.' In other words, writing transforms speech in a way which seemingly 'disconnects' it from its origins.

While in spontaneous speech, the 'tool' function predominates, and we use words as a means in negotiating meanings with our interlocutors. In writing, however, 'we are obliged to create the situation, to represent it to ourselves. This demands detachment from the actual situation' (Vygotsky, 1962: 99). In our texts, by the use of syntactical devices to interlink the pre-determined meanings of words, we can create an imaginary, *intralinguistic* realm within which to situate ourselves. Talk in relation to such textually created realms is thus about what 'might be' rather than what 'is'. If it is to be factual, then (as Garfinkel, 1967, makes clear) it must include within itself procedures for *warranting* reality-claims as true claims. I shall, in criticizing Bhaskar's claims about emancipation, make much use of this tool/text, this speaking/writing distinction in language use introduced by Vygotsky.

Vygotsky's metapsychology is then, like Bhaskar's realism, fundamentally concerned with (i) the *nature* of the natural world; (ii) people's *mastery* of it; and (iii) with the degree to which people, to the extent that they are natural beings, can master their own (socially manifested) natural powers, 'internalize' them, and themselves (as individuals) control and direct their expression. If we are to take his psychology seriously (and *I* of course think we must), then we must formulate a strange and special kind of hybrid, contexted, 'two-way flow' psychology, concerned to study: (i) a prosthetic outflow of activity, from people out towards their already partially structured surroundings, in which they can 'give' or 'lend' them further structure according to their use of the 'instruments' available to them in their activities (a making); (ii) an inflow of activity in the other direction, from an already partially structured and self-acting environment into the people within it, a flow of activity which they must interpret hermeneutically to grasp the nature of the situation in which they are placed (a finding); *and* (iii) a special *zone of activity* in which the relations between these two processes take place and are studied. For it is in this 'zone' (Vygotskians feel) that culture is 'appropriated' from nature, and cultural products are 'reappropriated' by nature in becoming embodied.

Bhaskar's social ontology

Returning now to compare Bhaskar's account of social activity and human agency with Vygotsky's. Central to it is his 'naturalistic' claim that the real things constituting the subject matter of the human sciences are *structures* and *social interactions* (understood ultimately in terms of *rules*). He makes this claim in relation to an image of social life formulated in his *transformational model of social activity* (TMSA) in which:

> Society is both the ever-present *condition* and the continually reproduced *outcome* of human agency: this is the duality of structure. And human agency is both work (generically conceived), that is (normally conscious) *production*, and (normally unconscious) *reproduction* of the conditions of production, including society: this is the duality of praxis. Thus agents reproduce, *non-teleologically* and *recursively*, in their substantive motivated productions, the unmotivated conditions necessary for – as a means of – those productions; and society is both the medium and the result of this activity'. (1989: 92–3)

On the basis of this model, Bhaskar (1989: 93) formulates what he claims are, or should be, the subject matters of the different human sciences:

> TMSA respects a methodological difference between the *social sciences*, which abstract from human agency, studying the structure of reproduced outcomes; and the *social psychological sciences*, which abstract from reproduced outcomes, studying the rules governing the mobilization of resources by agents in their everyday interactions with one another and nature. If the object of the former is *social structure*, that of the latter is *social interaction*. They may be linked by the study of *society* as such, identified as the system of *relations* between the positions and the practices agents reproduce and transform, which is the subject matter of the social science of sociology.

But it is at this point that I part company with Bhaskar. As someone who has grappled with Chomsky, and the many others who claim that social interaction is best understood in terms of systems of rules, I feel a certain unease with this outcome – rules are not just followed, but are also created, challenged, ignored, etc., all in perfectly intelligible ways without the need for rules to regulate such activities. How is it, when there is so much in Bhaskar with which I agree, that he can reach conclusions which I find so disagreeable?

The crucial (and I think wrong) step he takes – on the basis of claims like those about the duality of praxis he makes above – is a claim (which he slips in, by the way, in the course of making both a very important and very real distinction), that if social activity consists, at least paradigmatically in *work* on, and the transformation of, given materials; and:

> If such work constitutes the *analogue* of natural events, then we need an *analogue* for the mechanisms that generate them. (1989: 78, my emphases).

And this, I think, is the crucial but wrong step he takes. But then an important distinction immediately follows:

> If social structures constitute the appropriate mechanism-analogue then we must at once register an important difference – in that, unlike natural mechanisms, they exist only in virtue of the social activities they govern and cannot be empirically identified independently of them. Because of this they must be social products themselves. (1989: 78)

Precisely! But if they are social products, social constructions, why not treat them as such? Why treat them in terms of a mechanistic analogue? Why not formulate an account of the *real* politico-moral transactions people conduct between themselves in their actual, everyday affairs together, rather than a mechanism-analogue of them?

The answer I think is perfectly clear: Bhaskar's account here (ideologically) preserves a particular vision of what proper knowledge is, and the kind of professionalized science-based society in which its production is privileged – the view formulated in *A Realist Theory of Science* (Bhaskar, 1975). Indeed, to question his views further: Do descriptions in terms of mechanisms (clearly, humanly made entities) give a properly radical role to the natural, that is nonanthropomorphic, aspects of social activities and human agency? In other words, to both repeat and to add to the question Chalmers (1988) asked, but now in a different sense: Is Bhaskar's realism realistic, and also, is it properly naturalistic? And my answer to both parts of this question is 'No'.

What Bhaskar represses: Embodied agency and textual productions

Now I cannot explore all the reasons for giving this reply here, nor all the implications of it. But the following comments seem to me relevant: (1) TMSA is a model of people as scientists, and it is simply not a legitimate move (in terms of Bhaskar's own claim, that society consists in a structure – I would say an ecology – of differentiated practices and positions), to assume that all kinds of social activity can be understood on analogy with just one. (2) Further, on the model of people as scientists, he characterizes human agency in terms of individual people initiating change in a purposeful way; that is, in terms of people *causing* outcomes by manipulating the circumstances of those outcomes, by producing certain kinds of 'closure'. Although he is far too tasteful to say so, this (as Vygotsky says explicitly) is an interest in *mastery*, an interest in the production of one-way relations of domination. But there is another form of human agency manifested in the socio-historical processes Vygotsky discusses, in which, in the course of always open, two-way relations of interdependence, something at first created only in the *spontaneous*, contexted activities between people, is later 'privatized' or 'internalized' by individuals, for use under their own personal, decontextualized, *deliberate* control. (3) Characterizing the genesis of human actions, paradigmatically 'as lying in the reasons, intentions, and plans of human beings' (1989: p.78), mystifies (in favour of individualistic scientists) the socio-historical nature of these always open, spontaneous, contexted, originating activities. (4) The (ontological) part played by *embodied* forms of knowledge, also remains mysterious in Bhaskar's account; rather than an intransitive dimension, a dimension of (moral) intransigence would seem more suitable in characterizing social activities – for it is not a person's material nature that determines which, of all the things they might do, they feel able to do, but their *social identities* ('I couldn't do that, it wouldn't be me' we say). (5) Although critical realism might provide a framework for the evaluation of new spontaneous everyday social activities, if it is in such activities that human emancipation must start, it is difficult to see how transcendental realism provides even a 'guide' for their recognition, let alone a plan for their construction. (6) Finally, and perhaps most importantly, especially to the extent that realists in general (but not so much Bhaskar himself) have attacked the neo-conservativism (they say) is implicit in poststructuralism and social constructionism, is the neglect of the *textual* nature of the productive and reproductive process in science.

Bhaskar takes it that the most important practice supporting a science is its 'methodology': the assumption that (proper, scientific) knowledge is only acquired as a result of systematic thought and orderly investigation. But this 'methodology' only has sense, and only makes sense, within a context of other activities and practices (Chalmers, 1988). Central among these is the production of *written texts*. All professionally conducted science moves from text to text, usually beginning with the reading of already written texts, and ending in the writing of further texts. And as we have already seen in the discussion of Vygotsky above, within the many forms of linguistic communication, the written text has a special place. This is because it can be used as a means by readers (with an appropriate prior training), to construct a meaning solely by reference to the linguistic resources they possess within themselves. It is a carefully interwoven sequence of written sentences, structured within itself to an enormous degree by essentially intralinguistic or syntactical relations. Thus it can be said to be a (relatively) de-contextualized form of communication.

The relevance of all this for us, as professional scientists, is: that whatever else a *scientific* theory is, it is always and inevitably something written and published within the context of a publicly available text. Furthermore, to the extent that all theoretical writing claims that things are not what they ordinarily seem to be, but are 'in reality' something else, the terms of a theory are not intelligible in the same way as terms in ordinary language. They need a special form of introduction: if we want to be taken seriously in our scientific claims, we need to be 'instructed' in how to see various social phenomena *as* having a certain psychological character, for example, to see them *as* social structures or classes, *as* social representations, *as* rules, *as* attitudes, *as* beliefs, etc. – as Bhaskar 'instructs' us in how to see social life as consisting in structures, etc. But in addition to these considerations, we must also add that science is conducted within a context of argumentation (Billig, 1987; Popper, 1963). Thus all the claims we make are made against the background of other previous textually expressed claims – we must struggle for our emancipatory claims within a rhetorical context of argumentation in favour of other claims.

None of all these activities, however, seems to have a place in Bhaskar's account of science, and of emancipatory social activities. As a consequence, his realist account lacks a certain reflexiveness (could his position/practice possibly be as a rhetor rather than a philosophical underlabourer?). But also, he fails to take Rorty's Wittgensteinian warnings seriously – that is, Rorty's claim that 'it is pictures rather than propositions, metaphors rather than statements, which determine most of our philosophical convictions' (Rorty, 1980: 12). But as we know, texts are nothing if not the medium *par excellence* of fiction, of story-telling. We only have to read any science fiction novel to know that what is presented and experienced as an account of an actual (but in fact imaginary) reality works, so to speak, to 'manufacture' the sense of reality it conveys. What if, because we (wrongly) believe that such texts 'represent' the true subject matter of our science, we (wrongly) accord such representations, as Bhaskar himself continually warns, more prominence *scientifically* than the social activities and practices making their production possible? Then we can become the victims of a corporate or institutional self-deception, in which much of what we take to be the subject matter of our science is imaginary in the same way as the 'worlds' created by science fiction. This *is*, I think, the trap that

Bhaskar – in his claims about the reality (in the intransitive dimension) of structures and rules – still falls into.

A social ontology of 'formative activities' and 'ethical logistics'

Where do these arguments leave us? Where might the crucial differences between a critical realist and a (critical) social constructionist account of social activity lie? The central tension lies in attempts to conceptualize the relation between the activities of 'making' and 'finding'. Both realists and constructionists face this problem: Should one be privileged over the other (Shotter, 1990a)? Bhaskar seems to suggest not (and I would too). He puts the problem thus:

> Paradigmatically, we *make* facts and, in experimental activity, closed systems; but we *find* out about (discover and identify) things, structures and causal laws. We could stipulate these as 'necessary truths'. But it is better to realize that there is an inherent ambiguity or bipolarity in our use of terms like 'cause', 'laws', 'facts' and so on, and to be prepared whenever necessary, to disambiguate them, distinguish a transitive (social or making) from the intransitive (ontological or finding) employment of these terms. (1989: 150, my emphases)

The difference between us is, that while we both accept the inherent making/finding bipolarity of terms such as 'cause', etc., he suggests that they should be disambiguated in terms of his transitive/intransitive distinction (which favours, I think, 'finding' and 'closure'); while I favour not trying ahead of time to prejudge the issue (a bias in favour of 'openness' and 'making') – a bias which raises again of course all the problems to do with the politically contested nature of important aspects of social life Bhaskar's realism claims to solve. It is not the place here to discuss these problems in further depth. Suffice it to say that I think the tension is inescapable, and that practically, we must live with the dialectic between 'making' and 'finding'; indeed, they entail each other. But it is in the (political) contests as to which should be privileged over the other, that much new innovatory and emancipatory thought is generated (Shotter, 1989a).

Conclusions

In summary, then: it is Bhaskar's claim that ontological and epistemological talk must be distinguished, which makes his position quite novel. This distinction must, I think, be upheld just as much by social constructionists (if they are to be critical constructionists), as by realists – and here in this book, I have sought to describe the nature of an ontology of contested conversational events, an ontology derived from an investigation into what it is that makes conversation as we know it possible for us. But, as we have seen, if we pay close attention to the particular philosophical ontology Bhaskar proposes, we find that it is not derived from a transcendental analysis of the conditions necessary for ordinary, everyday social life to be possible, but *by analogy* from a conditions of possibility analysis of those required for scientific experimentation. Thus, those of us more directly concerned with the activities of ordinary, everyday social life – and who wonder, like Bachelard, how an intelligible world is fashioned from seemingly dreamlike, disorderly material – may find that, instead of the 'things' ontology Bhaskar proposes, an ontology consisting in an 'ecology of formative activities' is much more suitable. That is, instead of as the products of 'generative mechanisms', both the intended and unintended outcomes of social activity might be better analysed as issuing from processes of joint action in which a certain 'ethical logistics' is at work in the management of their negotiated outcomes – a 'logistics' conducted within the context of a political economy of access to 'ontological resources'; that is, access to the kind of social interaction required if one is to have the opportunity to develop, and to be a certain kind of person. Hence, instead of an ontology of social 'structures' and psychological 'rules' characterizing its *material* 'resistances' and 'enablements', an ontology of *morally contested* 'intransigences' and 'empowerments' embodied both in people and the social practices within which they have their social identities may be a more revealing social ontology (Shotter, 1990b). None of all this could have been said, however, without the 'enablements' provided by Bhaskar's own work in this area. He has fashioned a wholly new context for argumentation about social ontology, and because of this, his 'voice' merits enormous critical attention in all the human sciences, in the new (!?) 'tradition of argumentation' now developing.

Note

1. Bhaskar takes the term from Rorty. In seeking to 'de-divinize' our ontologies, Rorty (1989: 198) is urging that 'we try not to want something that stands beyond history and institutions'.

5
Social Life and the Imaginary

> A *picture* held us captive. And we could not get outside it, for it lay in our language and language seemed to repeat it to us inexorably.
>
> Wittgenstein, 1953: no. 115

> Communities are to be distinguished, not by their falsity/genuineness, but by the style in which they are imagined.
>
> Anderson, 1991: 6

At issue in the discussion of Bhaskar's work is what is involved in free and open discussion. In this chapter, I want further to discuss the processes of joint action in which, and by which, people construct between themselves 'organized settings' of enabling/constraints 'into' which to direct their future actions, and how it is that sometimes those settings can become more constraining than enabling. This discussion will also make clear why the search for alternatives to systematic, monological theories as appropriate outcomes of research in psychology – a search begun in Chapter 2, in which the importance of 'psychological instruments' was broached – is so very necessary. For, such forms of research, in ignoring the cultural settings from within which it is conducted, ignore also features of those settings constraining the nature of the arguments possible within them. Here, in bringing these settings to the fore, I want to emphasize, not that contest over their nature is simply unconstrained, but the opposite: to emphasize the fact that they contain 'developmental tendencies' – to do with the kinds of society people within them envision – that constrain what are felt to be relevant debates. To capture the nature of these still incomplete, developing tendencies – some of which are more 'realized' than others at a certain point in time – I want to introduce the concept of the 'imaginary' to enable talk about what is not yet wholly 'real', but yet is not wholly 'fictitious' either.

Earlier, I introduced the idea that 'social constructions' can be seen as originating and being given an acceptable linguistic formulation, in a two-way, socio-historical process, in which people (i) at first act out from a 'grounding' within their everyday social lives, (ii) where those actions, to the extent that the other people accept them, act back upon that background to give it further form – it is, I claimed, a process of giving form to feeling, a process in which what is at first a mere felt tendency can be realized as a new social institution, such as the possible turn in psychology from an individual, mechanistic cognitivism to a social, discursive form. But how might we characterize the nature of these as yet unintelligible tendencies or feelings present in the background of our social lives if (assuming my criticisms of Bhaskar's realist account to be correct), they cannot be represented as an already existing well-formed 'generative mechanism' (to use his terminology)? What I want to argue here, is that we need to make use of a couple of further categories, positioned between the real or the factual, and the nonexistent or the fictitious, to help us talk about the emergence of social constructions: categories of the partially real, (i) the *imaginary* and (ii) the *imagined.* In other words, I want to suggest that the organized settings people create between themselves give rise both to felt tendencies that cannot be wholly grasped in mental representations, but that these tendencies can nonetheless be thought about as imaginary entities. They have a degree of real existence due to their 'subsistence' in people's social practices, and to that extent are able (like fictitious entities) to exert a *real* influence upon the structure of people's activities. But, to the extent that the felt tendencies are incomplete, and open to further specification or determination in a whole number of different ways, they possess a degree of ambiguity or vagueness that prevents their complete specification; they do not yet wholly exist. Thus linguistic formulations as to their nature are always 'essentially contested' (Gallie, 1955–56). The most important 'objects' of this kind are what we talk of as our 'self' and our 'world', or our 'society'.

Such imaginary objects as these can play important roles, both in maintaining the multiple, partial structurings of daily life, and in maintaining its openness to further articulations. While any attempt to *complete* them as real objects destroys their nature, and can lead to an enclosed (mechanical) form of social life. And this can happen when such tendencies are literalized[1] in terms of an image or model; that is, as imagined or imaginable entities. It is this, I want to argue, that tends to close off discussion and debate, and indeed, can lead to a special state of affairs that can be called 'entrapment' (Stolzenberg, 1978).

Entrapment in untrue but incorrigible 'certainties'

In beginning this discussion, let me first distinguish the hurly-burly of everyday life (the multiplicity of partial orderings in everyday life), from the devices and institutions of the State, as well as from the economic mechanisms of production, distribution and exchange. These latter, as rule-governed[2] patterns and structures of *official* social life, clearly exist and are empirically identifiable as such. But what I want to argue is that the unofficial, everyday hurly-burly of social life is not best thought of as consisting in particular, fixed and empirically identifiable structures and activities. It lacks, I want to claim, any fully developed nature at all; it is only partially structured and open, to a certain limited extent, to further development, to further shaping or reshaping by those involved in its conduct. Hence, in our arguments about the nature of things, we must take it that our statements (whether true, false or meaningless) are not always about real things: sometimes what they refer to is imaginary; and there can be true (and false and meaningless) statements about imaginary things – strange as it might be to say that. And furthermore, what I want to argue is that what is at stake in the further structuring and shaping of the imaginary character of our daily social life together, is what people are pleased to think of as their social *identities* (Anderson, 1991).[3] Who and what we imagine ourselves as being (or as trying to be) in relation to the others and the 'Otherness' surrounding us, is what determines the 'shape' of our motives and feelings, what we feel worth undertaking, and what we feel is intelligible and reasonable. Currently, as belonging to a nation, we feel ourselves in 'community with' a whole crowd of people that we will never actually meet, while a whole crowd of others lie beyond our nation's boundaries. Hence the importance, and the contested nature, of factors affecting the character of the hurly-burly of everyday life: for our uncertain task is, not only *to be* human beings, but to be proper and full members of our community, if only we knew what was entailed in being so. While many may live a life consciously 'alienated' from the State, as well as from the economic mechanisms of social life, it is in the practices of our daily lives that we form the images of what we take our 'real' nature to be. And they inform our nature to such a deep extent that, quite literally, we do not know how to argue for ourselves as being otherwise – even though we may often feel a deep disquiet at the adequacy of such images of ourselves and our lives together.

'Waiting for Godot' *as how it is*

Let me try to illustrate some of my reasons for wanting to argue in favour of the *imaginary* nature of everyday life, by beginning with a quotation from Samuel Beckett's *Waiting for Godot* (Beckett, 1956: 80). Vladimir, one of Beckett's down-and-outs, is addressing a great deal of confused discourse to Estragon, the other tramp, about whether they should stick to their apparently assigned task – to wait for Godot – or whether it is a proper part of their general human nature to help a fellow human being in distress, urgently calling for their help. Vladimir suddenly sees a way out of their confusion: they do not need to know whether they are responsible for representing the whole of mankind or not, because

> that is not the question. What are we doing here, *that* is the question. And we are blessed in this, that we happen to know the answer. Yes, in this immense confusion one thing alone is clear. We are waiting for Godot to come . . .

And *that* is how at first they justify to us and themselves their reluctance to help – just as Descartes appealed to a single clarity in justifying his claim: 'I think therefore I am.'

But the tragedy for Beckett's down-and-outs (and the comedy for us) is that the one thing they feel perfectly clear about – their supposed motive for most of their daily activity together, the one thing they feel would transform everything for them, the actual arrival of Godot – is an illusion. It does nothing for them; it is not an agency in their lives; in fact, they live their lives without its help. It is merely a talked-about-Godot, a stand-in, a surrogate, for an elusive being who never actually appears, and only subsists 'in' their talk. However, they (and we) might be tempted to say that nonetheless it exerts 'its' influence in their behaviour. But such a claim is false, it is the reverse of the truth: for it is a certain form of talked-about-activity, activity talked about as *waiting*, which *necessitates* their reference to a Godot, not the existence of a Godot which necessitates their waiting. No such Godot (at least in their experience) has ever existed. Thus, although they *explain* their activity to themselves by referring their supposed waiting to the supposed existence of a Godot, they actually get on in the meantime perfectly well without the existence of this Godot. It is an *imagined* Godot which plays a real part in their lives.[4]

Indeed, the final hollow laugh in all of this is, of course, that not only are they are self-deceived, but they collude in each other's self-deception: they not only accept one another's account of what it is that they are doing, they remind one another of their task. But the one thing which alone seems clear to them – that they are waiting for Godot – is not a correct account at all of what they are in fact doing. It is a socially constructed and socially maintained illusion in terms of which they together make sense of their lives to themselves, to which they feel they must subordinate themselves.

> *Estragon*: We're not tied?
> *Vladimir*: I don't hear a word you're saying.
> *Estragon*: [chews, swallows] Tied?
> *Vladimir*: How do you mean?
> *Estragon*: Down.
> *Vladimir*: But to whom?
> *Estragon*: To your man.
> *Vladimir*: To Godot? Tied to Godot? What an idea! No question of it. [Pause] For the moment. (Beckett, 1956: 20–1)

Their subordination is self-imposed. Indeed, time and again they have to remind each other of their *waiting* (for Godot). And when they forget, then they indulge in practices and activities, informed by other images and identities (the music hall, the circus, and so on), which – upon remembering their task and who they think they are – they must look upon as *diversions* from what they see as the proper, meaningful purpose of their lives: their waiting. For their waiting is what gives them their *identity*; it is who they 'are'. They do not know how to account for themselves to themselves except in its terms.

But we – as their audience, outside 'their' intralinguistic reality – can see that they deluded; what *they* say they are doing is *false*. We can see that they are doing more, much more than waiting: they are *living* (perhaps not very well and with not much enthusiasm), but they are nonetheless, before our very eyes, living out a number of different, particular forms of life. Yet *they* cannot 'see' that fact; they have imprisoned themselves within an account of themselves of their own devising. And *they, as the individuals they are*, prevent themselves from 'seeing' its inadequacy: not just because it is the only 'currency', so to speak, in terms of which they can conduct their joint endeavours, but because they owe their being who they are, their identity in relation to one another, to its continued use. Thus they feel, if they are to avoid a certain ontological disorientation, they must hold each other to its use.

The 'ex post facto *fact' fallacy and the illusion of clarity*

Yet clearly, in the middle of all their confusion, the clarity they appeal to is illusory. And although they lack a sense of confusion, although they do not *feel* confused, to us, they are in fact still confused: for they have clearly mistaken features of their talk (about some 'thing') for the features of the supposed 'thing' itself. And the fact is, that no matter how clear (in certain special moments of reflection) the existence of Godot may seem to them – as a special and separate being beyond themselves who gives a meaning to their lives – not only need Godot not actually exist, they clearly in fact possess no actual knowledge of Godot at all. Indeed, they wonder at first if another wanderer in the wilds, Pozzo, is Godot. They can (and clearly do) live without an actual Godot or Godots. Yet if asked, that is how they explain their conduct: they are waiting for Godot. Without their waiting – false though it may be as an account of what they are actually doing – their life would seem at least to them to lack any sense or meaning. But the only Godot known to them is a Godot 'subsisting' in their ways of talking about such a being between themselves.

And the lesson for us here is that we too are living like his down-and-outs: no matter how clear and definable the *topics* of our talk and discussions may seem to us to be, no matter how strongly we may possess a sense of their 'reality', often, we are merely talking about and studying things which only subsist in the speech we use for co-ordinating our activities with those of the others around us. We have 'given' or 'lent' the things we talk of a nature which – although that which grounds our talk may be such that it 'permits' or 'allows' such an account – they do not actually have. And when it comes to our talk about our own nature, then this issue becomes acute. We cannot 'give it up' and simply turn to an alternative, without a great deal of existential disorientation; yet, we must try.

For it is not just that our means of warranting, justifying, or explaining our actions to those around us – by reference to our supposed 'inner' *mental states*, to 'motives' and 'feelings' supposedly 'in' us somewhere – is false and hides from us the proper relation of our actions to their context, to their surrounding circumstances. Neither is it just that it supports the illusion of an individualistic, ahistorical, decontextualized form of human agency which falsely ignores the role of our relations to others, especially those of our predecessors who fashioned the current 'organized setting' into which we now act. The nature of the falsity involved is even deeper and more dangerous than that: it is to suppose that our essentially unknown and unknowable human nature, that all our meanings, can be captured within a circumscribed and well-defined, systematic discourse; it is to mistake the imaginary entities, that *subsist* only in our stories about ourselves, as actually being who we are. Thus, while the social constructionist approach suggests that our nature is such that it is always in the making, that it is never complete, that new aspects of our being are already emerging from the background to our lives, by contrast, our current attempts to capture ourselves in a range of identifiable, well-defined 'images' or 'models' of our own making, in systematic discourses, suggests otherwise. Such images (or more properly 'we') can create *a sense of* – an illusion of – fixity and completeness about ourselves; we can 'lend' ourselves a nature which, although it is 'permitted' or 'afforded' by what we already are, only represents one small aspect of what in fact we are, and might next become.

But once we come to view the world from within the confines of an orderly, systematic discourse, the claim – that something defined within that discourse essentially underlies all our actions – seems undeniable; no one seems able to formulate a doubt about it within terms acceptable the followers of the system. What is at work here is a special kind of self-deceptive fallacy to which one becomes prone when one's ideal is that of constructing, and thinking within a formal system. It is fallacy of a hermeneutical kind, to do with interpreting the meaning of statements, or states of affairs, retrospectively,[5] from within such systems, and ignoring the socio-historical processes of argument and contest which are involved in their formulation as such. Following

(Ossorio, 1981), I shall call it the '*ex post facto* fact' fallacy. The temporal sequence of events involved is as follows:

1 Firstly, a situation is described which, although we do not realize it at the time, is *open* to a number of possible interpretations.
2 We are, however, then tempted to accept one of these descriptive statements as true.
3 The statement then 'affords' or 'permits' the making of further statements, now of a better articulated nature, till a systematic account has been formulated.
4 The initial interpretation (already accepted as true, of course) now comes to be perceived, *retrospectively*, as owing its now quite definite character to its place within the now well-specified framework produced by the later statements.

In other words, the original situation has now been 'given' or 'lent' a determinate character, within the terms of the system, which it did not, in its original *openness*, actually possess. This, I think, is a fallacy which operates on a grand scale in the social sciences, where we always attempt to make sense of social and psychological phenomena within *well-defined systems* of terms – that is, systematic discourses. It is what makes it seem that such systems can be detached from their origins in people's social activities, and exist in some free-floating sense 'outside' them.[6]

Someone who has studied its nature in relation to the genesis of the scientific fact is, as I have already mentioned, Ludwik Fleck (1979). As we saw earlier, in attempting retrospectively to understand the origins and development (and the current movement) of our thought, we describe their nature within our to an extent now finished and systematic schematisms. Thus, as he goes on to say:

> Cognition modifies the knower so as to adapt him harmoniously to his acquired knowledge. The situation ensures harmony within the dominant view about the origin of knowledge. Whence arises the 'I came, I saw, I conquered' epistemology, possibly supplemented by a mystical epistemology of intuition. (Fleck, 1979: 86–7)

But the trouble is, once 'inside' such systems, it is extremely difficult to escape from them to recapture the nature of our original, open and indeterminate thoughts, the thought to do with the system's development. We can become as Stolzenberg (1978) puts it, 'entrapped'. Where, the attitudes and habits of thought which prevent those within the system from recognizing its inadequacies arise out of them ignoring what Stolzenberg (1978: 224) calls 'those considerations of standpoint that have the effect of *maintaining* the system'. In other words, their plight arises, not just from them ignoring the fact that they have located themselves within a particular discursive or intralinguistic reality (sustained by a discourse couched within a particular idiom), but also from the fact within that their (self-contained, systematic) way of talking does not 'afford' or 'permit' the formulation of questions about its relations to its socio-historical surroundings. Syntax masquerades as meaning to such an effect, that 'We predicate of the thing what lies in the method of representing it . . . ' (Wittgenstein, 1953: no. 104).

'Things' implicit in idioms

Indeed, in mathematics, as Stolzenberg points out, the idiom we use is to do with 'finding' answers to mathematical problems, as if somewhere, in some special Platonic realm, the answers to problems we have not yet solved already exist – just as in psychology and the social sciences, we also attempt to talk of a special realm of reality which already exists independently of our involvement in it. And it is our initial, uncritical acceptance of this way of talking, what he calls our 'initial acts of acceptance as such in the realm of ordinary language use', which produce our entrapment. For:

> As soon as we allow ourselves to accept that talk 'about answers' and 'about statements' is, in some literal sense, about 'things' that stand in some relationship to us . . . it also appears to make sense to ask whether 'knowledge of the answer' is a *necessary* condition for 'the existence of the answer'. And it is precisely here that we may feel an irresistible temptation to say 'No, it is not'. (Stolzenberg, 1978: 242)

Yet what is it which *tempts* us to answer in that way? It is *not* a property of mathematical reality (wherever that Platonic realm might be), but of the logical syntax of the *idiom* within which the mathematical talk was couched in the first place. And, as Stolzenberg goes on to show, the 'intuition' which seems to tempt us is a little confused and seems to face us with a problem: 'By accepting that at least *after* we have carried out the procedure there is a "thing", the answer, that we then confront, we find ourselves faced with the question of whether the act of carrying out the procedure is one of "creation" or "discovery" ' (1978: 242). How shall we decide between them?

> Once we have, unwittingly, committed those acts of 'acceptance as such' concerning ordinary language use that make these pseudoquestions appear to be genuine ones, it does indeed seem to be hard-headed, and perhaps even solipsistic, to refuse to accept that the act of carrying out the procedure is one of discovery and not creation. Why? One reason is that, whereas the act of carrying out the procedure is obviously repeatable, that 'thing' we call 'the answer' is unique. If the act of carrying out the procedure literally produced the answer, then by carrying it out twice we would get two answers; and we see this as plainly counterfactual. (Stolzenberg, 1978: 243)

But notice what Stolzenberg is saying here. He is not actually saying anything factual, but he is merely pointing out how the logical in a special place, the imagination, in the heads of individuals, but in, for instance, the mathematical sense of subsisting, like $\sqrt{-1}$, only 'in' the procedures occurring, ultimately, between people. A sense of their supposed 'reality', their existence independent of the wishes and opinions of individuals, is carried by 'their' apparent ability to 'necessitate' a certain structure in our social interactions. Whereas, the true state of affairs is that it is a certain talked-about way of interacting – as in the Godot example above – that necessitates referring to them as if they must be actually existing things.

The imagined and the imaginary

Let us at this point return to the claim made above: that because discourses work to produce rather than simply to reflect the 'objects' to which the words uttered within them seem to refer, we need a way of talking about their transitional status, their only as yet partial existence, and the possibilities they contain for their own further realization: we need the category of the imaginary. But to say this, we now realize, is itself to say something ambiguous, to make a claim with an unclear meaning. Do we mean that – to the extent that our ways of talking fundamentally influence what we can 'see' in the world – if we are to produce a right way of seeing the world we must take care to discriminate between what is merely *imagined* and what is not, if we are to fashion a right way of talking? Or, do we mean by the *imaginary* something much more fundamental?

The imagined

To explore the first possibility for a moment: it is, for instance, still all too easy to make use of a single, certain, fixed and unrecognized image (metaphor) as an implicit frame in giving *order* to almost all our talk about talk. For example, with regard to the nature of communication, as Reddy (1979) points out, one such metaphor is the CONDUIT metaphor: with the metaphor of THE MIND IS A CONTAINER for ideas, COMMUNICATION IS SENDING[7] an idea from out of the mind of one person, through the 'conduit' of language, into the mind of another – we can find it at use most obviously when we tell someone 'You must *put* your ideas *into* words.' Within the framework structured by this metaphor, communication is easy; it leads us to expect 'success without effort' as the norm in our attempts to communicate; that is, as long as writers or speakers 'express themselves properly'. In other words, the only explanation the conduit metaphor offers for failing to 'find' the right thoughts 'in' what someone says, is that we must not have observed the right rules of communication.

grammar of the idiom used in mathematics is interwoven wit
everyday forms of talk: thus our ways of assessing what
mathematical fact fit in with, so to speak, our everyday practic
assessing what facts are. Thus, although such a problem 'is n
more than a fantasy produced by language' (Stolzenberg, 1978:
is still a peculiarly difficult fantasy to detect.

It is at this point that Stolzenberg's account meets with Wittgen
for just as Stolzenberg is critical of the contemporary mathemat
concept of mathematical 'reality', so Wittgenstein is critical
contemporary concept of mind. Like Stolzenberg, in discussin
'philosophical' problems about the supposed nature of ment
cesses and states can arise out of a way of talking, Wittgenstein
no. 308) also points out the importance of the first step (the firs
acceptance):

> The first step is the one that altogether escapes notice. We talk of p
> and states and leave their nature undecided. Sometime perhaps
> know more about them – we think. But that is just what commit
> particular way of looking at the matter. For we have a definite co
> what it means to know a process better. (The decisive moveme
> conjuring trick has been made, and it was the very one we thou
> innocent) . . .

This first step is important because it is at this point, during a p
decontextualized reflection upon a problem, that an idiom, a
talking structured by a root metaphor, is chosen in which to fo
it – and then all our self-created problems begin.

What Stolzenberg and Wittgenstein make clear is that 'hi
talk about what we take to be realms of reality at high
abstraction, are some very ordinary, everyday influences, in
which work to determine the sense made by such talk (
intelligibility of the abstract relations talked about). For exa
Stolzenberg points out, mathematical talk is currently made se
if it were talk about 'objects and their properties', and that
talk about 'procedures and operations', it would make
different kind of sense, and suggest quite different ways of w
claims to mathematical truth.

This is where the spontaneous, responsive nature of joint
important: while it can create social realities, partially structu
settings created by people's past activities which work as
enabling/constraints for their current activities, it does
unintended consequence, in a way that none of individuals c
can trace back to their own actions. There is thus a *tendenc*
such outcomes as having an 'objective reality' (see the sectio
action in Chapter 2). But as I have already argued, many
such realities are *imaginary*, not in the sense of being real thin

A second image of communication, as Reddy also points out, is of it as giving people partial, step-by-step INSTRUCTIONS for noticing and making *differences* in their attempts at MAKING SENSE of what is happening around them, including the 'instructions' they are given. With a change to this image, the implications in the image of communication as SENDING are radically altered. Within this order of things, as each partial instruction is received, and a difference made or noticed, it is not easy to 'make' sense of what people say. The 'instructions' for making sense are always incomplete. The addition of further specification of what might be meant is always possible. Partial miscommunication, or divergent understandings – 'Oh, I thought he meant X, what did you think?' 'I thought he meant Y.' 'Oh, really!' – are not abnormal. They are tendencies inherent within any activity of making something according to instructions. Partial communication, *possible* meanings are always to be expected. They can only be overcome by continuous effort and large amounts of situated verbal interaction aimed at testing and checking whether a possible understanding is an actual understanding intended.

Although the first image is a classic one, most people now, I feel sure, are far more happy with the second rather than the first. Most now *would* want to argue that, unless effort is expended in the negotiation of meanings, we mostly fail properly to communicate, and much of our argument is conducted in a context of misunderstanding and mutual bewilderment – but are we right? And, is that how 'official reality' works?

Indeed, isn't it still the case for us, that when we write our professional papers and texts, we still unconsciously assume (like Humpty Dumpty) that when we use a word, it means what we want it to mean, nothing more, nothing less; we assume that we have mastered at least the discourse in our professional neck of the woods – else we could never be even partially satisfied with anything we write as being an adequate expression of our 'thoughts'? The fact is, not that one of these images is right and the other wrong, but that *both* these images are at work at different times to order, frame, regiment, or thematize our talk – although, irrespective of the fact, in these poststructuralist times, that many of us now think that it is the second that should be primary, it is still the first that is privileged. It is privileged because within professionalized academic disciplines, systematic, coherent talk is still privileged. That is a part of what it is to have been socialized into one's discipline – to have become a 'licensed' practitioner of it. We have learnt how to discipline or thematize our talk in terms of a certain limited set of images. No wonder Wittgenstein (1953: no. 115) felt it a philosophical discovery to announce: 'A *picture* held us captive. And we could not get outside it, for it lay in our language and language seemed to repeat it to us inexorably.'

But what if, 'against the grain' of our thinking, so to speak, we were systematically to privilege the second image of communication as an 'instructing', rather than the first, of it as a 'sending'? Although such an image of it as involving the continual 'making and perceiving of differences' would seem to go much more 'with the grain' of social constructionist thought, eventually, I feel, we would again find ourselves wanting to make the same complaint: that we were being held captive by a picture, by something *already imagined*, and prevented from making our own meanings as we saw fit, in relation to a particular, practical context. This, however, leaves us in a difficult position; one in which we must say that no one single image as such is adequate to our needs. It is at this point that we need to move from the imagined to the realm of the imaginary.[8]

The imaginary

Now, it could be said,[9] that the point about *talk* of the imaginary is that we need a way of talking about entities which have the following properties: (i) they are incomplete, ongoing, on the way to being other than what they are – in short, they are unimaginable and extra-ordinary; (ii) they are nonlocatable, either in space or time, but can nonetheless have 'real' attributes in the sense of functioning in people's actions in enabling them to achieve *reproducible results* by the use of socially sharable procedures; (iii) they 'subsist' only in people's practices, in the 'gaps', 'zones', or 'boundaries' between people; (iv) to this extent (see my remarks above about our 'makings' in bridging such 'gaps'), we must talk of them as 'negotiated', 'political', 'contestable', or 'prospective' (Myhill, 1952) entities, ones which exist 'in' the world only to the extent that they can play a part in people's discourses – in short, their function is to make a way of human being, a form of life possible;[10] (v) such entities are the *means* of its formation; (vi) however, their 'structure' can never be made wholly 'rationally-visible'; indeed, it makes no sense to talk of them as having a 'spatially surveyable, complete structure'; that is, their partial structuring can only be revealed in 'grammatical' investigations;[11] (vii) in short, such entities – like words themselves (cf. Volosinov above) – are sources of continuous, unforeseeable creativity and novelty. As such, they are not in themselves either good or bad. But they do provide the 'thematics' in terms of which novel statements, perceptions and actions are lent their intelligibility.

A typical imaginary entity is, of course, $\sqrt{-1}$, which indeed now is called an imaginary number.[12] On consideration it will be found to have all the properties mentioned above, except perhaps (now) the lack of a *contested* nature – it is certainly a current source of mathematical novelty. However, in this connection, it is worth remarking that when they were first 'discovered', they were called 'impossible' numbers. Only later did they become 'imaginary', when complex numbers were shown – by Hamilton, for instance, in 1837 in his *Theory of Couples* – to have a hidden meaning: although they cannot exist as mathematical objects, they can nonetheless play a 'real' part in mathematical procedures; not in the sense of correspondence with reality, but in the sense of achieving *reproducible results* by the use of socially sharable (mathematical) procedures. The imaginary number functions as an originary source in mathematical research; an entity which in bridging a 'gap' is a focus of tension, conflict and further mathematical invention.

But perhaps some of the best examples of both imaginary and impossible objects, which nonetheless can generate in one a sense of their 'reality', are currently to be found 'in' keyboard-mediated interactions with computer-generated displays (Greenfield, 1987; Sudnow, 1983). Greenfield (1987) discusses a video arcade maze-game called *Castle Wolfenstein.* Castle Wolfenstein does not exist, yet nonetheless, children in interacting with the computer display come to gain such a grasp of its 'structure' (an architecturally impossible structure, actually), that as Greenfield shows they can draw out its Escher-like plan. What is especially interesting about this game is that as children become experts in the game, the forms upon the screen become a structure of passions for them; a whole new structure of (obessional?) passions and desires is developed. Furthermore, these desires are related to the child's identity within the game – his or her game-self – with affects and motives related to the child's momentary 'position' within the Castle. The whole enterprise is structured by the child's desire for mastery within the game. It is in the reconstituting of motivational and affective forces that one important aspect of the imaginary lies.

Regarding another aspect of its features, Davis and Hersh (1983: 400–5) discuss interacting with a computer display generated by the equations for a 4D-hypercube. They describe how, by interacting with the display long enough, by turning 'it' – that is, the set of projections of the 4D-cube on the 2D-screen – around on the screen, they gained a *feel* for 'it' as a unity. However, this is not only an imaginary object, it is an *impossible* one too – in the sense that no reality yet known to us will permit or afford it; no reality we know of is open, as yet, to being interpreted within the scheme of possibilities it allows. Yet: the gaining of an intuitive grasp of its nature is, clearly, perfectly possible. And as

Davis and Hersh say, regarding such 'imaginary objects': 'These imaginary objects have definite properties. There *are* true facts about imaginary objects.' But in what sense are these results true? It cannot be a matter of correspondence with reality, as in the testing of physical or empirical truths. It can only be a matter of achieving *reproducible results* by the use of socially sharable (mathematical) procedures.

But as Davis and Hersh point out, like Stolzenberg, this means giving up the idea that mathematics is *about* objects, existing in an ideal realm in the same way as in physical reality. Indeed, they go on to argue that it means that even in mathematics, not only is there no undisputable concept of what a 'proof' is, but also that *convincing* proofs do not just consist in the application of a procedure, but also in *persuasive testimony* (sometimes implicit) that the procedure was correctly applied. Without at least the possibility of such testimony, the 'proof' is incapable of commanding universal assent. And my point here is the same: that our ordinary, everyday talk abounds with references to such imaginary things – many of them also impossible in the sense mentioned above. Like Escher drawings, they have the property of being *incomplete* in any one perspective; and while they may seem open to further specification (of an already specified kind), other perspectives present in the 'object' prevent it. Their truly incomplete nature is such that, as Wittgenstein (1980: no. 257) says: 'Here *is* the whole. (If you complete it, you falsify it.)'

Thus, what all this amounts to is that the realm of the imaginary is not itself like a kind of image, a device for framing, regimenting or ordering social life. It contains sources both of novelty and contest. By adding it to our categories for talking about the nature of things, we can begin to talk of complex[13] entities, on the way to being other then at the moment they already are. For instance, I have already talked about 'traditions of argumentation', they are just such complex and reflexively contested entities. As MacIntyre (1981: 207) puts it: 'A living tradition . . . is an historically extended, socially embodied argument, and an argument precisely in part about the goods which constitute that tradition.' 'Traditions, when vital, embody continuities of conflict' (1981: 206). This is a very different idea, of course, from what we used to think of as a tradition. In the past, one of our great image-schematisms for talking about a tradition has been of it as a picturable STRUCTURE, meaning by that, of course, a hierarchically structured, *closed system* of knowledge, consisting in a static network or system of interconnected parts which is supposed to provide its members with ready-made solutions to problems. The realm of the imaginary, however, although it can be talked of – on the basis of the feelings it engenders – is not picturable.

Intralinguistic realities and being taken seriously

This point reaches its full import in the context of Vygotsky's (1986) account of the development of our mental abilities. Where, to remind ourselves of his claims, it is not so much our knowledge, in terms of the *contents* of our minds, that is important, as the *means*, or the 'psychological instruments', we use in 'instructing' ourselves in our activities. The importance of the *imaginary* emerges when the 'instrument' in question is not an empirical object as such, but is an entity that exists only 'in' a form of communicative activity, in a way of talking. For, as we all know, as our linguistic abilities increase, it is not difficult as adults to create whole fictional realities that, although we know them to be impossible (as in many science fiction novels), give us a sufficient sense of reality to move us in many ways. In other words, as adults, we reach a stage in our use of language in which, as we speak, we can create a new artificial, intralinguistic or imaginary context (in the procedural sense of imaginary referred to above) for our own further activities, and thus talk about *possible* rather than our *actual* circumstances.

However, if there is a decrease of reference to what 'is' with a consequent increase of reference to what 'might be', then what is said requires less and less grounding in an extralinguistic context – for it can find its supports almost wholly within the new, linguistically constructed, imaginary context. In other words, if a person wants to be perceived as talking factually, they must *warrant* their talk about what 'might be' as being about what 'is', by making use in their talk of what can be called 'a rhetoric of fact' (Smith, 1978); that is, they must, in addition to the structure of the state of affairs in question, show that certain checks have been, or could be carried out, which warrant their claims: that it is a state of affairs which is, for instance, (1) 'permitted by', or 'grounded in', circumstances; (2) independent of one's wishes; (3) the same for everyone (or could be); (4) dependent upon practical experience; and that the checking procedures used (5) are teachable; (6) were indeed applied aright; and (7) take into account the unique, local, and contingent nature of the circumstances; and so on. And one must provide *opportunities* in one's talk for the challenge of these warrants by others. And only if they fail to take them up, or if they do, one can refute or otherwise discredit their counterclaims, can what one says be accounted as factual.

By the use of such methods and procedures, adults (unlike children) can construct their statements as factual statements *in the course of their talk*, and adult forms of speech can thus come to function with a large degree of independence from their immediate context. While we may be just like computers, in that our powers of reasoned production outrun our powers of recognition (Myhill, 1952), unlike them, we do not have to test all the outcomes of a way of proceeding ahead of time; for we can, so to speak, check them out on the spot, in the course of their occurrence – this is the nature of human accountability, and what makes us (in the end) different from computers. We can assess the worth of a performance, not in terms of its antecedents, its origins or the procedures of its production, but we can *justify* in terms of its *present* appropriateness to its circumstances.

But there is even more to it than this – if, that is, one is to be seen as a morally autonomous, socially competent person in the giving or stating of one's accounts, thus to have one's account taken seriously: there is the question of one's immediate relation to one's audience. A part of what it is to be seen as offering worthwhile accounts, is to be seen as offering something which is, in the circumstances, fitting; that is, something which is socially and morally fitting. So what is at stake here in speaking in a properly accountable manner is, not just whether what is being claimed is simply perceived as being warranted, nor whether it can also be accounted as appropriate to the circumstances, but also, whether it is being said with a proper respect for the audience to whom it is being said: hence, not only must speakers show in their speech an awareness of their 'place', their relatedness to the others around them, their status and the rights it allows them and the duties it places upon them; but they must also construct opportunities accordingly in the course of their talk to be challenged in terms of their awareness of their 'placement', and know how to respond if others take up those opportunities.

Thus to act in an accountable manner, or to give an account of one's actions, is not to accompany one's actions with a description of their structure, to give a 'picture' of them in some way. It is not to do the same thing again but now in other terms; it is to do something else in addition to what one has already done: it is to add a certain kind of further specification to one's actions. By use of the sense-making procedures available to one in one's society, one's actions are 'given' or 'lent' an intelligible and legitimate form; one which shows how they should be treated according to the requirements of the medium of communication in operation in one's society. In other words, no matter how vague and incomplete and open to interpretation they are (and remain), they are 'lent' an imaginary completeness which allows them to be treated as actions of an identifiable kind: they become actions appropriate to the reproduction of a particular form of social life and of social identity. They are 'given' a character, an imaginary character – about which many true facts may be established – but which they do not in themselves in fact have.

Conclusions

In reviewing the importance of the category of the imaginary, let us first review what is involved in moving from a modern to postmodern science of psychology. Amongst the many other shifts it involves, there is a shift from the standpoint of the detached, theory-testing onlooker, to the interested, interpretative, and procedure-testing participant-observer; from one-way action to two-way interaction; from an interest in theories of underlying processes to an interest in accounting for the actual practices in everyday life. Indeed, this latter shift bespeaks a shift in our understanding of what we take rationality to be: there is now a growing recognition that the pursuit of formal rigour is not necessarily a route to rational soundness (Toulmin, 1982b). Indeed, many would now suggest that there is a need to develop methods of inquiry which allow for the warranting (or discrediting) of claims to truth in the course of an investigation's development (Barnes, 1982; Bernstein, 1983; Billig, 1987; Nelson and Megill, 1986; Rorty, 1980) – in which claims about what 'might be' can only be defended as claims about what 'is', by the proper inclusion of what, as mentioned above, might be called 'a rhetoric of reality', a rhetoric which finds its grounding in the as yet unrealized tendencies in a culture's current background activities: in its realm of the imaginary. And this is perhaps a part of what one must learn, in the future, if one is to be taken seriously as a socially competent investigator in one's own right – to take as much account of the partially real, as the already real.

But our conclusions must go deeper than this: for they bear also upon the current Western conception of what it is to be a person, and may be expected to change our attitudes to ourselves in two ways: in both (1) how we talk about our reasons for our actions, and (2) about our supposed self-contained nature. (1) Currently, we believe that what it is to be a person, is that we possess an inner psychic unity (which we call our 'self'), and that it is from our self that all our motivations issue, and that it is within our self that all the reasons for all our actions can be found. If the account here is correct, then we are corporately and incorrigibly self-deceived in these beliefs. But the incorrigibility of the self-deception involved consists in more than just our way of talking about ourselves being corporately maintained; it arises out of the fact that in its maintenance, we construct – in our academic psychology – imaginative surrogates or stand-ins for ourselves, of which such facts are true! But what this means is that many of our ordinary, common-sense ways of accounting for our everyday actions are false – many of our motives are the products of our activities, not the other way around. Primarily, in this view, just as we talk of Godot because we wait, not of waiting because of Godot, so (for instance) we talk of motives because we act, not of acting because we have motives – crazy though it may sound to say it. While our talk of motives may act back upon the disorderly activities of our social lives to 'lend' them some order, the search for 'motives' as such is illusory. It is an attempt to explain our self-formative activities in terms of a product of those self-same activities. (2) If we turn away from this project, and turn instead to an attempt to recognize how we construct (along with others) the contexts which give rise to such self-formative activities, then we can turn to a study of how we socially construct our selves. But as a result, the current Western view of the person as possessing an inner psychic unity can be expected to change to a more pluralistic conception, to a view which recognizes that 'I's in being 'me's must inevitably be intermingled with the 'you's of many 'others'.

Indeed, in this respect, it worth remarking that in our complex (post)modern societies, have begun to talk of members as being and as relating themselves to one another in what we might call relational terms, or in terms of similar differences – rather than simply in either just differences, or just similarities. Thus in America, instead of just blacks and whites, we are now beginning to talk of Hispanic-Americans, of Afro-Americans, and will have soon (no doubt) to talk of Euro-Americans; people who have different cultures within the common culture; people who everyday must bridge the tense 'gaps' between 'othernesses'. In other words, what we now want (and need) is a way of thinking about our communities which affords us the possibility of imagining (thus to formulate intelligible claims about), our relations to one another in terms of similarities (classes); in terms of differences (the politics of gender, ethnicity, identity, etc.); which allows us a unique individuality, while also allowing us to understand our fellowship with all of humankind; and which contests the terms and territories of each.

An image literalized as a picture will not do. In the past we have talked of POLITICS AS A DIALOGUE, but it is an image which has not always served us well – interpreted, as it has been, both within the 'text' of liberal individualism, and the image of society as a fixed STRUCTURE of classes, or of relations of domination. Some noting this, as I have done here, might argue for Rorty's (1980) image (following Oakeshott) of SOCIETY AS CONVERSATION; or, if it is thought to be an insufficiently differentiated activity, for SOCIETY AS AN ECOLOGY OF INTERDEPENDENT REGIONS OF DIFFERENT DISCOURSES, with, of course, in between such regions, 'zones of uncertainty' making up a society's civil society. But to repeat what I said above about images: they always function to order, frame, regiment, or thematize our talk; they work to privilege one version of things over another.

What, then, has been the aim in all this talk, if others will immediately want to be critical of it? To fashion an idiom, a practical idiom, an informative and instructive way of talking, suitable for the practical tasks, not only of making sense of how we make sense together, but also for understanding how we might act in a responsible and accountable manner (which allows for us both to be taken seriously, and to be called to account by them), while still maintaining the partially structured, but nonetheless open nature of everyday social life. And this is the point of the category of the (unpicturable) imaginary: while there might be other ways of achieving the same end, it allows us to proceed in our arguments without, ahead of time, entrapping ourselves in any particular picture. It motivates the imaginative effort required in trying to grasp the nature of a social world in action, a world of creative form-producing (formative) activities, a world in conversation, or within a conversation. And this is the goal, as I see it, of any investigations of a postmodern, social constructionist kind, attempting to account for the nature of our mental life.

Notes

1. I take this term from Rorty (1989), who talks of the open, indeterminate meanings of a metaphors becoming limited or closed by the metaphor being *literalized* in an image or model, e.g. as we move from the general metaphor, in psychology, of human beings as basically thinking beings, to the computer model of thought.

2. As Garfinkel (1967: 22–3) points out, no set of rules in itself is in fact sufficient to sustain an official institution in existence; the *ad hoc* judgments of those within it are also required to 'see the system' in its procedures.

3. I am very influenced here by Anderson's book, but in my terminology, I would want to talk more of nations as *imaginary* communities, and less of them as *imagined* ones. As I see it, the whole idea of nationhood – with the new transition away from State towards ethnic, cultural, and regional nationalisms – is still in the imaginary phase; it has not yet 'crystallized out', so to speak, into any clear images of what a nation is.

4. The 'mind' too is, I maintain, a talked-about-entity like 'Godot', a rhetorical device, talk of which serves to sustain a particular, ideologically structured form of life.

5. Much as in linguistics, one studies only patterns of already spoken words, and not the activity of words in their speaking.

6. This process is also discussed of course by Marx and Engels in their account in *The German Ideology* of how the 'ruling illusion' of 'the hegemony of the spirit in history' (Hegel) is produced.

7. I shall use this useful upper-case way of indexing metaphors, introduced by Lakoff and Johnson (1980), at other points in this chapter.

8. I have not yet had a chance to examine Castoriadis's work in any detail, but I am aware that he thinks that 'the imaginary ultimately stems from the originary faculty of positing or presenting oneself with things and relations which do not exist, in the form of representation (things and relations that are not or have never been given in perception), we shall speak of a final or radical imaginary as the common root of the actual imaginary and of the symbolic. This is, finally, the elementary and irreducible capacity of evoking images.' And that he too sees its necessity as arising out of the 'gap' between signifier and signified: 'The decisive grip the imaginary holds on the symbolic can be understood on

the basis of the following consideration: symbolism assumes the capacity of positing a permanent connection between two terms in such a way that one 'represents' the other. It is only at very advanced stages in lucid rational thinking that these three elements (the signifier, the signified and their *sui generis* tie) are maintained as simultaneously united and distinct in a relation that is at once firm and flexible' (1987: 127). Until that advanced stage, its nature remains uncertain.

9. I phrase it this way, for some (including myself in other contexts) might say that even to phrase the issue this way, in terms of 'entities', in terms of 'things' (nouns) rather than of activities, practices, etc., i.e. verbs, is still to privilege a language of constancy and substance, rather than a language of flux and change.

10. And to imagine a language is to imagine a form of life . . .' (Wittgenstein, 1953: no. 19).

11. 'The main source of our failure to understand is that we do not *command a clear view* of the use of words. Our grammar is lacking in this sort of perspicuity . . . ' (Wittgenstein, 1953: no. 122). It can only be discovered from a study, not of conventions of usage, nor from isolated examples of supposed correct usage, but of how 'it' necessarily 'shapes' those of our everyday communicative activities in which it is involved, *in practice*; an influence which is only revealed in the 'grammar' of such activities. Hence Wittgenstein's (1953: no. 373) claim that: 'Grammar tells us what kind of object anything is . . .'

12. First, we can note that in one interpretation, the dimension of real numbers can be identified with actuality, and the imaginary dimension with possibility. In electrical engineering, it is the realm of the imaginary that makes 'movement' between actualities a possibility.

13. An allusion to complex numbers *is* intended.

6
Linguistic Relativity in a World of Events

> If you ask A to explain how he got B's agreement so readily [as to what he was referring to in his talk], he will simply repeat to you, with more or less elaboration or abbreviation, what he said to B. He has no notion of the process involved. The amazingly complex system of linguistic patterns and classifications, which A and B must have in common before they can adjust to each other at all, is all *background* to A and B.
>
> Whorf, 1956: 211, my emphasis

In this chapter, I want to connect with some of the themes already explored in the previous chapter – to do with how we might talk about the only partially formed features of still developing social realities in a world of events and activities, rather than things and substances. But here, I want to do so from a slightly different perspective, one which explores more deeply the different formative powers of different ways of speaking, and the importance of Whorf's (1956) linguistic relativity thesis to these issues. Indeed, it seems to me that Whorf's work has been misunderstood in the past in at least these two ways: (i) as being to do only with what linguists would call syntax, rather than with what Wittgensteinians would call 'logical grammar'; and (ii) as being to do with *patterns* of already spoken words, rather than to do with the 'shaping' power of words in their speaking.[1] Indeed, this misreading of Whorf, is (it seems to me) itself a case in point of the very principle of linguistic relativity at work. We can (perhaps) see this, if we examine how he himself introduced its nature to a lay audience. He began by mentioning the revolutionary changes that have occurred in the world of science and the new ways of thinking they have introduced, and then went on to say:

> I say new ways of THINKING[2] about facts, but a more nearly accurate statement would say new ways of TALKING about facts. It is this USE OF LANGUAGE UPON DATA that is central to scientific progress. Of course, we have to free ourselves from that vague innuendo of inferiority which clings to the word 'talk', as in the phrase 'just talk'; that false opposition which the English-speaking world likes to fancy between talk and action. (Whorf, 1956: 220, his emphases)

In fact, just as for Austin (1962) so also for Whorf: you can (actively) do things with words. It is this that seems to have been missed in past readings (and speakings) of Whorf. And it will be through an account of the formative function of talk (that I shall elaborate below) that we will be able to 'see' (to use an inappropriate metaphor) Whorf's work in a new light.

In this connection, if we turn to more recent times, to Rorty's claim, in his *Philosophy and the Mirror of Nature* (1980: 12), that 'it is pictures rather than propositions, metaphors rather than statements, which determine most of our philosophical convictions', we can see that claim also as a version of linguistic relativity. He is suggesting that, traditionally, our philosophical talk about mind and language has been shaped by a whole set of visual or specular metaphors, and that it is these metaphors, rather than the nature of our mental activities themselves, that have determined the forms and dimensions of what we feel it important to debate in our philosophical investigations. Where, 'the picture which holds traditional philosophy captive is that of the mind as a great mirror, containing various representations – some accurate, some not – and capable of being studied by pure, non-empirical methods. Without the notion of the mind as mirror, the notion of knowledge as accuracy of representation would not have suggested itself' (Rorty, 1980: 12). If we want to change our philosophical 'views' (sic) of the world, 'we have to get the visual, and in particular, the mirroring, metaphors out of our speech altogether' (Rorty, 1980: 371). Thus as Rorty sees it (says it) – and I have argued this also, especially in the previous chapter – intellectual progress is not a matter simply of winning *the* argument, but of changing the agenda of argumentation by changing the metaphors, the vocabulary in terms of which academic, intellectual argument is conducted (Rorty, 1989). And this is, of course, precisely my aim here.

Here, as in previous chapters, I want to explore the implications of an account of language in which language is *not* primarily a device for 'picturing', 'depicting' or 'mirroring' (truthfully or otherwise) an already existing language-independent reality, but is primarily a formative device for *use* by people in coordinating their individual actions (Mills, 1940; Wittgenstein, 1953). Thus, rather than simply representing 'reality', speaking and writing should here again be 'seen as' (talked of as)[3] 'giving', or 'lending' a form or structure to a state of affairs, situation, or circumstance appropriate to it having currency, so to speak, in the way of life in which the language is used. In other words, something which is only partially specified and thus open to further specification, is given further specification linguistically, *but only according to communicative requirements*; that is, only in a way that promotes, as Mills (1940) says, 'the coordination of diverse action', or, in Wittgenstein's (1953) terms, 'going on', in the living of a certain 'form of life'. Thus our ways of speaking and writing work *practically*, to formulate the topics of our discourse and to give them a structure appropriate to our forms of life, which otherwise they would in themselves lack.

Covert grammar, rational-invisibility, and illusions of discourse

Such a view of linguistic functioning – of speaking and writing as not working by the use of already fixed codes simply to represent 'reality', but of them as being continuously creative or formative processes in which we construct the situation or context of our communication *as we communicate* – is, for us, to repeat, utterly revolutionary. As Harris (1980, 1981) points out, it calls in question one of the great myths of our time, a myth which since antiquity has been a part in one form or another of the Western tradition. In that myth, it is supposed that words stand for things either 'out there' in the world external to the language-user (in what Harris calls the 'reocentric' version of 'surrogationalism'), or (in its 'psychocentric' version) for things to be located internally, 'in the mind' of the language-user. And what I want to do in this chapter, through an examination of Whorf's (1956) work upon the languages of the American Indians, is to illustrate what it might be like *not* to think, or talk, in this way about ourselves. But to demonstrate how a quite different way of talking about ourselves – in terms of events (or as Whorf says 'eventing') – could lead to us experiencing ourselves in quite a different way. As a preliminary to this task, I want to do four things.

The first is to attempt to make clear that, when Whorf spoke of grammatical categories, he did not always mean what linguists now talk of as syntax, that is, recognizable patterns of already spoken words – often he meant something quite different. He distinguished between what he called overt and covert grammatical categories – what he also called PHENOTYPES and CRYPTOTYPES – in the following manner. Overt grammatical categories, or phenotypes, are syntactically marked in some explicit, formal way within the sentence in which they appear, where their formal nature is determined by their place in the formal patterning of that sentence. Covert categories, or cryptotypes, are quite different. 'The class membership of the word is not apparent until there is a question of using it . . . then we find that this word belongs to a class of words requiring some sort of distinctive treatment . . . This distinctive treatment we may call the REACTANCE of the category' (1956: 89). He called such a category a CRYPTOTYPE because, as a 'hidden' category, 'they easily escape notice and may be hard to define, and yet may have a profound influence on linguistic behaviour' (1956: 92). For instance, 'names of countries and cities in English form a cryptotype with the reactance that they are not referred to by personal pronouns as object of the prepositions "in, at, to, from". We can say "I live in Boston" but not "That's Boston – I live in it" ' (1956: 92). Instead of 'in it' or 'at it' we say 'here' or 'there'. As I see it, this is what Wittgenstein (1953) would called an aspect of 'logical' grammar. And when he says 'grammar tells us what kind of object anything is' (1953: no. 373), it is by examining the *reactance* related to our talk of 'it', that we are able to make clear to ourselves what that 'it' is for us. That is a part (see Chapter 3) of Wittgenstein's method of doing philosophy. And this is the reason for my claim above: that to interpret Whorf's talk of grammar in a merely syntactic sense was an inadequate interpretation. The *reactance* occasioned by the use of a word only shows up in the context of its use, in its speaking.

Second: Following on from this, the account of language I have given thus far in this book represents our 'basic' ways of speaking as working 'instructively' – in their speaking – to invoke or provoke in us, as both responsible listeners or readers in a certain society, a creative process in which we determine what it is that is officially 'rationally-visible' to us (Garfinkel, 1967). Their *reactance* is such as to suggest that it is this, rather than that, kind of thing we are talking about. In other words, our 'accounting practices' work to 'instruct' us in how to 'see' an otherwise indeterminate flow of activity as having this, rather than that, kind of form to it (a form which otherwise it would not in itself have). Our 'seeing' is 'in-formed' by the terms in the dominant discourse of the day. But it is worth mentioning before we go any further, that by the same token, those self-same, official accounting practices will also work to render other aspects of what occurs 'rationally-*in*visible' to us.

To elaborate: in our everyday lives we are, as I have already said, embedded within a social order which, morally, we must continually reproduce in all the mundane activities we perform from our 'place', 'position', or status within it. Thus we must account for all our experiences in terms both intelligible and legitimate within it, and currently, we live in a social order that, officially, is both individualistic and scientistic. Everything which occurs must be made sense of in its terms. It is because of this that we have concentrated far too much attention upon the isolated individual studied from the point of view of an uninvolved observer. And ironically, what has been rendered 'rationally-invisible' to us in us making sense of our world in this way, are the sense-making procedures made available to us in the social orders into which we have been socialized. These are procedures which, as I have said, have their provenance in the history of our culture, and in terms of which, as Garfinkel and the ethnomethodologists have shown, we perceive the flow of activity around us as 'visibly-rational'. We do not, however, see them as procedures which we ourselves perform – as the epigraph quote from Whorf, above, illustrates – they are seen in other terms: as the operation of cognitive mechanisms 'in' individual people; as structures with their own dynamic which determine people's observed behaviour. It is in these terms too, that language appears not as a formative activity, but as a kind of logical calculus within individuals; indeed, it is impossible to 'see' language as formative in such terms. In this view, communication *is* simply a matter of A telling (transferring information) to B in his or her talk. Indeed, another aspect of the rational blindness induced in us by our current individualistic modes of accountability, is our failure to attribute sufficient significance to the second-person standpoint in life, to 'you's, to the 'involved' or 'participatory' standpoint in which what are thought to be 'I's *meanings* are perceived and understood as such; that is, from within the situation containing them both, the situation which third-person external observers are 'outside' of. It is only second-person listeners who have the right to expect first-person speakers to be as they present themselves as being (Goffman, 1959).[4] Thus, unlike third-person outsiders, *they* present speakers with a context of enabling-constraints that they must *act into*, if listeners are morally to undertake the duty of attending only to what speakers intend them to attend to.

Third: An even more important phenomenon, perhaps, and certainly more bewildering, as we have already to an extent seen, is the imaginary entities our ways of speaking convince us exist. These are illusions which arise from *projecting* back into the phenomena of our concern, our methods of representing it – so that it appears to us as if we *are* simply 'mirroring' in the structure of our representations the structure of reality. This tendency leads us, as Goodman (1972: 24) says, to 'mistake features of discourse for features of the subject of discourse'. I have already discussed aspects of this problem in Chapter 5, but here I would like to take that discussion further.

Consider the following examples: (i) We speak of understanding as a 'mental process' and wonder what goes on in our heads which enables us to do it, and we set out to attempt to discover its nature. 'But', says Wittgenstein (1981: no. 446),

> don't think of understanding as a 'mental process' at all.—For *that* is the way of speaking that is confusing you. Rather ask yourself: in what kind of case, under what circumstances do we say 'Now I can go on'. . . That way of speaking [in terms of 'mental processes'] is what prevents us from seeing the facts without prejudice . . . *That* is how it can come about that the means of representation produces something *imaginary*. So let us not think we *must* find a specific mental process, because the verb 'to understand' is there and because one says: Understanding is an activity of the mind.

The idea that there *must* be a process in our head arises, not from what we know about our own inner mental processes, but from the influences of our own ways of talking upon us.

Another obvious illusion is (ii) the feeling that every 'thing' must possess a fundamental, underlying, systematic structure, amenable to a single logical description – the true description of what the thing 'is'. But *is* there always such a structure there to be described? Goodman (1972: 30–1), in discussing 'the way the world is', argues not:

> There are very many different equally true descriptions of the world . . . no one of these different descriptions is *exclusively* true, since the others are also true. None of them tells us *the* way the world is, but each of them tells us *a* way the world is.

For, not everything is a fully completed, objective thing; many 'things' are incomplete, and on the way to becoming something other than what they were when they were last observed – the world included. And what Goodman says of the world, Wittgenstein (1980, I: no. 257) says of things in general:

> Mere description is so difficult because one believes that one needs to fill out the facts in order to understand them. It is as if one saw a screen with scattered colour-patches, and said: the way they are here, they are unintelligible; they only make sense when one completes them into a shape.—Whereas I want to say: Here *is* the whole. (If you complete it, you falsify it.)

Thus, as I have suggested before, it is in the very nature of our surrounding circumstances, that they can only be partially specified and lack a final specification as to their actual structure.

Fourth: However, as an incomplete process, practical activity is still open to, or able to take on, or to be lent, further specification. It seems to 'invite' one or another kind of completion; and this, as Goodman and Wittgenstein suggest, *is* what often happens in our attempts to describe it: we describe an incomplete process by its supposed final product. William James (1890: 196) describes this tendency as 'the psychologist's fallacy':

> The *great* snare of the psychologist is the *confusion of his own standpoint with that of the mental fact* about which he is making his report . . . Both it itself and its object are objects for him. Now when it is a *cognitive* state . . ., he ordinarily has no other way of naming it than as the thought, percept, etc., *of that object*. He himself, meanwhile, knowing the self-same object in *his* way, gets easily led to suppose that the thought, which is *of* it, knows it in the same way in which he knows it, although this is very often far from being the case. The most fictitious puzzles have been introduced into our science by this means.

And this is my point here: unless we become sensitive to the manner in which our ways of speaking form and shape the topics of our discourse, we shall often be investigating *fictions* of our own devising without recognizing them as such. Psychologists are attempting to discover how people *would* perceive the world *if* it was as they depict it to be: as if full of 'things' and 'substances'. But is it? In an attempt to answer this question, I would now like to turn to a study of Whorf's (1956) writings, and in particular what he had to say about a very different world from ours: the Hopi world of events, or 'eventing'.

Metaphors we (English-speakers) live by

In his chapter on 'the relation of habitual thought and behaviour to language', Whorf (1956: 138) explores two questions: (1) Are our concepts of 'time', 'space' and 'matter' given in substantially the same form by experience to all men and women, or are they in part conditioned by the structure of particular languages? (2) Are there traceable affinities between (a) cultural and behavioural norms, and (b) large-scale linguistic patterns? To both questions, Whorf answers 'Yes'. Let me turn first to what he has to say about the use of nouns and noun phrases in talking about things in general.

The world of the Standard Average European (SAE) language[5] is, Whorf claims, a world of matter or substances, of things, in general thought of as 'stuff'. We have two kinds of nouns for use in talking of such stuff: individual (or count) nouns and mass nouns. Individual nouns are used in speaking of bodies with definite outlines: 'a tree, a stick, a man, a hill', while mass nouns are used for homogeneous continua without implied boundaries. However, as Whorf points out, we perceive few natural occurrences in .his way, as unbounded extents: 'air, water, rain, snow, rock, dirt, grass, and sea' perhaps, but the distinction is more widespread in language than in the observable appearance of things. For, in the context of their occurrence we perceive most such substances as possessing a definite outline. However, their outline can be different in different contexts. The mass noun has to be further individualized by the use of additional linguistic devices. This is partly done by the use of the names of *body-types*: 'stick of wood', 'piece of cloth', 'pane of glass' and so on; but also by introducing the names of *containers*: 'glass of water', 'bag of flour' and so on. These very common container formulae, in which 'of' has an obvious, visually perceptible meaning ('contents'), influence our feeling about the less obvious body-type formulae, says Whorf: 'sticks', 'pieces', 'panes', etc., seem to *contain* something, a 'stuff', 'substance', or 'matter' equivalent in some way to the 'water', 'flour', etc., in the container formulae. The formulae in both cases are similar: *formless item plus form*. Our ways of talking are such as to require us to talk of many things in terms of such a binomial structure; that is the only way in which they can be 'given' or 'lent' an intelligible character. Hence, says Whorf, for SAE people, the philosophical ideas of 'substance' and 'matter' are instantly acceptable as common sense; they represent in general the ways in which we already talk in particular 'about our reality'.

Nowhere is the power of linguistic analogy in the creation of imaginary entities more apparent than in the creation, among the stuff and substances of our universe, of the formless stuff we call 'time'. Such terms as 'September', 'morning', 'noon' and 'sunset' are with us nouns, and they have little formal linguistic difference from other nouns, says Whorf. There is for us some 'thing' to which such phase-nouns, when we use them, seem to refer. In constructing it, we also apply here – in talking of 'a moment of time', 'a second of time', 'a year of time', etc. – the same linguistic formula of *formless item plus form*. We imagine that, just as 'a bottle' contains a quantity of liquid, so 'a summer' actually contains a quantity of time, marked out by 'beginning' and 'end' boundaries (which then puzzle us as to when exactly they occur). But in Hopi, all such phase terms, like 'morning', 'winter', etc., are not nouns at all but, says Whorf, a kind of adverb. Nor are these 'temporals' ever used as nouns, either as subjects or as objects. Thus they would not say, as we do, 'in the morning', but 'while morning-ing'. Indeed, as Whorf says, Hopi is a timeless language in the sense that, what we feel must be explicitly recognized as features of the passage of time, are not recognized as such in Hopi. Neither is there any 'thingifying' of time as a region, extent, or quantity; nothing is suggested about it in Hopi, says Whorf, other than the 'getting later' or 'latering' of it.

More recently, Lakoff and Johnson (1980) have made many of the same points as Whorf about our English ways of talking; they have explored, as they put it, 'the metaphors we live by'. They also discuss *container-metaphors*, as well as what they call *orientational metaphors* (such as consciousness is UP; unconsciousness is DOWN), *structural metaphors* (such as TIME IS MONEY – Don't waste time) and ontological metaphors (such as THE MIND IS A MACHINE – My mind just isn't operating today). In discussing time, they point out that the major metaphor used is that of TIME PASSES US, which gives rise to the two subclasses of TIME IS A MOVING OBJECT and WE MOVE THROUGH TIME, such that it is not inconsistent for us to say both 'In the following weeks . . .' *and* 'In the weeks ahead of us . . .' – which initially might seem to be contradictory, implying that the future is both behind and in front of us. Like Whorf's, their work also demonstrates the ineradicably metaphorical nature of *our* ways of talking.

The essence of metaphor is, they say (1980: 5), 'understanding one *thing* in terms of another' (my emphasis). There is, however, both a superficial and a deep sense in which this claim may be understood.

Superficially, it can be read simply as meaning a shifting or displacement of words from a supposed literal to a metaphorical context of usage: a form of words which already makes sense in one context is used to make a similar kind of sense in another. But they make a deeper claim, that 'metaphor is pervasive in everyday life. Our ordinary conceptual system, in terms of which we both think and act, is fundamentally metaphorical in nature', they say (1980: 3). In other words, the otherwise utterly undifferentiated flow of activity in which we are involved is always given or lent an intelligible form linguistically, a form which enables one to perceive it as 'accountable'; that is, as an organization of 'commonplace events'. In this deeper sense, then, while there may be what one might call canonical or paradigmatic linguistic usages, there are no literal usages – if by literally speaking one means describing what is there independently of the shaping function of language.

Metonymical forms of talk

Is it the same for the Hopi? Not quite, Whorf claims. While full of figures of speech, of course, their language, he says, has neither the need for nor analogies upon which to build a concept of existence as a duality of *formless-matter plus things-with-forms* (that is, bodies and quasibodies made from, consisting of, or containing, the basic substances of the world). The general character of the Hopi cosmos is marked out by the use of verb or predicator forms (if 'verb' is the right term to use here in discussing a language not one's own), not by nouns and nominals. 'The Hopi microcosm', says Whorf (1956), 'seems to have analyzed reality largely in terms of EVENTS (or better "eventing")'; and he goes on to describe the different natures of the 'eventing' of events:

> events are considered the expression of invisible intensity factors, on which depend their stability and persistence, or their fugitiveness and proclivities. It implies that existents do not 'become later and later' all in the same way; but some do so by growing like plants, some by diffusing and vanishing, some by a procession of metamorphoses, some by enduring in one shape till affected by violent forces. In the nature of each existent able to manifest as a definite whole is the power of its own mode of duration: its growth, decline, stability, cyclicity, or creativeness. Everything is thus already 'prepared' for by the way it now manifests by earlier phases, and by what will be later, partly has been, and partly is in the act of being so 'prepared' (1956: 147)

While 'planning for the future' is one of the central activities in *our* form of life, and is the activity towards which science is thought of as contributing, for the Hopi, Whorf claims, it is 'preparation'. Hopi preparation, however, is quite different from our planning. Both involve thinking. But we talk of our thinking as having to do with us constructing or formulating – as a result of a means–end, cause–effect analysis – a plan (or theory, or set of principles, etc.) which we then have 'to put into practice' in some mysterious way. The mysterious hiatus between theory and practice arises for us because, given our ways of talking, 'matter' is only changed and fashioned by other matter impinging directly upon it, and it is quite unnatural for us to think of our thought as pervading and as being able to affect the world around us directly in any way. What is unnatural for the Hopi, however, is the thought that it does not! While our thought takes place in an *imaginary space* – 'in our minds', we say, 'somewhere privately within us', either 'in the forefront or the back of our minds' – the Hopi world has no such imaginary space. The corollary of this, as Whorf points out, is that thinkings and feelings to do with 'eventings' in the world are located there, out in the world in which the eventing takes place – as a natural part of the whole into which they are interwoven.

Thoughts and feelings are thus, for the Hopi, treated as directly connected to events in the world in some way: if one's thinking – about the health and growth of some plants, say – is good, then it will be good for the plants, if bad, then the reverse. But the kind of thought meant here is not 'theoretical' thought, the preliminary formulation of possibilities in imaginary space, but 'practical' thought, the invoking of the appropriate imagery, the thinking of oneself 'into' the context of the possibly required practical activities, the conducting of appropriate 'thought experiments', the attempt to increase one's awareness of what actually 'is', to rid oneself of goals irrelevant to the task in hand, and so on. That kind of thought power is, says Whorf, the force behind ceremonies, prayer sticks, ritual smoking, etc. 'The prayer pipe is regarded as an aid to "concentrating" (so said my informant). Its name, *na'twanpi*, means "instrument of preparing" ' (1956: 150). Those who gather around to smoke the pipe before peace negotiations are already, in practice, halfway towards a more common, cooperative form of life. Such a form of activity – of working within a present situation, thus to accumulate within a part of it a sufficient influence to affect an aspect of the whole – is, we might say, metonymical: a part is taken as representative, or as invoking the whole. But if, as Whorf implies, everything is in some sense everywhere in the Hopi world, then it is entirely reasonable to hold that what one does in one part of a field of interwoven activities, ripples out, so to speak, and affects what happens in the totality. In metonymic ways of speaking, a feather invokes the bird, an eagle's feather all the eagle's qualities, such that to possess such a feather gives one access to all the eagle's qualities in some way; just as we, being speakers of English (SAE) and possessing some of the requisite linguistic skills feel we possess access to English as a whole.

Practically speaking

The importance of preparing activities to the Hopi are indicative, as Whorf makes clear, of their timeless notion of time. While we spatialize time in a three-tense system of past, present and future, they use only a two-tense system of earlier and later, a system which, as he suggests, seems to correspond better with the feeling of duration[6] as it is experienced. For, conscious experience, even for us, does not obviously seem to contain a past, present, and future, but a complex unity: 'EVERYTHING is in consciousness, and everything in consciousness IS, and is together', says Whorf (1956: 143–4). There is, however, a distinction in consciousness between that with which we are in immediate *contact* (what we are seeing, hearing, touching) – the 'present' – and what is not a part of our immediate circumstances. Within that second category we may distinguish between what we can *remember* – the 'past' – and what we can *imagine*, intuit, believe, or fancy – the 'future'. All these – what we are in contact with, remembering and imagining – are all in consciousness together. But whereas we order our conscious experience by talking of it in spatial terms, the Hopi make use of no such ordering devices; time for them enters into the above scheme by it *all* 'getting later' (or 'latering') together. Thus for them, everything which has ever been done is accumulated and carried over into the present event, while what it is becoming affects what it is also. It is, says Whorf, as if the return of the day was felt as the return of the same person (or group of persons, which in a sense, a practical sense, it is), not as 'another day' like the appearance of another and entirely different person.

All this implies that the answer to at least Whorf's first question, as to whether *our* concepts of 'time', 'space' and 'matter' are *not* given to all humankind in essentially the same form, is 'No'. The Hopi, in some sense, live in a space and time quite different from our space and time. Furthermore, whatever the space–time or time–space they do live in is, 'it' seems to be furnished quite differently from ours. It seems to be full of activities in which they can (to an extent) participate, rather than of things external to them. Such a form of life appears quite incomprehensible to us; we cannot easily assimilate it to any already familiar, *organized* common sense scheme of understanding. Indeed, our difficulties with it are manifested, as Harris (1980: 18) says, in our modern theories of language, for they present

> a revealing anatomy of the difficulties inherent in an essentially literate society's attempt to conceptualize something it has forgotten, and which it cannot recall from its cultural past: what an essentially non-written form of language is like.

But nonetheless, there are enclaves of understanding within our own 'reality' which appear to be very similar – as I shall illustrate in a moment below. Yet we fail to notice this. Why? As Whorf points out, the major reason is that the philosophical views characteristic of Western thought – especially Cartesian mind–body dualism – receive massive support from the form plus substance dichotomy (indeed, as a case in point, body–mind dualism is still as prevalent as ever, especially in artificial intelligence research). While holistic, monistic, relativistic and contextualist views of reality, similar to those of the Hopi, have been formulated by philosophers and scientists, they remain incomprehensible in everyday life.

For a case in point, we can turn for a moment to mention the fate of the attempt by Pepper (1942) and others (such as Rosnow and Georgoudi, 1986) to canvass a movement in psychology called *Contextualism*. The 'root metaphor' of contextualism is, says Pepper (1942: 232), 'the historic event', where, just as in Whorf's account of Hopi, the contextualist does not mean by such a term 'primarily a past event' (if indeed there is such a 'thing' to which to refer). It means, he says, an event that is 'alive in its present', it is 'the event in its actuality . . . when it is going on *now*' (1942: 232), and he continues in his writing to attempt to specify his meaning more exactly. However, we can feel the tension in his writing between his feeling that an 'event' is not a 'thing', and his need to write as if there is something (some 'thing') already there that his writing is 'about'. For although, in giving instances of the contextualist root metaphor 'we should', he says, 'use only verbs', he himself continually slips back into the use of nouns and noun phrases, such as 'the ever changing event', rather than being prepared simply to say, for instance, that it is 'eventing' which concerns him. Why? Could it be that he feels such a new way of talking would not be accounted intelligible within the social institutions in which he wants to have his say? We shall find that it is as easy for Pepper to jump out of his language as to jump out of his skin, that his language speaks him more than he speaks it. And inextricably embedded in its nature is a certain metaphysics – of things and substances – making it very difficult for a way of talking based in verbs to be acceptable. Given the difficulty in grasping what it is that contextualists are talking 'about', it is not surprising that it shows little sign at the moment of 'catching on'.

Why is this? It is not because such a view is refuted by *the* facts – indeed, as we now realize, there is no way in which 'facts' as such could ever 'refute' a way of speaking, for it determines what are to be 'accounted' as facts. Nor is it because, contrary to what often is claimed, they are counter-intuitive. While Newtonian notions of space, time and matter are often said to be intuitive, and relativity is cited as an example of how mathematical and scientific investigation can prove intuition wrong, is *that* actually what Einstein's discovery (invention?) of the theory of relativity proves? Laying the blame on intuition, says

Whorf, is wrong: 'Newtonian space, time, and matter are no intuitions. They are', he says, using a specially selected word (1956: 153, my emphasis), '*recepts* from culture and language. That is where Newton got them.' In other words, as recepts (to give the dictionary definition of the word), they are mental images without an intellectual basis. What they represent as being 'in' the world is 'in' our way of representing it. They arose out of our current ways of speaking, and that is why – unlike the contextualist vocabulary of 'events in their going on now' – they were so easily accepted back into them.

As Whorf (1956: 152) says, if intuition is not to blame, the reason why relativistic and contextualist views find it so difficult to gain acceptance is that 'they must be talked about in what amounts to a new language' – one which, so to speak, seems to go against the grain of our current ways of talking. They require, apparently, a language of verbs, a vocabulary of activities; seemingly, we must talk in terms of 'eventing', etc., in an attempt to make a new kind of sense. But must we? Are our current ways of speaking really inadequate?

For Newton, space and time were *absolutes*, there independently of how one might talk about them or investigate them; they were not hypotheses ('Hypotheses non fingo'), nor were they terms to be used in constructing a frame of reference relative to events. In other words, the words 'space' and 'time' were taken as denoting 'its', existing independently of any activities or events taking place within them. But what if, along with Whorf, we now take 'space' and 'time' as belonging to us, so to speak, rather than to our world, and investigate them as involved in 'fashions of speaking', serving the social purpose of coordinating diverse action?

In everyday practical contexts of usage, rather than use such terms to represent absolute and abstract entities, we often say such things as: (1) 'There's no space in our relationship for such things', (2) 'I must make time for that', (3) 'He's spaced-out, man', (4) 'We've too much time on our hands', and so on. In other words, we use the words 'space' and 'time' in constituting actual and concrete features in and of the context in which they are used. We indicate by their usage, perhaps (to take the examples above in turn), that: (1) certain activities will invite sanctions; (2) that we're under pressure, that too much should not be expected of us, but we'll still try to do it; (3) that he's disorganized, that there is a lack of logical coherence in his behaviour and he is not to be relied upon; (4) we're bored, not engaged in anything interesting, so we're open to suggestions, and so on. How we live practically is not best described as taking place in a three-dimensional space of things in motion through a fourth space-like dimension, time, but in a 'time–space' of 'nonlocatable' regions and moments, offering us various invitations and prohibitions, etc., *relative to our current activity*.

It is difficult for us, however, not to assign places in space somewhere, in which we feel the 'things' we speak of are located. Yet as Wittgenstein (1981: nos. 486 and 497) says:

> 'I feel a great joy'—Where?—that sounds like nonsense. And yet one does say 'I feel a joyful agitation in my breast'.—But why is joy not localized? Is it because it is distributed all over the body? Even where the feeling that arouses joy is localized, joy is not . . . 'Where do you feel grief?'—In the mind.—What kind of consequences do we draw from the assignment of place? One does not speak of a bodily place of grief . . .

The answer will occur to us, he suggests (1980, I: no. 129) if we ask: 'But what does behaviour include here? Only the play of facial expression and gestures? Or also the surrounding, the occasion of the expression?' In other words, talk of place does not imply geographical localization, but is, in fact, of the circumstances surrounding our expression. For example, while we might say to someone 'The love I feel for you is in my *heart*', that is not where we should look for the import of their statement. In practice, its implications are 'in' the subsequent context between that person and oneself the statement helps to create. Such circumstances can be intelligibly described perfectly well in the ordinary language available to us currently. In other words, the establishing of a special language for the description of 'eventing' is not as necessary as Whorf thought. What then is required?

Only, seemingly, the recognition and restoration to legal tender, so to speak, both of some currency we already possess, as well as the restoration of people's rights to coin more, as and when they require it. The establishing of these new ways of sense-making is difficult, not because they are contrary to fact, nor because they are counter-intuitive, nor because they require description in a wholly new language, but because they require the reconstruction of the official accounting practices (our 'basic' ways of talking) in terms of which we maintain our 'official' realities – our official forms of life. For it is these that currently rule ways of talking in terms of events and 'eventing' out of court.

Theories and accounts

What I have attempted to set out above, then, is an *account* of something to which currently we are somewhat rationally blind: namely, our own accounting practices, and the part played in them by the rhetorical and tropological functions of language in giving articulable form to otherwise unformulated feelings. Accounts are such that, in the context of their telling, they are 'self-specifying' in that they work to construct or to specify further that context or setting within which, and by use of which, their telling *makes* sense. The rhetorical essence of an account is that in its telling it works practically to inform or to instruct recipients of it – to the extent that they accept it – as to how they *should* make sense of the circumstances around them. In other words, it informs them as to what kind of person they *should be*. Unlike theoretical statements, they do not usually need any explanation as to their meaning. Even if they prove unacceptable to those to whom they are offered, their import is understood.

As already mentioned, I have called the kind of knowledge required to be able to talk and to understand in this self-specifying way, knowing of the third kind: it is a knowing *from within* a discursively constructed situation; that is, from within an event. As such, it is a form of knowledge whose nature cannot be described theoretically, in ways amenable to evidential support. Even to try to do so would be paradoxical: for we want an account of it in practice, a contexted understanding of it from within the context of its use, and to assume that its nature could be described theoretically would still be to assume that it could be described in a context-free way – hence my insistence that what I have provided here is an account of our accounting practices and not a theory of them. Thus it cannot be judged as to its truth or falsity, for it is not formulated so as to be amenable to evidential support; it can only be judged practically, as to whether it is instructive or not, and whether it 'accord[s] with the practice of the person giving the description' (Wittgenstein, 1980, I: no. 548), that is, 'it is not a kind of *seeing* on our part; it is our *acting*, which lies at the bottom of the language-game' (Wittgenstein, 1969: no. 204).

Because few are prepared to grant the importance of the above distinction between theories and accounts, and often claim that anything that guides empirical research must be 'a theory', let me set out the main differences between the two more explicitly below. Strictly, to be amenable to evidential support, theories ought to have the following properties: (1) explicitness; (2) abstractness; (3) discreteness; (4) systematicity; (5) completeness; and (6) be thus predictive. While few theories meet these conditions (and many argue, as I have said, that to insist on these conditions is to be over-fastidious as to what theories are), accounts have no such pretensions: (1) an account is not explicit but is open to interpretation; (2) it is not abstract but works by the use of examples (or paradigms); (3) its elements are not discrete but are context-dependent; (4) it is not systematic, for its elements are intentionally not rule-related to one another; (5) also its descriptions are incomplete; and (6) though it shapes our expectations, it is not predictive in any precise way. Only in the requirement that it be coherent and be understood as a whole, is it like theoretical talk; it cannot itself be grounded in evidence, for it works to shape what we will interpret as evidence.

Thus, being presented with a theory is quite different from being presented with an account. The categories provided by a theory can be used to reorganize one's perception of events, events that already make one kind of sense, can be seen as fitting into another, *already pre-established* framework of interpretation. But the sense in which one listens to or reads an account is quite different: if the facts it provides so far are unsatisfactory in some way – that is, incomplete, contradictory, or even bewildering – one waits for later facts and uses them in deciding the sense of earlier ones. What sense there is to be found is *not decided beforehand*, but is discovered or disclosed in the course of the exchange in which the account is offered. Thus, to give an adequate account of what something 'is', neither a *theory* nor a *model* of it will do. For we must not talk about it as really being something else, as requiring an unusual description in special *theoretical* terms. Nor must we talk about it as being *like* something else which, in other respects, is not actually like it at all. For both these ways – using theories or models – provide only partial, or biased, ways of 'seeing' it from the 'outside', from a standpoint unconcerned with the form of life from within which it is being observed. Our task – if an adequate understanding of something rather than its effective manipulation is at issue – is to 'see' what confronts us as 'what' actually it is within the form of life within which it has its being.

To give an account of something, to formulate practical knowledge of it as a topic, we must collect together in a certain kind of way what we *must already know*, in order to be the competent, autonomous members of our society we are. But to do this, we do not have to collect evidence as scientists; as presumably socially competent persons ourselves, we ourselves can be a *source* of such evidence (Cavell, 1969). Drawing upon the knowledge we already possess, what we need is an account of what we know about the topic in question, in the ordinary sense of the term 'account': as simply a narration of a circumstance or state of affairs. Something which in its telling 'moves' us this way and that through the current terrain of our practical knowing, so to speak, sufficient for us to gain a conceptual grasp of it – it is a view 'from the inside', much as we get to know the street plan of a city by living within it, rather than by seeing it all-at-once from an external standpoint. It is a grasp which allows us to 'see' all the different aspects of it as if arrayed within a 'landscape', all in relation to one another, from all the standpoints within it; it *narrates* a topic to us as a system of common 'places', as a whole given form by a set of topics or tropes.

That is: primarily vague, but not wholly unspecified states of affairs or processes, are specified further within a medium of communication, *according to the requirements of that medium*, which is the reproduction of the pattern of social relationships in which it has its currency. Thus the features of what we represent in our forms of communication are more in our forms of communication than in what we represent by them; the basic nature of our language is formative or rhetorical rather than representative or referential. We have, Wittgenstein says, been held captive by a picture, the picture theory of language, which suggested to us that our language was not so much for communication as for representing in its structure the structure of the world. I have argued here the opposite: that we project into the phenomena of our concern features of our methods of representing it. It is our dominant mode of accountability which suggests to us a world of locatable, isolable, individual mobile entities in cause and effect relation to one another. Recognition of practical discourse would entail the recognition of the nonlocatability of many psychological phenomena. For example, as Wittgenstein (1980, I: nos. 903, 904 and 905) says about our attempts to centre our psychology 'in' the 'minds' of individuals:

> why should the *system* continue further in the direction of the centre? Why should this order not proceed, so to speak, out of chaos . . . It is thus perfectly possible that certain psychological phenomena *cannot* be investigated physiologically, because physiologically nothing corresponds to them . . . Why should there not be a psychological regularity to which *no* physiological regularity corresponds? If this upsets our concepts of causality then it is high time they were upset.

In other words, if we were able practically to accept the consequences of living in a world of events rather than of things, then we really would find ourselves in a world that is utterly strange to us, even though it would be the world of our own everyday, conversational life. And, instead of the 'mental states' we currently talk of as the *cause* of our behaviour, they would appear as one of its consequences.

Conclusions

Like Wittgenstein, Whorf forces us to see that the basic 'being' of our world is not as basic as we had thought; it can be thought of and talked of in other ways: as a world of activities and events, rather than of substances and things. Like Wittgenstein also, he does this through 'grammatical' studies that explore what is felt by native speakers to go with what – and, irrespective of whether his account of Hopi grammar is 'true' or not, like a good piece of science fiction writing, it enables us to imagine other ways in which we might make sense of our own forms of life. While currently we spatialize time and talk of it as a dimension of measurement, and think of ourselves as living somewhere upon that dimension 'in' an historically changing world, the Hopi (truly, or merely in Whorf's version) dynamize space and talk of it as space in which their thinkings and feelings are in responsive contact with the influences at work in their surroundings. For us to think of ourselves in this way – as like a compass needle, thoughtlessly but sensitively registering changes in a surrounding magnetic field – goes against the grain of our thought about ourselves as the agents of our own actions; but we *can* think it, nonetheless. What goes against the grain for the Hopi, according to Whorf, is the opposite: the thought of themselves and their desires as separate from what goes on in their world. But no doubt in the Hopi world too, as in ours, there are two sides to the question; they could, no doubt, be provoked into 'thinking' (?) the opposite. But to repeat: while what we talk of as our 'thought' takes place in a special, inner, *imaginary space* – 'in our minds', we say – the Hopi 'world' contains no such inner, imaginary space. For them, as for the rhetorical–responsive version of social constructionism being outlined here, the supposed 'thinkings' and 'feelings' we talk of as having to do with the 'eventings' in our world, have to be located there, out in the world in which such talk takes place – as a part of the whole into which it is interwoven. To locate it in 'the mind' is to locate it in something imaginary rather than real.

By the same token, it is worth reminding ourselves of what Whorf said about the rhetorical–responsive power of language to create in us an incorrigible sense of the 'reality' in which we live, a 'reality' that aspects of which our 'mind' can 'intuit'. What we talk of as our 'intuitions' are, he said, *recepts* from culture and language. What our ways of talking represent as being 'in' the world are 'in' our way of representing it. They are 'rooted' in our current ways of speaking – whose primary function is the forming of different forms of life – and they work 'developmentally' to supplement, to specify or to articulate such ways of talking further. But it is also worth noting, that it is only in working outwards, from within such intralinguistically constituted 'realities', that we can make intelligible contact with that which is due to *other than* our recepts from language. And it is this possibility – of making contact with an otherness different from ourselves – that saves us from being wholly entrapped within intralinguistic realities of our own making. For, as we have seen, in dialogue with the others around them, different people can come to understand their differences. While such dialogues do not allow an instant, monologic, computational kind of understanding, they do allow the slow, back-and-forth development of a contested but negotiable practical understanding. Further, such contests and negotiations are not of an 'anything goes' kind; but neither are they are not grounded in any predetermined, outside, systematic standards. To repeat: they are 'rooted' in the developed and developing conversational contexts within which the practical negotiations take place. Thus, within a dialogical perspective, the problem of linguistic relativity takes on a quite different, nonvicious character. The different ways of being in the world of different peoples, although not easy to interlink, are not for ever incommensurable.

This does not mean, however, that we are at last in a position to discover that final form of life that we all, as human beings, *should* live. For our task in the future is just as much a task of making as of finding. Each time we encounter a limitation upon our ways of knowing others (or ourselves) – as we did in revealing our entrapment by the traditional epistemological paradigm – we must try to identify it by contrasting our knowledge practices with alternatives, thus to respect the being of others (and ourselves) more effectively. And this is a process to which, of course, there is no foreseeable end, either in theory or practice. But distinguishing that which is due to our talk from that which is not becomes possible only if we can grasp the nature of our part in the construction of our own intralinguistic realities. And it is as an aid in this task that I think the value of Whorf's work lies.

Notes

1. I will both offer textual support for these claims, and more fully explain what I mean, later in the chapter.
2. Whorf characteristically capitalized words he wanted to be especially noticed.
3. This is the last time I shall self-consciously mark the importance of our vocabulary here. For, I cannot wholly purge my writing of visual metaphors; it would make my writing even more tortured, peculiar and multivoiced (i.e. full of qualifications and 'second thoughts'), than it already is. But nonetheless, readers should remain vigilant in noticing their pervasive presence.
4. Goffman talks of the context of self-presentation as having a *moral* nature, in terms of involving different rights and duties for speakers and listeners.
5. He lumps English, French, German, and other European languages all together in SAE (1956: 138).
6. 'Hopi', he says (1956: 216), 'may be called a timeless language. It recognizes psychological time, which is much like Bergson's "duration", but this "time" is quite unlike mathematical time, T, used by our physicists. Among the special properties of Hopi time are that it varies with each observer, does not permit of simultaneity, and has zero dimensions; i.e. it cannot be given a number greater than one [talked of as split into numbered parts]'.

PART III

CONVERSATIONAL REALITIES

7

In Search of a Past: Therapeutic Re-authoring

> 'Look, I've spent ten years trying to dispose of the past by committing it to paper. Uselessly, of course, otherwise I wouldn't be here' [says Fraser to his psychoanalyst].
>
> Fraser, 1984: 186

We have now assembled a large number of 'tools' for use in accounting for the processes of joint action in which social constructions, or reconstructions, are produced. It is now time to demonstrate their application. In this chapter, what I want to talk of is the nature of 'living' dialogue, the nature of the process in which two unique human beings, occupying unique places or positions in the world, with two unique biographical projects, come together to make some kind of contact with each other, motivated by the very fact that, due to their differences, there is a possibility that they might fulfil in each other what singly they lack. And here, I want to talk of this process in the context of psychotherapy.

In a number of recent papers, Anderson and Goolishan (1988, 1990, 1992) have been critical of systems theory and constructivist approaches to family therapy for not providing a place anywhere for different people's unique experience, for ignoring the client's 'point of view'. They want to open up a 'space' for a form of conversation within which the first-person voice of clients can be heard, a space within which it is possible for clients to express 'who' they *are*, a space in which they can communicate in some way what it is like *to be* them and how they experience their uniquely troubled world. And with this concern, I am completely in agreement, for I shall take it that the basic practical-moral problem in life is not what *to do* but what *to be*; and, that the basic problem in psychotherapeutic dialogue is, how can one help another to reshape, to re-author, what they *have been* in the past, to enable them to face what they *might be* in the future with hope rather than fear, dread, or despair . . . 'If you [professionals] could have talked with 'the me' that knew how frightened I was', as Anderson and Goolishan (1992) had one client say to them, in complaining about his previous treatments, 'If [therapists like] you had been able to understand how crazy I had to be, so that I could be strong enough to deal with this life threatening fear, . . . then we could have handled that crazy general [his delusion]', he said. And Anderson and Goolishan feel it important to take such claims seriously.

Thus, rather than only with the usual scientific virtues of the truth or accuracy of 'theories', they are also concerned with whether their 'account' is *adequate* to the state of affairs in question, with whether they have been what Lorraine Code (1987) calls 'epistemically responsible' in their formulations; that is, with whether they know enough about other people in order to conduct their personal relationships with them 'well', such that they can judge, for instance, whether an utterance will be hurtful or supportive to another or not. It is simply epistemically irresponsible to claim, in virtue of one's expertise, ahead of time, that one already knows the rules for hurtful and supportive utterances. Thus, what Anderson and Goolishan want is a way of accounting for psychotherapeutic events which respects the being of their clients, an account 'in' which their clients 'can recognize themselves', in which their 'voice' can be heard.

But this concern with adequacy is not the only major change of emphasis we must make in turning away from purely scientific concerns to those of, what could be called, just ordinary rationality. Their concern with 'accounts' rather than 'theories' must be extended to 'narrative accounts'. Indeed, if the living of a life does involve a contexted, temporal working out of conflicting forces, it is all but impossible to represent the tension and movement, the 'motivations' and 'desires' at work in such a process, in terms of a set of timeless theorems derived from abstract, context-free principles. Thus, instead of theoretical structures, there is a turn to storied forms, to see: (1) not only if they can function as the required intellectual device for collecting together an otherwise disconnected, fragmentary set of events into an intelligible and 'instructive' whole; (2) but also – just as 'theory' used itself to play a role in our theories about ourselves – to study the role our storytelling might play in the stories we tell ourselves about ourselves.

Rhetoric: Communication without shared understandings

In pursuit of this aim, in *their* attempts to understand the linguistic nature of the psychotherapeutic process, Anderson and Goolishan (1992) think of themselves as taking an interpretative, hermeneutical 'turn' – but one of a special kind. For rather than, as in many other forms of psychotherapy, including psychoanalysis (as well as in normal, everyday life activities) – where therapists make interpretations and construct stories against a background of what, on the basis of their professional or common-sense knowledge, they think *ought normally* to be the case – Anderson and Goolishan have proposed what they call a 'not-knowing' approach,[1] an approach which allows the client to 'make' a to-an-extent-new biographical narrative, rather than to have imposed upon them one of a theoretically already determined kind, 'found' for them by the therapist. The 'not-knowing' approach involves the adoption by the therapist of a particular 'position' in relation to clients – the concept of a 'position' will have to do a lot of work in what follows, and it will be elaborated further as we go on: here, it means the adoption by the therapist of both a way or method of listening to what clients say, and also, a special way of responding to it, a sustained attitude which 'invites' clients to try to say what their world is like to them; rather than as in everyday life, where we struggle to institute *our* form of life in the face of other people's. The 'not-knowing' approach works to institute a form of partial togetherness, in which the client is able to manifest, in relation to the therapist, their genuine otherness.

But for it to afford this, this mode of communication must, I think, be 'rooted' in certain 'special moments': moments in which therapists share with their clients, not so much understandings as *feelings*, thus to establish with them something of a common ground, a shared (sensory or sensuous) basis in terms of which *both* can intelligibly contribute in their different ways to the joint authorship of a (new) biographical account of the significance of just those very feelings. And the nature of these special 'moments' is one of the things that I want to discuss.

However, if we are to understand their nature, we shall require more than the resources available in the hermeneutical interpretative approach: we shall need some of those made available in recent *rhetorical* approaches as well. For the hermeneutical approach – which in its application makes use of what is called 'the hermeneutical circle' – is concerned with a back-and-forth 'movement' between initial encounters with parts or fragments of meaningful behaviour, or with things said, and the fashioning of them into a coherent whole, a whole which, retrospectively (that is, when you look back on it) is publicly intelligible in itself. In other words, the back-and-forth movement ultimately gives rise to a *shared*, decontextualized, self-contained understanding. Hermeneutics has its place (and its dangers, as we shall see) in our biographical concerns. But our more immediate task, is that of trying to understand prospectively, how conversation and dialogue can still proceed, *before* shared understandings (and the knowledge that goes with them) have been achieved! – how each fragment of A's behaviour has a meaning for B, in B's context, which is not necessarily its meaning for A. To arrive at genuinely *shared* understandings, at some knowledge – at, for example, a shared understanding of what I mean by the rhetorical aspects of language as distinct from its hermeneutical and interpretative features – we must grasp what a pre-shared-understandings form of communication is like. This is a form of communication in which, although B acts on their understanding of A, and vice versa, there are no moments of common evaluation, of common feeling between them, no 'our world' in common between them.

Thus, the view I shall take (which is one I also share with Anderson and Goolishan), is that the human world in which we live is best thought of as a whole 'multiverse', or 'social ecology', of unique but dynamically interdependent regions and moments of human communicative activity. And in such a multiverse (surprising though it may be to say it) language is neither primarily for the representation of the world, nor for the achievement of shared understandings: it is used much more practically. As I shall view it, it is primarily for the coordination of diverse social action (Mills, 1940), for materially 'moving' people.

In this view, genuinely shared understandings are infrequent, and only achieved with a great deal of special interpersonal work to do with their formulation, testing, judging and criticizing. For understanding is not a simple, once and for all achievement: as Anderson and Goolishan say, 'understanding is always a process "on the way" and never fully achieved' (1988: 378). It is a temporally developed and developing event, in which what is understood is constructed from vague fragments in a process of negotiation – both two-way between participants, and back-and-forth in time – involving: assumptions about the biography and purposes of the speaker; tests of these and other assumptions; the use of the circumstances of the utterance; the waiting for something later to make clear what was meant earlier; and the use of many other 'seen but unnoticed' background features of everyday social life; all deployed according to agreed practices or 'methods' of testing, formulating and judging. Thus, only gradually do we come to a shared understanding, to a grasp of 'the matter' being talked about. But it is developed and developing over the whole course of the exchange in which it is produced, and furthermore, its significance (for those involved) can only be known '*from within* this development' (Garfinkel, 1967: 40).

But if this is so, if shared understandings are so infrequent, how can conversation intelligibly proceed at all? Well, thinking practically, thinking about coordinating or interlinking different social actions, we can think of the function of every utterance as working, in terms of the speaker reacting to what others have said previously, in relation to whom or what the speaker is trying *to be*; that is, how he or she is trying to 'place', 'position', or 'situate' themselves in relation to the others around them. Thus actual 'living' utterances, ones which make a difference in our lives, must take into account the (already linguistically shaped) context into which they are directed. As Bakhtin (1986: 91) puts it:

> Any concrete utterance is a link in the chain of speech communication of a particular sphere . . . Utterances are not indifferent to one another, and are not self-sufficient; they are aware of and mutually reflect one another . . . Every utterance must be regarded as primarily a *response* to preceding utterances of the given sphere . . . Each utterance refutes, affirms, supplements, and relies upon the others, presupposes them to be known, and somehow takes them into account . . . Therefore, each kind of utterance is filled with various kinds of responsive reactions to other utterances of the given sphere of speech communication.

In other words, in the essentially noncognitive approach I want to outline here, our *different ways* of speaking become important because it is assumed that the primary function of speech is to 'give shape' to, and to maintain, reproduce, or transform certain modes of personal and social relationships, to 'position' people in relation to each other. Thus, in this view, if it seems undeniable in our experience that at least some words do in fact denote things, they do so, I would argue, only from within a pattern of social relations already constituted by ways of talking in which these words are used, used for materially 'moving' or 'repositioning' people in some way. But in what way?

Rhetorical-poetic uses of language

It is here that the rhetorical (and poetic) function of language becomes relevant. There are two aspects to rhetoric that I would like to emphasize, one more familiar than the other. (1) The familiar aspect of rhetoric is to do with the *persuasive* function of language, the capacity of speech bodily to 'move' people, its power to affect their behaviour and perceptions in some mysterious, noncognitive way. It is its capacity to affect people's 'feelings' which we shall find below to be of great importance. (2) The other, more unfamiliar, aspect of rhetoric, however, is related to the more poetic aspect of language (Gr. *poesis* = making), to do with 'giving' or 'lending' a *first form* to what otherwise are in fact only vaguely or partially ordered feelings and activities. And it is this: the realization that, even in the face of the vague, indescribable, open, fluid and ever changing nature of human life, language can work 'to make it appear as if' it is well ordered and structured, its form-giving or form-lending aspect, which is for us, I think, rhetoric's most important characteristic.

For the moment, let me concentrate upon just the first of these aspects. To illustrate what can occur in such 'a moving moment', I want to make use of a line from Samuel Beckett's *Endgame* (Beckett, 1986: 118). It is Hamm's vehement, angry, accusatory, but also self-pitying line, which comes after his account of why he had offered only minimal help to a poor man in the snow. He loses his patience with the man for still retaining a hope for a better future, and he says to him (and to all of us as well): 'Use your head, can't you, use your head, you're on earth, there's no cure for that!' – a powerful line, I think you'll agree. But what does it mean? What does it do? It doesn't tell us anything we didn't in some sense already know.

It imparts no new knowledge. But it does 'move' us in the sense of morally 're-positioning' us in relation to our own situation, so that we come to 're-see' it in a new perspective. It breaks the flow of our mundane thoughts and interests, and, in contrasting with them, confronts us afresh with a realization, a consideration, an occasion, perhaps, for a re-evaluation of our lives. In Wittgenstein's terms, it does not so much 'say' anything as 'show' us (or 'remind' us of) something about ourselves. It reminds us of something we already know but – with other more mundane interests in mind – were ignoring; reminding us of it clashes with and thus problematizes our everyday circumstances; it thus provokes us into seeing them as being 'other than' what at first they seemed to be, into seeing new (but in this case tragic) possibilities within them. And if Hamm were a real person, it would also tell us something about him. As it is, we feel it tells us something about Beckett the writer – his tragic vision, what his world is like for him.

Feelings

But what is the nature of our being such that we can be moved like this? To grasp the nature of these 'moving' utterances, we must do more than just formulate some new concepts; we must also practice a bit of conceptual psychotherapy upon ourselves, and allow ourselves to be a little bit changed in *our* being. Thus our 'psychotherapeutic' task is to recognize the deeply embedded, implicit metaphors lodged in the language in terms of which we currently unthinkingly think, and to replace them with others: for instance, we hardly need Rorty's (1980: 12) reminders – about pictures and metaphors being more important than propositions – for it to be 'clear'(?) to us that much of our talk about our ways of thinking and knowing makes use of a vocabulary of 'visual' terms. But what if, instead, we were to imagine ourselves blind, and as having to make sense of our surroundings by feeling our way forward like blind people, through the use of long canes? Then, for instance, we might find talk about knowledge – in terms of 'knowing our way around' (Wittgenstein, 1980, I: no. 549); or, as being able 'to go on' (Wittgenstein, 1980, I: no. 446) without stumbling or meeting insurmountable barriers – as not metaphorical, but as literally what knowledge is for us.

In wanting to talk in this way about our mental lives, I have been greatly influenced by, among others,[2] William James (1890) who, in his famous 'The Stream of Thought' chapter, talks of '*signs of direction* in thought, of which we nevertheless have an acutely discriminative sense, though no definite sensorial image plays any part in it whatsoever' (1890: 244), and who then goes on to say this:

> Now what I contend for, and accumulate examples to show, is that 'tendencies' are not only descriptions from without, but that they are among the *objects* of the stream, which is thus aware of them from within, and must be described as in very large measure constituted of *feelings of tendency*, often so vague that we are unable to name them at all.

So when I talk of feelings, it is such feelings of tendency that I mean – 'a feeling of what thoughts are next to arise, before they have arisen' (1890: 247) – to quote James yet again. What has already been said gives rise to a difficulty, an agreement, a challenge, a criticism, a description, and so on. 'Each utterance refutes, affirms, supplements, and relies upon the others, presupposes them to be known, and somehow takes them into account', to repeat Bakhtin's (1986: 91) comment above. Where these are all examples of what some other philosophers might call the *intentionality* of mental activity: the *sense* it contains of intrinsic interconnectedness with the otherness around it. And indeed, it is precisely this kind of language of 'feeling' – of being able to feel the 'shape' of the 'othernesses' around us through the use of various 'means' and 'devices' – that will help us to understand why narrative constructions can be such powerful psychotherapeutic instruments.

Fraser: In search of a past

To make just some (but not all) of these issues less abstract, let me mention a particular case. For some time now I have been both moved and intrigued by an account of his own (successful) psychoanalysis, written by the British oral historian, Ronald Fraser (1984) – he is well known in England for his 1979 book *Blood of Spain*, recording people's experiences of fighting in the Spanish Civil War. When he was three (in 1933), Fraser's Scots father and wealthy American mother went to live in a Manor House in the south-east of England (the Home Counties) where his father embarked upon the life of the energetically idle rich: fox-hunting, shooting and entertaining, whilst his mother began to have love affairs. The account is intriguing, because he combines oral history material gathered in the early 1970s from the servants of the estate amongst whom he grew up (the period 1933 to 1945), with accounts of his psychotherapy sessions.

At the beginning of the analysis, '*P*' (the analyst) asks Fraser 'What exactly are you hoping for?' And Fraser replies 'Mmm . . . To consign – no, to recreate an uncertain past . . .' [pause] 'With sufficient certainty to put it behind me.' He wants just to be rid of the trouble it causes him. He describes his initial conflict, his unease, the dis-ease within his self or selves that his life on the estate produced within him as follows:

> *F*: It's not surprising, perhaps, because there were two worlds, two houses within those same walls . . . Two Manors, under different roofs, . . . the old at the rear . . . where servants, nanny and children [Ronald and his brother Colin] lived; and the superimposed and imposing new Manor at the front, which belonged to the parents . . . 'I belonged without yet belonging'. (1984: 4–5)

That, at least, was a general formulation of his problem.

But as the analysis progresses, it seems to be rooted in a more specific feeling, one which *at first* he formulated as that of his mother as having abandoned him – but which, as we shall see, indicated that something else was at stake, something much more to do generally with sources of security and a sense of belonging. But the feeling, when he thinks of it as being directed toward his mother, was expressed thus:

> *P* [the analyst]: You've never forgiven your mother for leaving you with Ilse [the German nanny], have you?
> *Fraser*: No! I've never forgiven her for not being the kind of mother I wanted – an island in the sea from which a child can set sail on its own, always sure there's a refuge to which to return to. (1984: 97)

He had said this after what I think is the crucial analytic exchange. It goes like this:

> *F* [Thinks: Since her [his mother's] death I have hardly thought of her, and says]: 'I mustn't tell Ilse I love my mother for fear I may lose her, Ilse . . . Does that make sense? . . . What's it mean to be looked after by someone who isn't your mother while your mother is actually there?
> [long pause]
> *P*: Having two mothers, I suppose . . .

The words strike me with great force.

> *F*: Two mothers! Split between each, neither sufficient in herself. Why have I never seen this? . . . Two mothers and I'm torn between them . . .
> *P*: . . . you split them – into the good and the bad mother.
> *F*: Oh . . . [long silence] I split them! Not they me . . .

But what the analyst does is to 'move' Fraser to confront himself with the objective fact that although his mother didn't help him as much as she might have done, and that, in fact, others on the estate looked after him better, much better, they too placed demands upon him to judge her.

But Fraser had not wanted (did not know how) at first to accept this. Later, as Fraser said (1984: 184) to *P* about his mother: 'I wanted to love her, not destroy her . . .' He had wanted to have her in a central place in his life; she was the one he had tried to be an "I" for; she was the one for whom he had tried to be someone. And 'How can one write about one's past without an 'I' as the focus?', he had asked *P* earlier (1984: 90).

And this, I think, is crucial. It is to do with how Fraser thought of himself as 'placed', 'positioned' or 'situated' in relation to all the others around him: he was someone who was abandoned, someone who did not belong. Thus, in trying as he thought to be someone for his mother, he was trying to attain a 'feeling of belonging' – where 'belonging' means, I imagine, something like possessing the confidence possessed by the members of a ruling class, where whatever one might do wrong, you never lose your membership – they look after their own; while 'not belonging' means, I think, something like this: the carrying around of a hidden weight of anxiety that one is going to be judged and not only found inadequate, but, as a result, banished from further participation. Thus, he had set himself an impossible task: what he was trying *to be* was someone who, from the position of not belonging, was trying to re-collect the fragments of his biography as someone who did belong. Thus, if not for her, for whom else could he *be* someone? To 'move' him from this original position required a rhetorical use of language.

In the next session he says to his analyst (1984: 184):

> *F*: I've reached the bottom line: to accept the destruction and start again . . .

(And he writes) 'In the inner darkness I look across the years in silence until I hear him say':

> *P*: Without accepting it you wouldn't find parts of the lost ones in you again. It's like mourning . . .

And the analysis begins to draw to a close when Fraser begins to understand how his quest *to be* someone can, perhaps, be satisfied by other formulations. Thus he realizes how – not to be rid of his past – but how he can reconstitute his biography (those events 'inscribed' or 'embodied' in him, in his being as a person) as a corpus of knowledge he feels he can rely upon.

> *F*: Yes, I seem to have made my peace with the house [he says].
> *P*: Well, your people live on in you perhaps more than you want to believe. Your mother, father, Ilse . . .

F: Perhaps they do . . . and silently I feel them gathering, coming together, until they fill the emptiness around me . . .
P: It was the unity of love you yearned for.
F: Instead of the fragments, yes. The dead live on in us, despite everything, don't they? *Like people in books whom you can return to time and again* . . .
P: Sure . . . [pause] (1984: 186, my emphasis)

And that, I think – the phrase 'like people in books you can return to time and again' – is the clue we need to understand what has actually happened to Fraser in his analysis, and I shall make more of it later. But, just for the moment, if we were to ask Fraser himself, 'How did the testimony about your mother (and all the others with whom you were involved) help you in "coming to terms with" your past?', then, at one level, he gives us a very nice answer. I would like to quote it because again it emphasizes what we usually fail to notice. For, as he says to his analyst (1984: 187):

F: But all we've done here is to examine the fragments. We've never seen the totality, the causal relationships between them.
P: [and his analyst replies] I doubt that one can ever be so precise . . . You want to be the subject of your history instead of the object you felt yourself to be.
F: The subject, yes – but also the object. It's the synthesis of the two, isn't it?
P: The author of your childhood then, the historian of your past.
F: That's what I intend – to write about it from the inside and out . . .

And that is, of course, what he does in the book. In other words, what he says here emphasizes – in talking about wanting to be both the continuing subject (the author) and the (developing, well-crafted) object of his own history – is not that the child is the father of the man, but just the opposite: that people who feel free (of the anxiety of 'not belonging') and are able to orient toward the future with hope and confidence, are themselves the authors of the children they once were (Crites, 1986). And Fraser was able (with a very little necessary help, and much work) to remake his 'I', the 'position', the single point of view from which, from now on, he would recollect the fragments of feeling he would require as a *resource* in his future biographical projects.

Biographical fragments as a practical corpus

But what was Fraser's new way of being? How did he re-relation himself to his past, if he didn't get rid of it? Well, to grasp the nature of the difficulty he was in, let us return to the hermeneutical approach, but now, to bring out one of its central dangers, what Donald Spence calls (1986) 'narrative smoothing': it is a danger because a nice coherent, well-organized narrative, with everything in its place, *prevents* the appearance of alternative *circumstantial* possibilities, amongst which, if we are to be the authors of our own lives, we must be free to judge. In other words, it diverts our attention away from the fact that in our practical-moral activities, we are embedded in a context, and quite often, our circumstances surround us with possibilities. Our attention is diverted, because, in a hermeneutical construction, all the fragments which have occurred are decontextualized, and made into a *orderly or systematic whole* – often with, as Freud put it, the insertion of the 'missing portions' which *must* have 'originally' been there if things are to be orderly. This is the 'finding' of a narrative, and Freud, as we all know, used the archaeological metaphor.[3] Once we have found this correct whole, people's past actions are thought of as taking on their *proper* meaning within *its* context.

But this, I think, is absolutely wrong. What their actions take on there is not so much meaning as *intelligibility*; that is, they become capable of being grasped reflectively and intellectually. The order has been *constructed* and the missing portions supplied, by drawing upon a 'grammar' implicit in our life and language, by drawing upon features implicit in our 'accepted' ways of coordinating our actions with one another – and to the rational intellect, such a grammar gives the appearance of a proper meaning. But it is, I shall say, a 'counterfeit' version. It has been 'minted' wrongly; it has the wrong origins. For it has issued from a desire for a single, particular way of ordering social life – which for Freud, concerned as he was with psychoanalysis as a natural science ('What else can it be?') was in terms of individuals achieving mastery and possession of essentially socially produced resources. This is what it debases: its own proper minting and currency in the 'hurly-burly' or 'bustle' of practical, everyday life events (Wittgenstein), in which there is no order, no one single, complete, proper or true order. 'A faithful account of . . . the context of discovery will very likely have the appearance', says Spence (1986: 231), 'of a disconnected series of fragments strung together. Surprise, bewilderment, and faint glimmers of understanding probably all circle around one another during the average [analytic] hour in much the same way as they appear during a dream state . . . '

But if this is so, the *true* meanings of the events in the living of our lives cannot be properly understood within the confines of any order, narrative or otherwise. They are only to be found in the not wholly orderly, practical living of our lives. And this was Fraser's discovery: that if he was to be a 'maker' of narratives, the author of his own childhood, the historian of his past, he had to find a new 'position' for himself in relation to his own past. What he needed to do was *not* just to carry *the* narrative of his past into the future, as if it were the only proper one, but to be able to draw upon the fragments of his own past as and when he pleased, as a practical-moral resource, to re-collect from them enablements (and constraints) of moment by moment relevance in judging how at present to best proceed in the realization of who he felt he should be in the future. This is why I emphasized his account of how he now felt about those he had known, that they were 'like people in books you can return to time and again'. No longer imprisoned within a single narrative, he realized he could treat his own biographical fragments as, to use a phrase of Alan Blum's (1971: 301–2), 'a practically conceived corpus of knowledge'.

Conclusions

In other words, to sum up, first for Fraser and then for the therapist: from Fraser's new position, as now the author of himself, his life becomes both a temporally developed and developing event, understood as such in a two-way, back-and-forth process of construction, oscillating in fact between the tasks of formulating two interlinked narratives: one a retrospective, re-collective, hermeneutically constructed narrative, and the other a prospective, pro-jective, rhetorically formed narrative – two quite different narrative forms, each modifying the other. It is a mistake to think that the kind of understanding we seek is the 'proper' narrative of our past lives, or that we need a well-ordered script to carry us into the future. Each prevents us from being present at that moment of judgment when, in contact with the circumstances around us, we must recollect those aspects of our past relevant for our future. If we are to continually reconstitute our past in terms of the 'lure' of our future projects, we must continually, at least to some extent, reconstitute ourselves (Crites, 1986). Thus the 'I', who at any one moment we are, is poised in that tense bridging position (the 'present' moment), and must link an indefinite number of remembered episodes from that present point of view, while being oriented toward a future project, while – and it is this which we all forget – also noticing what is made available to us by way of the new opportunities in our current circumstances. Fraser's problem was that he could not live with what he himself had so far made of his own biography; it did not make sense to him, or for him; he could not easily use it; it limited rather than liberated him; he did not feel at home in it; it did not enable him clearly to 'see' how to 'project' himself into the future.

This was Fraser's problem: but what was it like for the psychotherapist? If we ask, What *practically* happened in Fraser's analysis? I think we must reply along the following lines: (1) That first, the analyst discovered the central feeling of insecurity and lack of belongingness at the heart of Fraser's 'dis-ease' with his life, and discovered also the well-formed narrative, and the 'position' within it from which Fraser had tried to collected the fragments of his past together to form them into coherent biography, and how his wanting to be an 'I' for his mother, not only made the task impossible, but made the biography practically unusable. Up until this point, the analyst faced 'finding' *the* well-made narrative within which Fraser had entrapped himself. (2) Then, the analyst faced the task of finding the biographically engendered source *feeling* which that narrative, indeed accurately, but in fact inadequately, formulated. (3) At this point, his task changed from primarily a hermeneutical to a rhetorical one: he had to 'move' Fraser to a new 'position' from which to make sense of his own biographical data, by first leading him himself to discredit his old position, and by second, helping him to 'make' a new 'position' and thus a new biography for himself.

In all of these activities, narrative instruments are in use in one way or another; hermeneutically and rhetorically. However, because there is no principled way in which we can decide which should have priority over the other, I want to end by emphasizing again the importance of the rhetorical-poetic, the 'doing' rather than 'stating' aspect of language use – for it has not so far been given sufficient prominence in our theories of language. It provides us with the resources we need to 'see' the 'movements' involved in 'doing' communicating. It enables us to 'see' the movement between the retrospective and prospective aspects of the process of understanding at work: the differences between attending to what has already been said and the context to which it gives rise, and attending to the activity of saying something further, in which one person materially 'moves' or 'affects' another by their utterances *in that context*. By 'moving' us to new 'positions' in relation to our own storytelling, it has enabled us to 'see' how . . . we might 'move' ourselves to new positions by our own storytelling . . . which is, of course, one of the great powers, and one of the great dangers, of all storytelling.

Notes

1. Therapists, if they are to adopt the 'not-knowing' position, must adopt a position which is very frightening to those of us trained as academics. For they must think of communication as working, not as primarily in terms of shared understandings, but – in rhetorical terms – as originating in vague, not-yet-cognitively-formulated *feelings*, of 'sensed movements' or 'sensuous re-positions', to which, as a recipient, they must reply in some way; but in what way, if it is not to do with trying to establish what they think life *ought* to be like? Whatever they answer, it is their task to 'feel' in the course of it, the unique other who confronts them, what it is like to be him or her. Thus, as well as re-thinking the nature of communication, they must also re-think the nature of their

knowledge (of the other) as beginning with a whole sequence of vague, fragmentary feelings that, over time, they must integrate into a 'felt' totality, a whole which functions as a 'basis' in terms of which a linguistic formulation of its nature can be judged for its adequacy. Thus, in switching to a language of 'feeling', they must stop thinking in terms of visually 'seeable things', in terms of patterns, structures or systems as spatially *complete* entities, with all their parts simultaneously present. They must begin to think of 'experiencing historical events', which develop, of course, over time, and whose 'parts' at one moment in time owe their character to what has happened in the past, and what might happen in the future. Hence, they can no longer think of them as primarily spatial, but they must think of them as having primarily a temporal existence, as like conversations, which are almost always incomplete until the last words are said, and which even then may be resumed the next day. And perhaps what will be most difficult for them, trained as they have been to a high degree as academics, to think and to act autonomously, with a 'plan' or 'picture' in mind, they must grasp what it is like just to 'feel one's way forward', to just creatively respond to their circumstances – as we do in fact do it all the time, in sensing, say, the 'shape' of a problem in something that someone has just said, and in formulating a question which we hope will clarify things, But it is still not something we make rationally-visible to ourselves in our explicit accounts of what we think our knowledge is.

2. Bartlett (1932: 206) talks of all remembering as beginning with 'very largely a matter of feeling, or affect'.

3. In their search for 'it' – the proper narrative – therapists ask clients what the client of Anderson and Goolishan (1992) that I mentioned earlier called 'conditional questions'. These are questions, the client felt, that functioned to check out whether the client knew what he was *supposed* to know (on the basis of the therapist's theory). This client became very sensitive to such questions; hence his characterization of them.

8
Real and Counterfeit Constructions in Interpersonal Relations

> Narrative is a primary cognitive instrument – an instrument rivaled, in fact, only by theory and metaphor as irreducible ways of making the flux of experience comprehensible . . . [But we must abandon] the idea that there is a determinate historical actuality, the complex referent for all our narratives of 'what actually happened', the untold story to which narrative histories approximate.
>
> Mink, 1978: 131, 148

The temptation to make sense of our activities by recontextualizing them within an artifical, coherent or orderly context of our own devising is very great. As individuals, we would like to be able to grasp their meaning clearly, ahead of time, thus to be able to plan what to do for the best in our lives, and their placement in an orderly context allows us to do that. We met the temptation in Bhaskar's account of scientific realism in Chapter 4, in which he claims to be able to identify ahead of time the structures of social life that constructionists would maintain are, in reality, still contested; we met it also in Fraser's attempt to make sense of his own identity, in terms of the all too coherent story he had devised for himself about his own past; and we shall meet some of these temptations again here, especially as they relate to problems in psychotherapy. While many claim that human activities cannot be represented in the static, logical structure of a scientific theory, they are tempted, by the dynamic plot structure of a good story and the 'sense of reality' it seems to generate, that it can be accurately represented by an appropriate narrative structure. But, if our reality really is the turbulent, heterogeneous, developing affair I am assuming it to be in this volume, then that temptation must be resisted. We cannot avoid using narratives, metaphors or theories, but what we can avoid is becoming entrapped within their confines by claiming any one of them to be the single *correct* narrative, metaphor or theory. They are instruments, not depictions. I first wrote this chapter to honour the life and work of Don Bannister on being asked to participate in a memorial conference for Don Bannister, called 'Metaphors in Life and Psychotherapy', held in London in 1988, and I have retained it in its original form here. I was especially happy to have been asked to participate in this event, and I began by explaining why.

Psychology and psychotherapy: Anxiety and storytelling

When I began to study psychology in 1959 (unbelievably nearly 30 years ago), I slowly began to realize that I didn't like its mechanical nature very much, nor the fact that it touched upon very little in life that seemed important to me. But I stuck at it – learning theory, operant conditioning, statistical decision theory, psychophysics, computer simulation, transformational-generative grammar – until I could not bear it any longer. And I began to feel a great deal of anxiety and depression about whether I could ever become a 'proper' psychologist or not. But, as David Smail (1984: 82) has put it, very perceptively I think:

> Far from being a mechanical fault, a 'symptom', a 'dysfunction' or an indication of 'maladjustment', the experience of anxiety constitutes an assertion of the real nature of our subjective engagement with the world. To fall prey to anxiety is, at least partially, to fall *out* of self-deception, since the phenomenon of anxiety is an insistence that the subject's experience be taken seriously, that the person's *actual* predicament cannot and will not be ignored.

And that doubly is exactly how I felt: first, that not only did psychology not take people's experience seriously, but secondly, that I could not continue any longer in the self-deception that it did. Indeed, there are a large number of important distinctions – especially a whole realm of judgments, central to the conduct of our everyday life affairs, to do with assigning and attributing responsibility – that it flagrantly and arrogantly ignored. A set of ethico-political or humanistic concerns which Broadbent (1970), for instance, dismissed in his William James lectures in Harvard in 1970 as 'the last kicks of a dying culture'.

But what to do? I set out in a 'Duplicated' paper my 'objections', my 95 'Lutheran' theses. But then what? More was needed than just to nail them to a convenient door. Well luckily, no ideology so completely dominates a social order, or an academic disciplinary order, that it does not give rise within itself to intimations also of a counter-order, to hints of possibilities for other, quite different ways of being – a point of importance also for psychotherapy to which I shall return in a moment. And for me at that time two people stood out like beacons for their humanity and heart, and untiring energy (it always needs energy), in trying to devise different ways in which to be a psychologist – opposed to that of being an individualistic 'external' observer, concerned (like some Machiavellian Prince) only with predicting and controlling the behaviour of their 'subjects'. One of them is here today, and that is Rom Harré; the other was Don Bannister. I sent my 'objections' to them both, and they both responded in ways which justify the myths that we are now beginning to construct around them (for Rom Harré's response, see Shotter, 1990a). Don not only invited me – a complete beginner with no track record at all – to contribute towards the volume on *Perspectives in Personal Construct Theory* he was editing at that time (Shotter, 1970: my first 'social constructionist' text), but also later on to help think about forming an association to mediate between academic psychologists and psychotherapeutic practitioners – so that both could learn from each other; the association that became what is today the PPA (the Psychology and Psychotherapy Association).

Now the difference between Don and me – to modify a current expression – is that he put his actions where his mouth was. Whereas I hung back, and like Browning's *Grammarian*, decided not to live 'until I knew how to live', Don put the implications of his critique into practice in many different ways. Not least, as I think Miller Mair is going to tell you in his talk, in exploring other media of communication than 'scientific' ones – in both the investigation and the presentation of psychological problems as they make their appearance in human experience. So, although still prepared to pay lip-service to the idea that 'science' required one to set out one's theories as a set of quasi-mathematical or geometrical propositions (with corollaries, etc.), Don also began to tell stories – about scientists, for instance, who gradually come to realize in the course of their investigations of a certain green slime, that its aim in life is to investigate them! His way of telling us about what *reflexivity* actually means in practice. Or, as Miller Mair (1988: 126) put it in his magnificent paper at the Leeds Symposium in 1986, Don also

> told a new story about what was generally regarded as the most florid madness [schizophrenic thought disorder]. He led us to consider this quintessence of meaninglessness as *a way of living*, not some malfunctioning of the body. He demanded that we take this bastion of the psychiatric world-view and open it up to a different reading, telling a tale of tactics in living rather than of dumb necessity.

Thus schizophrenics, while undeniably suffering from a disturbed physiology, can be seen nonetheless as like all the rest of us human beings, as just trying to make the best sense they can of their disturbed circumstances. And Don, like Oliver Sacks (1986: 4), who has said that:

> it must be said from the outset that a disease is never a mere loss or excess – that there is always a reaction on the part of the organism or individual, to restore, to replace, to compensate for and to preserve its identity, however strange the means may be . . .

alerted us (some twenty years earlier) to the 'drama' or the 'odyssey' involved in our human attempts *to be* somebody. And also, in less propitious times than those now available to Sacks, that the way to communicate the emotional power, and the moment by moment changes in sensibility and situation entailed in being 'in' the middle of that drama, is through the telling of it as a story.

Yet – and here is the 'hanging back' of the Grammarian coming out – and yet, does the story really capture what actually was involved in the living of it? Can we go even deeper – not to reject theories for accounts, or to reject accounts for stories, as being useless to us – but on the contrary. To penetrate into the process of talk and telling itself: (1) to say something about the resources upon which such activities as theorizing, accounting and storytelling draw upon; (2) to say something about the different uses they each serve in the ecology of our everyday social lives at large; and also (3) to say something more about the experience of living which even a story does not tell? I think we can, and this is the issue I want to discuss in the rest of my talk today. To give you a prelude to the line I now want to take, let me give you three quotations. One is from someone whose name I shall reveal to you only later; it is:

> Quite often we do not succeed in bringing the patient to recollect what has been repressed. Instead of that, if the analysis is carried out correctly, we produce in him an assured conviction of the truth of [a] construction which achieves the same therapeutic result as a recaptured memory.

I reproduce this here because I first want, I'm afraid, to raise some issues to do with what I think are some very real dangers in telling stories.

My second quote is from Umberto Eco's *The Name of the Rose* (Eco, 1984), and to an extent, instead of my paper here today I could just read you pages 491 to 493 of that book, for essentially, what I want to say here is what he says there. The quotation is:

> There was no plot, and I discovered it by mistake.

And it is to do with the necessity, nonetheless, notwithstanding all the dangers of telling stories, of telling stories.

The third quotation is from Miller Mair's paper about storytelling (Mair, 1988: 136), in which he talks of Don as saying that he was 'arrested' by a phrase that he (Miller) had used in a paper about listening to people's personal concerns in psychotherapy – the phrase, and this is the quotation, is:

> . . . in the context of this, their one and only life.

And I want to ask, of course, why this *is* an arresting phrase – because I also find it arresting, as I'm sure you do too. There is something special about such phrases [as I mentioned in the previous chapter] and I think we should explore what it might be.

To 'tally with what is real in him'

So, to turn to my first issue: the dangers in storytelling. Freud, you will recall, was anxious to rebut the criticism that psychoanalysis was, to quote him, 'nothing more than a particularly well-disguised and particularly effective form of suggestive treatment' (Freud, 1973: 505). For if such a charge was true, as he himself said, 'we should have to attach little weight to all that it tells us about what influences our lives, the dynamics of the mind or the unconscious' (1973: 505). Indeed, the whole edifice of the causal theory constructed by Freud – to do with how infantile development shapes our adult personalities – would be at least suspect, and might have to be abandoned.

Well, not only do I in fact think that the charge *is* true, and that Freud is self-deceived in thinking that he had fashioned an appropriate criterion for assessing the objectivity of his claims. But that furthermore, the way that his criterion fails (as Marie Jahoda (1977) points out), reflects into the whole nature of scientific psychology, and renders it also vulnerable to the charge of resting upon similar self-deceptive foundations. But the self-deception is not just Freud's own. It points to a weakness in Western rationality, in what in the past we have taken our criterion of objectivity to be: namely, independence from the wishes and opinions of any of the individuals involved in the investigative processes concerned. But this, unfortunately, does not rule out corporately produced illusions and delusions, in which the social production of outcomes is attributed solely to individuals acting in isolation from one another. And the result of this is, that instead of such investigations working genuinely to help us in solving the problems we face – by providing us (as in any effective therapy) with new and empowering accounts of ourselves instead of disabling ones – they simply work to re-empower the individuals they serve to act once again as seemingly cohesive, self-contained individuals.

But this is done, however, at a cost: that of mystifying them as to the true nature of their historical, social, economic and political predicament. Instead of them becoming aware of the nature of the social relations in which they are involved – with its political economy of cultural resources people require if they are to develop their identities; they simply once again return to living 'naturally' within them, thus both to reproduce them in their actions and themselves as the kind of person 'naturally' able to act in the 'right' ways to do so. But the 'natural' or the 'pre-programmed anti-relational pre-understandings' which go to make up our Western individualistic, scientistic culture demand (among other things) – if we are to appear as normal, acceptable people to others – that we treat ourselves (and others) as attempting to master and control as much of ourselves and our surroundings as possible. But the cost of maintaining the illusion of mastery is to allow ourselves to be made the victims of various, seemingly natural, imaginary metaphysical agencies supposedly at work in them – variously called the *unconscious*, the *id*, the *superego*, the *Oedipus complex*, and so on. Similarly also in mainstream psychology: there, psychologists talk of similar metaphysical agencies to whom we are supposedly subject in the living of our lives: *locus of control*, or *self-efficacy*, or *mental representations*, and so on. Hence, 'authenticity' in the sense of a personal, private spiritual liberation becomes the imaginary value of life in a society in which the real relationships of class, race and economics are disavowed, and are replaced by the idealistic and impossibly split; that is, essentially schizoid values of personal responsibility and ownership, on the one hand, and claimed equality in terms of access to communal resources, on the other. In such circumstances, unable to liberate oneself in the material world through the liberation of others, one turns to the illusory liberation of the spirit – to supposed new 'new age' movements.

In making clear how all this applies to Freud, let me do so by examining what Freud claimed was a sufficient criterion for objectivity in rebutting certain charges made against him: that psychoanalysis works merely by 'suggestion', that it is just to do with the special relations possible between people, rather than with special states within individuals. 'These accusations are contradicted more easily by an appeal to experience than by the help of theory', he said.

> Anyone who has himself carried out psychoanalyses will have been able to convince himself on countless occasions that it is impossible to make suggestions to the patient in that way. The doctor has no difficulty, of course, in making him a supporter of some particular theory and thus in making him share some possible error of his own. In this respect the patient is behaving like anyone else – like a pupil – but this only affects his intelligence, not his illness. After all, his conflicts will only be successfully solved and his resistances overcome if the anticipatory ideas he is given tally with what is real in him. Whatever in the doctor's suggestions is inaccurate drops out in the course of analysis . . . (1973: 505)

Yet nonetheless, as Freud freely admitted, in *the transference* (as analysts like to call it) – the 'battlefield' upon which the analytic struggle takes place – 'new editions of old conflicts' are created. And the analyst-doctor finds that:

> In place of his patient's true illness there appears the artificially constructed illness, in place of the various unreal objects of the libido there appears a single, and once more imaginary, object in the person of the doctor. But, by the help of the doctor's suggestion, the new struggle around this object is lifted to the highest psychic level: it takes place as a normal mental conflict. (1973: 508)

This, as Freud (1973: 507) says, completes his 'picture of the mechanism of cure by clothing it in the formulas of the libido theory'.

And this reference to 'old conflicts', at least originally, was a major reason why the Freudian story about ourselves is supposed to have exerted such a fascination for us. For it is his account of our behaviour as being 'unconsciously motivated' by such conflicts – either inherent in the structure of family relationships or in the very nature of our biology – which is meant to have shattered our comfortable, bourgeois view of ourselves as able to justify all of our conduct to ourselves in wholly rational terms. But is it true? Are we 'unconsciously' motivated in many of our acts by 'repressed conflicts'?

Well, we think we are. And when we hear Evans-Pritchard's (1976: 150) account of how the African Azande make use of a 'chicken-oracle' in sustaining a workable social order, we smile knowingly when he says about his attempts to confront them with its failures that:

> I was met sometimes by point-blank assertions, sometimes by secondary elaborations of belief that provide for any particular situation provoking scepticism, sometimes by polite pity, but always by an entanglement of linguistic obstacles . . .

For we feel that we would not be so naïve. We may talk about the 'id' and the 'ego' and the 'unconscious', but we are talking about *real* things, or at least hypothetical things which have a great deal of evidence in their support. But I think we are being naïve – or at least in the past, we have been. And by having not been properly aware of the power of language, of the power of storytelling to 'lend' a *sense of reality* to wholly fictitious worlds, we have allowed ourselves to have been talked into accepting a *counterfeit* version of our social lives together – where what I mean here by the term 'counterfeiting' is the appropriation and use by individuals for their own purposes of certain special, communally constructed and sustained resources, which (like money) are the resources in terms of which the community in fact maintains itself as a community.

My reason for using this term is that I do not want to deny that the social realities within which we live are socially constructed; indeed, my purpose is just the opposite – to emphasize that fact. Thus, just as money has no reality except as a medium of exchange in the conduct of transactions – for its value is in its 'promissory' character: the degree to which those using it are prepared to honour the commitments implied in its use – so also with language. Problems arise, however, in arguing just what those commitments or promises are. And the degree to which we can avoid the responsibilities in which we have embroiled ourselves is, I think, what Freudian forms of talk are all about, and why I think that they are in many respects counterfeit.

The value of order and coherence

In trying to say exactly why I think they are counterfeit, I could go into a great number of details, to do with, for instance, all the current controversies about the history of the 'seduction theory' (Masson, 1984) and the way Freud (SE 1962: 3: 202–14) substituted for it his notions of 'infantile sexuality'; but not only have I no time for that, as important as it has turned out to be, it is not in fact relevant. What is, is to bring out the general nature of interpretative or hermeneutical processes, and to point out two things: one is the importance in them both of certain, particular unexamined, pre-understandings (to use a term of Heidegger's) in their constitution; and the other is the general assumption common to *all* such processes, that there is or was indeed a 'hidden' *order* already in existence awaiting explication – it is this last assumption that I now think most unwarranted. But to turn to discuss the point about particular pre-understandings first.

Here I want to draw upon a paper by Roy Schafer (1980) on 'Narration in Psychoanalytic Dialogue'. In this paper, he wants in fact to completely reinterpret psychoanalysis as a wholly storytelling enterprise, as concerned with what one might call a 'history of the present' rather than a 'history of the past'. At this point, however, let me leave that overall question on one side, and draw upon certain detailed aspects of his paper. In it, for instance, he points out what all recent philosophers of science have pointed out about the nature of *data* in science: that data are theory-laden. That:

> What have been presented as the plain empirical data and techniques of psychoanalysis are inseparable from the investigator's precritical and interrelated assumptions concerning the origins, coherence, totality, and intelligibility of personal action. (1980: 30)

And that as far as Freud was concerned, in his formal theorizing he made use of two primary narrative structures in forming his precritical assumptions. One begins with the infant and young child as a beast, otherwise known as the id, and ends with the beast domesticated, tamed by frustration in the course of development in a civilization hostile to its nature. The basic story is ancient; it has been told in many ways over the centuries, and it pervades what we consider, says Schafer, to be 'refined common sense' – about which more in a moment. The other narrative structure is based upon Newtonian physics as transmitted through the physiological and neuroanatomical laboratories of the nineteenth century. Both these structures exemplify a dominant commitment of Freud's, one which through all the twists and turns of his theorizing he never relinquished: a commitment to determinism, to showing how present behaviour is causally determined by past occurrences, a commitment to psychoanalysis as a natural science, a commitment he expressed in the now famous statement:

> Psychoanalysis is a part of the mental science of psychology ... Psychology, too, is a natural science. What else can it be? (SE 1964: 23: 282)

Thus for him, the claim by Jung for instance, that the origins and causes of neurotic conflicts are to be sought in the current circumstances of life – and that many supposed 'childhood memories' are adult fantasies, retrospectively projected back into childhood – was not just rejected; it made no sense to him within his own personal narrative. But what was that narrative?

Well, if we turn to *Civilization and its Discontents* we will find what I think are some very personal statements of Freud's to do with his own feelings about his relation to the world and to the others around him. For instance, he says there (1961: 26) that:

> Against the dreaded external world one can only defend oneself by some kind of turning away from it, if one intends to solve the task by oneself. There is, indeed, another and better path: that of becoming a member of the human community, and, with the help of a technique guided by science, going over to the attack against nature and subjecting her to the human will.

Freud's commitment to a 'natural scientific' *Weltanschauung* then, was not just a special professional commitment to objectivity, but he was clearly totally immersed in the Cartesian project of 'the mastery and possession of Nature' by individuals. He clearly did not know how *to be* otherwise. This is why, I think, that although Freud 'knew', in one sense, that psychoanalysis was a storytelling enterprise – for as I'm sure you guessed, my first quote about therapeutic results being achieved solely by *constructions* was from Freud himself – he was unable to admit the fact; he, because of who he was, had to persist with his natural scientific *Weltanschauung*.

But as Schafer points out: (i) not just Jung's concern with adults becoming *individuated*, but yet other narratives can be used to organize analytic data. For instance: (ii) Followers of Karen Horney can apply her Adlerian concern with the *ad hoc* strategies people develop for coping with their relations to other people; (iii) Kleinians can give an account of the child or adult as being in some stage of recovery from a rageful infantile psychosis at the breast; while (iv) Kohutians tell of the child driven in an almost instinct-like fashion to actualize a cohesive self; and soon, I'm sure, we shall have stories about (v) the postmodern, de-narrativized, decentred, fluid, yuppie-self, liberated from the burden of having to commit itself to playing any consistent part for very long – along with its supposed 'neurotic' search for some narrative structure somewhere to make sense of the labyrinthine turbulences of its life. Each narrative can be used as a device for eliciting, constituting, selecting and organizing (thus to guide further elicitation) psychoanalytic data.

But each narrative also constitutes in its telling, to the extent that we tell it to *ourselves* as well as others – as Schafer also makes clear – a 'telling-self' and a 'told-self', as well as the relations of this self to 'others', a self whose character is determined by its 'place' or 'position' in a discourse. And in Schafer's retelling of the psychoanalytic narrative, the psychotherapeutic function of psychoanalytic interpretation is to reconstruct all the fragments of the patient's *present* (not past) life given in the analytic sessions into a new narrative: 'The competent analyst says in effect,

> Let me show you over the course of the analysis another reality, commonsensical elements of which are already, though incoherently and eclectically included in what you now call reality . . . This second reality is as real as any other. In many ways it will be more coherent and inclusive and more open to your activity than the reality you now vouch for and try to make do with. On this basis, it also makes the possibility of change clearer and more or less realizable, and so it may open a way out of your present difficulties'. (1980: 50)

But, if this second reality does not cure patients by tallying with something real in their illness (as distinct from affecting them in their intellects), how does it 'move' them? Why doesn't talk of this new narrative just work to 'inform' them? Is it enough, as Schafer says, that it gives an alternative, yet still coherent account of life's little fragments? In other words, there are still a number of points to be cleared up: (1) the truth value of such narratives; (2) from whence they draw their power; and (3) their relation to reality.

If you complete it, you falsify it

It is suggested that they draw their power from their coherence. This, I think, is only partly true; metaphor as we shall see in a moment is important also. But let us first examine quite what is being claimed here. As we know, the basic nature of the constructive process involved is the taking of pieces or fragments of the patient's associations, and accounts of their dreams and memories, and so on, and of weaving them into a coherent whole. By giving each previously random-seeming event an intelligible part to play in that whole, this allows us to make sense of them. And, in guiding us towards the making of further important discoveries about the patient's life, it is thought to be compelling and persuasive. The famous hermeneutical circle involves a back-and-forth between 'the whole conceived through the parts which actualize it and the parts conceived through the whole which motivates them' (Geertz, 1975: 52). Except, I must add, Freud did not think of it as just a constructive process, but as *re-constructive* process, as being in fact like archaeology. In one of his earliest expressions of this metaphor, he says (SE 1896/1962: 3: 191):

> If [the archaeologist's] work is crowned with success, the discoveries are self-explanatory: the ruined walls are part of the ramparts of a palace; the

> fragments of columns may be filled out into a temple; the numerous inscriptions . . . when they have been translated and deciphered, yield undreamed-of information about the events of the remote past, to commemorate which the monuments were built.

But in another account of his method (SE 1923/1964: 19: 116), using a slightly different metaphor, he reveals why he thought it gave certainty; because for him, the process was like that of doing a jig-saw puzzle:

> If one succeeds in arranging the heap of [puzzle] fragments, each of which bears upon it an unintelligible piece of drawing, so that the picture acquires a meaning, so that there is no gap anywhere in the design and so that the whole fits into the frame – if all these conditions are fulfilled, then one knows that one has solved the puzzle and that there is no alternative solution.

In other words, partially at least, interpretations are persuasive not because of their evidential support but because of their rhetorical appeal; conviction emerges because the fit with the other pieces of the puzzle is good – where as Schafer shows, the puzzle is determined by Freud's precritical narratives – not because we have made a proper contact with the past.

It is interesting to compare this statement of Freud's with Wittgenstein's (1980, I: no. 257) remark [already mentioned in full in Chapter 6], in which he says:

> Mere description is so difficult because one believes that one needs to fill out the facts in order to understand them . . . they only [seem to] make sense when one completes them into a shape.—Whereas I want to say: Here *is* the whole. (If you complete it, you falsify it.)

But this is precisely Freud's tactic, for example, in *The Interpretation of Dreams*, in the famous case of the man dreaming that he was talking to his dead father. About the dream, the man had said that he was talking to his father 'in the usual way, but (the remarkable thing was that) he had really died, only he [the father] did not know it'. 'This dream becomes intelligible', says Freud (SE 1953: 5: 430), 'if after the words "but he had really died" we insert "in consequence of the dreamer's wish" and if we explain that what "he did not know" was that the dreamer had this wish.' But it is not Freud's tactic alone; we all do it, and life would be impossible if we didn't. Why? Because, I think, as C.W. Mills (1940) said, long before Wittgenstein pointed it out also, the fundamental function of talk is not to *represent the world*, but to 'coordinate diverse action'. And only certain kinds of talk will work to do this, will work to produce order. It is a concern with talking 'about' past things in a way that will produce order that is important. But again, why?

I should have known . . . there is no order in the universe

If I were to give you a totally haphazard account of a sequence of events, which, in the words of G.K. Chesterton, was 'just one damned thing after another', but, nonetheless, I assured you that it was in fact a *true* representation of what had actually happened, you would very likely say something like: 'Well, it might very well be true, but it makes no sense to me; I'm just as puzzled now what to do as I was before.' For, if we are to act in an *orderly* way, in a way intelligible to others like ourselves, we require an account which 'situates' us and suggests a socially acceptable 'line of action' to us. Only then, it seems, is it worth us asking questions as to the value of the account, in terms of the action it suggests. True representations which make no sense are, seemingly, useless to us.

Indeed, this is why I mentioned the quotation from Eco's *The Name of the Rose* earlier. It occurs towards the end of the book in the context of a discussion between William of Baskerville (the 'Sherlock Holmes' of the story) and Adso (his 'Dr Watson'). William has just been discussing the motives of Jorge, the villain of the piece. He says about him that:

> Jorge did a diabolical thing because he loved his truth so lewdly that he dared anything in order to destroy falsehood . . . [But] perhaps the mission of those who love mankind is to make people laugh at the truth, *to make truth laugh*, because the only truth lies in learning to free ourselves from insane passion for the truth. (Eco, 1984: 491)

But Adso tells him that he's only speaking like this because of his depression at the turn of events – the burning of the library and so on – and that he should have good cheer at defeating Jorge, 'because you exposed his plot' (1984: 491). But it is at this point that William says strangely that: 'There was no plot, and I discovered it by mistake' (1984: 491). Although in a moment he explains what he meant:

> 'I arrived at Jorge seeking one criminal for all the crimes and we discovered that each crime was committed by a different person, or by no one. I arrived at Jorge pursuing the plan of a perverse and rational mind, and there was no plan, or, rather, Jorge himself was overcome by his own initial design and there began a sequence of causes, and concauses, and of causes contradicting one another, which proceeded on their own, creating relations that did not stem from any plan. Where is all my wisdom, then? I behaved stubbornly, pursuing a semblance of order, when I should have known well that there is no order in the universe.'
>
> 'But in imagining an erroneous order you still found something . . .' [Adso replies].
>
> 'What you say is very fine, Adso, and I thank you. The order that our mind imagines is like a net, or like a ladder, built to attain something. But afterward you must throw the ladder away, because you discover that, even if it was useful, it was meaningless.' (1984: 492)

Meaningless? Surely not! What can Eco mean here? Surely, it was just because the fragments *are* put into an order – by the insertion of the supposedly missing portions which *must*, originally, have been there – that they take on a meaning! No it is not. What they take on there is not so much meaning as *intelligibility*; that is, they become capable of being grasped reflectively and intellectually. The order has been *constructed* and the missing portions supplied, not because they must have been there in reality, but by drawing upon a syntax, upon a 'grammar' implicit in our language; that is, by drawing upon features implicit in our 'accepted' ways of coordinating our actions with one another – where, to the rational intellect, syntax gives the appearance of meaning. But it is a counterfeit version, a version in favour of a single, particular way of ordering social life – which for Freud, as I have argued above, was in terms of individuals achieving mastery and possession of essentially socially produced resources. It is counterfeit, because, as Eco points out, in the universe – or as Wittgenstein would say, in the 'hurly-burly' or 'bustle' of everyday life – there is no order, no one single, complete order. Hence the *true* meanings of the events in the living of our lives cannot be properly understood within the confines of an order; they are only to be found in the not wholly orderly, practical living of our lives. And the meanings they have there are different from the meanings assigned to them within a story-world, with its one *coherent* order. In such imaginary worlds, as one very well-known creator of many such worlds, C.S. Lewis (1939: 156), said:

> The percentage of syntax masquerading as meaning may vary from something like 100 per cent in political writers, journalists, psychologists, and economics, to something like 40 per cent in the writers [like himself] of children's stories.

What retrospectively and intellectually seems an unintelligible fragment of a 'hidden order', is made sense of in everyday life in different ways, in different contexts, at different moments.

A whole cloud of philosophy in a drop of grammar

But how? By, I want to say, drawing upon the resources available to us in common sense. But what is the nature of common sense? If we are to believe our textbooks on 'scientific' psychology – which thank goodness we do not always need do – then while 'the informal knowledge' provided by not only common sense, but also by 'poets, philosophers, playwrights, and novelists', is 'brilliant and insightful . . . [and] often quite impressive', it 'seems both confusing and inconsistent' (Baron and Bryne, 1984: 4) – where, to prove their point, they exhibit the contrast between 'Absence makes the heart grow fonder', and 'Out of sight out of mind'. Thus, due to its confused inconsistency, it cannot 'by itself provide an adequate basis for understanding the complex nature of social relations', they say. Well here, I think they have got it quite right: it is confused and inconsistent. But unlike Baron and Bryne, and unlike Freud, who, because it is full of contradictory fragments think that an order must be imposed upon it, I think its confused, inconsistent nature is its strength.

Thus here, for my penultimate point, I want to turn to what I think is some of the most important work in social theory at the moment, and that is the work of Michael Billig and his colleagues in the Loughborough Discourse and Rhetoric Group, on what they call the 'dilemmatic' structure of common sense – that is, the impossibility, as they see it, of *ever* organizing common sense into a single order because of its essentially contrary themes and unresolved tensions (Billig, 1987; Billig et al. 1988). Their claims can be related to a number of others very similar. Wittgenstein (1980, II: nos 624–6), as I have already mentioned, saw everyday life as a 'bustle', which is 'indefinite' but nonetheless recognizable 'from the general impression it makes'. While Heider (1958: 2) says about it that, 'though unformulated and only vaguely conceived, [it] enable[s] [the human being] to interact with others in more or less adaptive ways'. Clifford Geertz (1983: 90) calls it 'immethodical', but points out that, despite all its disorder, it has as one of its major qualities 'accessibleness', or as Barthes (1983: 214) says, of what he calls 'the Image-repertoire', 'its power is immediate: I do not have to look for the image, it comes to me, all of a sudden', on occasion after occasion, called out at 'the whim of aleatory circumstances'. And finally, let me mention Merleau-Ponty's (1964: 88) phenomenological account of the act of speaking:

> The words and turns of phrase needed to bring my significative intention to expression recommend themselves to me, when I am speaking, only by . . . a certain style of speaking from which they arise and according to which they are organized without my first having to represent them to myself.

And he continues in a way which, although it is not directly relevant to my point here, I cannot resist quoting:

> There is a 'languagely' meaning of language which effects the mediation between my as yet unspeaking intention and words, and in such a way that my spoken words surprise me myself and teach me my thought.

My point in mentioning the comments made by all these writers about the nature of common sense and its vague and unformulated structure, is to point out that – although from an intellectual point of view it may seem unintelligible – this does not mean that it lacks point as a *practical resource*. Indeed, quite opposite is the case, and this is where Billig and his colleagues' work comes in. In rethinking the nature of ideology – the way in which the thinking of just a class or an elite within a society might come to 'infect', so to speak, the whole thinking of the society – they point out that the tendency in the past has been to treat ideological systems as indeed integrated *systems* of thinking, or, to use the psychological terms, as schemata, *par excellence*. In their account, they emphasize an ideology's dilemmatic aspects: the fact that within the ideology of liberalism there are, for instance, dilemmas to do with the relation between the individual and the collective, between egalitarianism and authoritarianism, between individual and social responsibility, between an agent's freedom of action and natural necessity, and so on. The fact is, even within an ideology, there is debate and argumentation, because, within each ideology, there is an irresolvable dialectic of themes and counter-themes – many of which are classic dilemmas which have been with us from the beginning of time. And what gives them their 'ideological' flavour is the dominant 'idiom' or 'vocabulary' of metaphorical containers within which we attempt, in our storytelling, to give them intelligible shape, for our ways of talking always benefit certain portions of society over others.

But yet again, and this brings me to my final point, we can raise the question: why are we 'moved' or 'arrested' by some formulations rather than by others? This is where my third and final quote is relevant: Miller Mair's phrase 'in the context of this, their one and only life'. Why is it that certain phrases *arrest* us and *move* us? The answer is simply, I think, because they are poetic. But what does it mean to say that? And here we move, I think, right to the origins of language itself, and into a controversial area in which it is possible to say very little which is sensible. But we can, I think, at least say this: first, that there are certain special moments which one shares with others – I shall call them *moments of common reference* – in which, as two people (two beings) regard one another *and* their common situation, they know from each other's 'attunements', as I shall call them, that they are each sensing it in the same way – just as one knows, for instance, in shaking another person's hand who is leading and who following, or that, perhaps, the person just does not come from a handshaking culture and doesn't understand what the activity is all about. The second thing is that in such moments, one's expressions can work to give a shared significance to such shared circumstances – and here Vico (whose views I'm essentially giving you here), mentions the way in which hunched shoulders and hesitant looks can come to signify fear – a fear first experienced in common with others when fleeing to the caves to hide, for instance (and only for instance), on the occurrence of thunder. In other words, to say that a phrase is poetic or metaphorical, is to say that it works to give form to something which in itself is essentially formless. But furthermore, in so doing, if it is to be 'moving' instead of just 'informing' then it has got to affect us not just in our intellect, nor in our illness, but in our living. And this is what Wittgenstein means, I think, when, in making essentially the same point as Merleau-Ponty, he claims that 'It is correct to say "I know what you are thinking", and wrong to say "I know what I am thinking" ' (Wittgenstein, 1953: 222). He is claiming my different ways of speaking about the thought of others and my own thought, can surprise me and teach me the differences involved here: that others 'show' us their thought 'in' their actions, while we do not 'show' our own thought to ourselves in this way. As Wittgenstein says (1953: 222), 'a whole cloud of philosophy is condensed into a drop of grammar'. Stories may tell us what in certain particular circumstances we *should* do to fit our actions into a particular order, but their danger is, that by revealing in their telling only a selection of the possibilities open to us, they can so easily conceal from us what that range of possibilities is.

9
The Manager as a Practical Author: Conversations for Action

> **The most essential responsibilities for managers . . . can be characterized as participation in conversations for possibilities that open new backgrounds for the conversations for action.**
>
> Winograd and Flores, 1986: 151

The topic of this chapter bears upon social-organizational *theory*, but there is no doubt at the moment that these are turbulent times (Gergen, 1990) both *for* and *in* organizational theory – many theories are offered, but few seem adequate or helpful. My comments below will not alter this state of affairs. Indeed, for theory or theories as such, they offer only bad news. For I want to argue, along with Winograd and Flores (1986), that it is not yet more or different theory that we need in management studies, but a better understanding of conversation and conversational realities. Indeed, the implication of my comments below is that, at least in management studies, we should demote theory stated in terms of propositions, rules or principles, right to the back room of our thought – leaving it on hand, perhaps, for just for an occasional recall, but no more. This is because I want to argue (following Vico – see below) that instead of modelling itself on the natural sciences – with their emphasis upon knowledge of the external world – management studies will fare better if it functions as a *humane study*, drawing upon the special knowledge we have 'from within' ourselves as conversationally competent human beings. For, by still treating management studies as a 'science', and by placing our central focus upon 'theories' (even though we have ceased to worry about whether they are true or false, and treat them only as 'tools of thought'), we hide from ourselves our lack of knowledge in at least two spheres of activity, crucial to an understanding of what is involved in the management of organizations.

For instance, we still do not understand the nature of the essential core ability to do with what it is that makes a manager a good manager. Clearly, it is *not* to do with finding and applying a true or false theory, but something to do with a complex of issues centred on the provision of an *intelligible formulation* of what has become, for the others in the organization, a chaotic welter of impressions.[1] In this sense, a manager can be seen as a 'repairer', as someone who is able to restore a routine flow of action that has broken down in some way, to give it an intelligible direction. Thus, rather than *as if* 'doing science', managers may best be seen as *actually* involved 'in the making of history'. For – although they must often function (as Marx said in general about people making history) 'under conditions not of their own choosing' – good managers, when faced with such unchosen conditions, can, by producing an appropriate *formulation* of them, create (a) a 'landscape' of enabling–constraints (Giddens, 1979) relevant for a range of next possible actions; (b) a network of 'moral positions' or 'commitments' (understood in terms of the rights and duties of the 'players' on that landscape); and (c) are able to argue persuasively and authoritatively for this 'landscape' amongst those who must work within it. If this is the case, if managers can within their own sphere of influence be seen as 'making history', then they must be more than just a 'reader' of situations, more than just a 'repairer' of them. Perhaps a good manager must be seen as something of an 'author' too.

But they cannot just innovate as they please, for the fact is, not just 'anything goes' – they cannot be authors of fictions, which bear no relation to what the unchosen conditions they face will 'permit', or 'afford'.[2] Their authoring must be *justified* or *justifiable*, and for that to be possible, it must be 'grounded' or 'rooted' in some way in circumstances others share. This leads us to a second crucial sphere of knowledge/activity in which the idea of the manager as a 'scientist' fails us. For in its provision of an abundance of tools for *thought* and *perception*, it hides from us its lack of provision of tools relevant to that other important side to any investigatory practice: that of being able to act from *within* a circumstance, *through* an instrumental aid, thus to know how further to act within it – the process of 'feeling' one's way forward, so to speak. Indeed, because a theory as such, strictly, is a third-person, external *observer*, systematic version of events, and is oriented towards influencing those events not from 'within', but only externally from without, such a theory can often seem to *exclude* action: thus a sense of being disempowered by one's own analysis is still possible even with the most complex and sophisticated forms of theory. What we need to understand is the nature and functioning of those kind of adjuncts, or (prosthetic) extensions to our organs of sense and action – which, as Polanyi (1958: 55) puts it, 'are not objects of our attention, but instruments of it' – *through* which we both act *and* know.

In fact, if we are to understand authorship, what we need, as I have argued above, is an account of people's use of language in these terms, an account which emphasizes (above its merely representative function) what might be called its *formative* power: the ability of people in otherwise vague, or only partially specified, incomplete situations (arising in the *joint action* between first and second persons), to 'give' or to 'lend' to such situations a more determinate linguistic formulation (with all the required properties listed above) – according to what they 'sense' or 'feel' that the only vaguely specified *tendencies* in the situation will 'allow' (Shotter, 1984). To refer to a systematic theory when facing a 'crisis' in human conduct, is to treat it as *like* a certain, already well-known state of affairs. While this may seem to help in enabling one to prepare one's reactions ahead of time, in ignoring the precise 'tendencies' in the situation, it may lead to one being surprised by the unexpected. In short, to be justified in their authoring, the good manager must give a sharable linguistic formulation to already shared feelings, arising out of shared circumstances – and that is perhaps best done through the use of *metaphors* rather than by reference to any already existing theories. In what follows, I shall merely fill in some of the background to this view in order to amplify it further.

Difficulties with the image of the manager as scientist

The problems outlined above, raised by training managers to orient themselves towards business problems as if they are scientific problems, is not new. These problems were all, for instance, outlined in Giambattista Vico's 1708 oration called 'On the study methods of our time', in which he attacked the introduction of 'the new geometric methods' of the Cartesians into the universities. Vico was a professor of rhetoric – then understood as the art of arguing, in an essentially indeterminate situation, as to which course of action, amongst those it 'affords', it is best in the situation to follow – and he was concerned that 'the greatest disadvantage of our [new] method of study is that, in expending so much effort on the natural sciences, we neglect ethics, and in particular that part which deals with the nature of the human mind, its passions, and how they are related to civil life and eloquence' (in Pompa, 1982: 41). With this in mind, let me first examine some of the difficulties raised by the image of the manager as a scientist using *theories*, as his or her main operational 'tool' – making use of Gareth Morgan's account as a stalking horse – thus later to cite some of Vico's comments against the background of difficulties with Morgan's views.

Although theory is central in any 'scientific' approach to problems, the crucial move outside of science, is the 'putting of theory into practice'. This is, so to speak, where the 'gap' lies; this is where the relation between an 'experimentally proved' theory and 'reality' is still not obvious. If we turn to one of the most successful books in this area at the moment – Gareth Morgan's (1986) *Images of Organizations* – we find two new trends in attitudes to theory evidenced. (1) One is the offering of a whole range of possible theoretical structures as throwing light on the nature of organizations – organizations AS MACHINES;[3] AS

ORGANISMS; AS BRAINS; AS CULTURES; AS POLITICAL SYSTEMS; AS PSYCHIC PRISONS; AS UNFOLDING, HOLOGRAPHIC, IMPLICATE ORDERS; AS INSTRUMENTS OF DOMINATION – with an explicit attempt to face the task of dealing with organizations as activities rather than as things, as 'developmental' processes rather than as final products, with them as partial and indeterminate tendencies rather than as exhibiting the operation of predetermined functions, and so on.

The other trend, is the offering of these possible structures, these 'images', not within the classical context for the presentation of scientific theories – in which evidence is presented for the *truth* of just one of these theories as corresponding with reality – but of them *all* as 'tools' or 'aids to reading' within the overarching metaphor of the ORGANIZATION AS A TEXT. Morgan takes this approach to the problem because, as he sees it, the problem of understanding organization is difficult in that 'we do not really know what organizations are, in the sense of having a single authoritative position from which they can be viewed . . . the reality is that we are *all* like blind men and women groping to understand the nature of the beast' (1986: 341) – hence the multiplicity of the aids he offers. For, 'effective managers and professionals in all walks of life, whether they be business executives, public administrators, organizational consultants, politicians, or trade unionists, have to become skilled in the art of "reading" the situations that they are attempting to organize or manage' (1986: 11).

Unlike his supposedly more 'pure' social scientific colleagues, Morgan can take this more pragmatic stance towards theory as, after all, his task is not that of training of scientists, but of 'effective'[4] managers and professionals. And there is no doubt that dissatisfaction with a science-based approach to professional and managerial training is rife. For instance, as is well-known, we have Schon (1983: vii) suggesting in his book on the reflective practitioner, that

> universities are not committed to the production and distribution of fundamental knowledge in general. They are institutions committed, for the most part, to a *particular* epistemology, a view of knowledge that fosters selective inattention to practical competence and professional artistry.

And as Schon sees it, that particular (inappropriate) epistemology – 'technical rationality' as he calls it – involves approaching socio-practical problems as requiring the 'application' of a science, the putting of 'a theory into practice', the learning of a certain limited set of conceptual frameworks for the solving of problems. Whereas, as he sees it, the problems faced by practitioners are of quite a different kind from those faced by the solitary 'thinker', attempting to choose between complex alternatives for the *solution* of a problem; it requires a skill, not of problem-solving, but of 'problem-setting':

> the process by which [corporately] we define the decision to be made, the ends to be achieved, the means which may be chosen . . . Problem-setting is a process in which, interactively [along with everyone who must solve it], we *name* the things to which we will attend and *frame* the context in which we will attend to them. (1983: 40)

Thus the task is not one of choosing but of generating, of generating a clear and adequate formulation of what the problem situation 'is', of creating from a set of incoherent and disorderly events a coherent 'structure' within which both current actualities and further possibilities can be given an intelligible 'place' – and of doing all this, not alone, but in continual conversation with all the others who are involved (see also Winograd and Flores, 1986). As a character, the 'manager' is clearly very different from that of the 'scientist', and clearly requires a very different kind of education.

Now, as I have already mentioned above, someone who foresaw the nature of these problems very clearly, and who spoke against the modelling all of a university's 'study methods' upon those of science, was Giambattista Vico. Besides speaking out on the many dangers to do with failing to grasp the proper nature of the relation between our knowledge, our theories and our actions – and the fact that we can only be said fully to know a thing, if we know how human beings came to make it as is, his *verum-factum* principle – to which I will return to in a moment, Vico also spoke out, in a way which might almost sound sacrilegious, against the single-minded search for truth in the following terms:

> Since the sole aim of study today is truth, we investigate the nature of things, because this seems certain, but not the nature of men, because free will makes this seem extremely uncertain. This method of study gives rise to the following disadvantages for young men: that later they neither engage in public life with enough wisdom, nor know sufficiently well how to imbue oratory with morality and inflame it with feeling. With regard to prudence in public life, we should remember that the mistresses of human affairs are opportunity and choice, which are extremely uncertain, being governed for the most part by simulation and dissimulation, which are both extremely deceptive. Thus those whose only concern is truth find it difficult to attain the means, and even more the ends, of public life. More often than not they give up, frustrated in their own plans, and deceived by those of others. We assess what to do in life in accordance with those passing moments and details of things which we call 'circumstances'. (in Pompa, 1982: 41–2)

For, in Vico's terms, the knowledge we need in dealing with those passing moments we call 'circumstances' is not knowledge formulated in terms of systematic and fixed principles, but *practical wisdom*, where clearly – and I want to go into this in more detail in a moment – compared with the kinds of knowledge of which we are all familiar, this is a distinct kind of knowledge, *sui generis*.

As I have already mentioned, it involves a special contextualized form of knowing, a knowing of a third kind which takes into account (and is only accountable within) the social situation within which it is known. Thus, says Vico (in terms which might seem to anticipate Foucault), the difference between the imprudent academic and the wise man is this:

> The imprudent academic, who moves from a universal truth straight to particular truths, uses force to make his way through the maze of life. While the wise man, keeping his eyes on eternal truth amid the turnings and uncertainties of life, follows an indirect route because straight ones are impossible, and prepares plans which will be successful in the long term, as far as the nature of things allows. (Pompa, 1982: 43)

Imprudent academics must use force because they act in accordance with how circumstances *ought* to be, according to their theories, rather than in accordance to what they actually 'are'. But what 'is' their nature, what 'are' human circumstances, and in particular, the circumstances within organizations, like?

Images and contests: Realism and constructionism

Given what has been said so far, it is now clear that there are *two* distinct ways in which we might attempt to answer this question: (1) We may still, like scientists, like uninvolved, third-person, external observers, attempt to produce *a theory* which 'fits' or 'mirrors' them (the circumstances) in order to manipulate them by manipulating their surrounding conditions. Or, we might approach the problem in a very different manner: (2) as like ordinary, everyday first or second persons involved in them, not trying to mirror or to picture them, nor by trying to say in what ways they are 'like' something already familiar to us, but by trying to make ourselves reflexively self-aware of the ordinary, everyday activities and practices by which we normally succeed in conducting our affairs effectively. Such an awareness allows us to sustain such conduct in a knowledgeable manner. These two approaches are very different in many ways, and I shall run through a catalogue of differences in just a moment.

But let me straight away bring out one fundamental aspect in which they are markedly different: in everyday life, much of what we talk about has a *contested* nature; that is, our talk is not about something which already actually exists, but is about what might be, what could be the case, or what something should be like. To take some rather grand but obvious examples: in our arguments about the nature of 'democracy', 'society', 'the person', 'the individual', 'the citizen', and many other essentially political concepts, we cannot assume that we all already know perfectly well what the 'it' is that is represented by the concepts we are arguing about. Political 'objects' such as these are not already 'out there' in some primordial naturalistic sense before our talk about them; we make them 'make sense' in the course of our arguments about them. They are, in W.B. Gallie's (1955–56) sense of the term, 'essentially contested concepts', that is, they are concepts whose proper clarification gives rise to endless disputes, philosophically. In other words, by their very nature, they are not amenable to resolution simply in empirical or theoretical terms; all proposed 'clarifications' of such concepts – to the extent that they can only be persuasive rather than 'proved' – are themselves a part of the practical politics of everyday life. The same is the case, I suggest, about many less grand but much more common notions about which we argue; for instance, the concept of 'our situation here and now', or 'our concept of our organization'. In other words, the fundamental aspect in which the two different approaches markedly differ is in whether one takes a *realist* or *social constructionist* stance towards the problem here in hand – and in my estimation, the realist stance although empowering in some ways (for individual managers) is disempowering in others (for organizations as a whole).

That is, if managers still think of themselves as like scientists, and take a *realist* attitude, they will talk as Morgan (1986) does of the difficulties they face as arising out of 'the *fact* that the complexity and sophistication of our *thinking* does not *match* the complexity and sophistication of the *realities* with which *we have to deal*' (1986: 339, my emphases). So, although they may accept that 'any realistic approach to organizational analysis must start from the premise that organizations can be many things at one and the same time' (1986: 321), in an attempt to increase the sophistication of their thinking, the fact must still be that 'we can see certain metaphors *fitting* certain situations *better* than others' (1986: 342, my emphases). Thus, no matter how fluid and flexible this approach may become – by the adoption of images taken from Bohm's (1980) notions of an implicate order, or Maturana and Varela's (1980) of autopoiesis, or Taoist or Marxian logics of dialectical change – the fact is that the manager is still cast in the passive role of someone who, before he or she can *do* anything, must first *find out* something; that is, as someone who must first think in order to do. As Morgan (1986: 322) puts it: their first step is to produce a *diagnostic reading* (using different metaphors to identify aspects of the current situation), while their second step is to make a *critical evaluation* (of the usefulness of competing diagnoses) – an evaluation which ultimately involves that mysterious ability of making, he says, a *judgment of the situation at hand.*

Now, it is not just that this, as I have already said, leaves the nature of the crucial core ability, of what it is that makes a manager a good manager, hidden, but among the abundance of tools for thought and perception it provides, it also hides the loss of the opportunity actively to enter into the 'shaping' of one's own circumstances. Indeed, as Morgan realizes (1986: 266), a sense of being disempowered by one's own analysis is still possible. For, even if we understand our lives in a complex and sophisticated way, as determined by the logic of unfolding oppositions, for instance, the fact is, we can still experience our everyday lives as

> shaped by forces over which we have little control. [Thus] a manager may feel that he or she has no option but to follow the rules of the market and general environment in shaping corporate policy. [Or] a worker may feel that job opportunities and career prospects are predetermined by his or her education or social background. [Where] in each case, the logic of 'the system' or 'the environment' is seen as being in the driving seat.

That is, we will experience it in this way if we continue to adopt a 'passive attitude' to social reality.

However, if we adopt a more active attitude, we can attempt to 'reframe' the tensions and oppositions underlying the forces shaping the system, 'and thereby influence their direction'. Thus,

> Dialectical analysis has major implications for the practice of social and organizational change. It invites us to think of ways in which oppositions . . . can be reframed so that the energies generated by traditional tensions are expressed in a new way. Dialectical analysis thus shows us that the management of organization, of society, and of personal life ultimately involves the management of contradiction. (Morgan, 1986: 266)

Well yes, I could not agree more. But Morgan having seen that this is a problem, what is the solution he offers? He merely offers improved reading skills. For, as he sees it, theory is still crucial because – even though he has already said that *organizations can be many things at one and the same time* – he feels that 'practice is never theory-free, for it is always guided by an image of what one is trying to do' (1986: 336) – thus as he sees it, the 'people who learn to read situations from different (theoretical points of view) have an advantage over those committed to a fixed position. For they are better able to recognize the limitations of a given perspective' (1986: 337). And indeed they do have an advantage. But as mere readers, they do *not* have an advantage over those who know also how to function as *authors*. Those who do not feel themselves bound to live according to any particular, already existing, well-formed images, but are able, so to speak, to 'get in touch' with the vague 'feelings of tendency' (James, 1890) within themselves to which their circumstances give rise, are much more free to 'lend' or to 'give' such tendencies an intelligible expression of their own choosing, thus to become more the authors of their own lives.

Two changes in our image of the nature of knowledge

If we are to understand how to live, not according to the already existing, well-formed images in our texts, but, so to speak, according to the vague 'feelings of tendency' we can sense within ourselves to which our circumstances give rise, then we must construct an account of what it is like to act as an ordinary person who is able, *in the course of acting*, to be aware of what is currently occurring, thus to use that awareness to inform their own further conduct in the situation. An understanding of its nature requires, I think, at least two changes in our current attitudes towards the nature of knowledge: one involves a movement from the form of knowledge acquired by observation to that acquired through 'feeling' discussed in Chapter 3; the other, a movement from knowledge acquired by 'finding' to that acquired by 'making'.

It is worth adding here, however, that with respect to our powers of 'making', Vico came to believe that they gave us a special access into the nature of human beings. For whatever the instrumental powers the natural sciences provided, there is a sense, Vico thought, in which we can know more about our own and other people's experiences and actions – in which we acted as participants, indeed as authors, and not as mere observers – than we can ever know about nonhuman nature which we only observe from the outside. This is his *verum-factum* principle. Thus he *reversed* the degree of certainty that one could expect from humane studies compared with the natural sciences, claiming that certainty was more possible in the science of history (as he conceived it) than in physics, because while we may have made its mathematical theories, we have not made its substance, and thus cannot know the physical world *per caussas*; that is, not merely that it is, but what it is, and how it came to be such.

> For to know is to grasp the genus or form by which a thing is made, whereas consciousness is of those things whose genus or form we cannot demonstrate. (Vico, in Pompa, 1982: 58)

> [Thus] history cannot be more certain than when he who creates the things also narrates them. Now, as geometry, when it constructs the world of quantity out of its elements, or contemplates that world, is creating it for itself, just so does our Science [create for itself the world of nations], but with a reality greater by just so much as the institutions having to do with human affairs are more real than points, lines, surfaces, and figures are. (Vico, 1968: para. 349)

Vico's claim here, that in essence 'logical necessity' exists only because logic is a free creation of the mind, is reminiscent of Einstein's well known statement: 'Insofar as the propositions of mathematics give an account of reality they are not certain; and insofar as they are certain they do not describe reality.'

Concluding comments

I began this chapter by claiming that the essential core ability to do with what it is that makes a manager a good manager, was *not* to do with finding and applying true or false theories – that is, being able to 'read' the situation they must manage for the 'images' which are hidden in them somewhere. It is instead to do with a complex of issues centred on the provision of *intelligible formulations* of what, for the others in the organization, had broken down into a chaotic welter of impressions. Their task in such situations is to give a shared or sharable significance to the already shared, but vague 'feelings of tendency', arising out of the circumstances in question shared amongst those in the organization, thus to restore a flow of action that had become unintelligible in some way. Thus essentially, the good manager, I wanted to suggest, should be seen doubly, not *as if* involved 'in doing science', but as *actually* involved 'in the practical making of history' – thus besides being a 'reader', or a 'repairer', a good manager should also be something of an 'author' too. But not as an author of texts, but a 'practical-ethical author', a 'conversational author', able to argue persuasively for a 'landscape' of next possible actions, upon which the 'positions' of all those who must take part are clear.

This claim essentially implies another: that an important aspect of management studies should not been seen as a science, but should be seen as an aspect of what traditionally is known as humane studies. Elsewhere, I have argued for the discipline of psychology to be seen in these terms also (Shotter, 1984). Thus, rather than an empirical-explanatory science working in terms of theories, I have talked of it as a practical-descriptive one working in terms of 'instructive accounts'; that is as providing 'prosthetic' (as well as 'indicative') aids to thought, perception, and action in this sphere: in which 'making' (or 'practical authoring') is at least if not more important than 'finding'. In attempting to give an 'instructive' account of the nature of the knowledge involved in this skill – the third kind of knowledge *from within* (or embedded within) 'circumstances' of which Vico talked – I have not introduced a new and systematic theory, but just a list (more or less) of possibly useful 'analytic devices or resources': the 'formative' power of language; the importance of 'feelings of tendency'; the nature of 'knowing-from'; 'practical authoring'; 'responsivity = answerability + addressivity'; 'breakdown and its restitution'; conversation vs. written texts; psychological instruments: 'prostheses and indicators'; rhetoric: justification and criticism; realism vs. constructionism; 'making' and 'finding'; and so on.

In the past, in assuming our procedures of inquiry to be secure, and our problems to be located (mainly) in the nature of our subject matter, we have indulged in a great deal of *metatheoretical* and *epistemological* discussion – we discussed *theories* because we felt accurate theories were the goal of our investigations. In the approach being canvassed here, our supposed objects of study are of less concern to us than the general nature of our investigatory practices. In other words, instead of metatheory, we become concerned with *metamethodology*: Primarily, we become interested in the procedures and devices we use in both 'socially constructing' the subject matter of our investigations, as well as how we establish and maintain a contact with it (this is the 'critical' aspect of the constructionism discussed). For the 'hook up', so to speak, between such devices and our surroundings, determines the nature of the data we can gather *through* their use. We thus move away from the individual, third-person, external, contemplative observer stance, the investigator who collects *fragmented* data from a position socially 'outside' of the activity observed, and who bridges the 'gaps' between the fragments by the imaginative invention of theoretical entities towards a more relational, interpretative approach, in which outcomes occur as a result of *joint action* (Shotter, 1984) between all the participants involved.

Another consequence of the *social constructionist* position taken here should be emphasized, a point usually hidden by the implicit 'realism' induced in the 'scientific' approach to these issues: it is the assumption that when we talk about such 'entities' as the 'company', the 'market', the 'customer', the 'product', the 'current situation', 'office procedures', etc., we all know perfectly well what these entities are that we are talking 'about'. We find it difficult to accept that 'objects' such as these are not 'there' in some straightforward, realistic sense. It is difficult to accept their contested status, that almost everybody involved has a different version of their nature; they only 'make sense' as they are given significance within a discourse. But to claim this: that even in the sphere of business our ways of talking work to produce rather than simply to reflect the objects of which we talk, is to make a very unfamiliar claim. We all still unconsciously assume that (like Humpty-Dumpty) when we use a word, it means what we want it (and take it) to mean, nothing more, nothing less. Indeed, if people all have different notions of what it is that they are talking about, that must be because some of them have got it wrong, or have misunderstood. Nowhere is this more apparent than in our talk about talk, in which we assume that words are *surrogates* (Harris, 1980) which STAND IN for the things in our world, and communication is a process of *telementation* (Harris, 1981) in which we put our ideas INTO words in order to SEND them to the minds of others. It is this, and other unrecognized image-schematisms implicit in almost all our talk about talk, that makes us blind to the fact that much of our talk is either conducted in a context of misunderstanding and mutual bewilderment, or requires much greater openness to the argumentative negotiation of meanings if it is to be better understood – in other words, our forms of communication at the moment lack a grasp of the nature of how they are best managed.

Notes

1. 'As with language in general, we cannot look to simple notions of truth and deduction. The energy "crisis" was not created by commercial acts of the oil companies, the Arabs, or the American consumer, but by those with the power to create consensus who looked at a long-term situation and declared it to be a crisis. The relevant question is not whether it is "true" or "false" that there is a problem, but what commitments are generated for (speaker and hearer) by the speech acts [utterances] that created it, and how these commitments generate the space of possible actions' (Winograd and Flores, 1986: 147).
2. I am influenced in my use of the word 'afford' here by Gibson's (1979) 'ecological' approach to perception in psychology. As he sees it, we do not perceive our visual surroundings like a camera, taking pictures: we perceive it 'for action', in terms of what actions it 'affords'.
3. Here, I am using the convention established by Lakoff and Johnson (1980), of signalling the explicit citation of a metaphor by the use of upper-case text.
4. 'Effective' here remains, of course, problematic.

10
Rhetoric and the Recovery of Civil Society

. . . civil society is the true focal point and theatre of all history.

Marx and Engels, 1977: 57

What I want to do in this chapter is to explore the importance of rhetoric and traditions of argumentation in the formation and shaping of forms of social life. However, rather than in the already well-formed central, institutionalized regions and moments within the social life of a group, I want to study its functioning in the more disorderly zones of activity existing between or outside them, zones which, in line with certain comments of Vico (1968), Marx and Engels (1977), and Gramsci (1971), I think we can identify with aspects of what they call the *civil society* of the group.[1] My particular purpose in doing this is to contribute towards the currently emerging debate – initiated in England by Marquand (1988), but perhaps already anticipated in America by Bellah et al. (1985), and now rife upon the continent of Europe also – about *citizenship*, and about the nature of the realm of public activity required for its sustenance. Although in more general terms, my concern could be said to be with the perennial problem in social theory to do with the relation between order and chaos. For what I want to do is to give a special place and function in social theory to a realm halfway between chaos and order, and to argue that humanly *adequate* social orders (that is, adequate in a sense to be discussed below) can only be created, sustained and transformed in appropriate ways, by continually drawing upon the resources made available to them in the zones of relatively disorderly activities in the conversational backgrounds within which they are embedded – in forms of playful discussion and gossip, as well as pastimes and entertainments, and a myriad other mostly unnameable activities, all usually dismissed as a waste of time.

In social theory in the past, it has been felt both that the intrinsic nature of our subject matter *must* be orderly, and, that our aim *must* be the production of order (why?). As result, we have not taken such disorderly conversational activities seriously. The very character of our disciplinary discourses has caused us to marginalize them. In other words, without us realizing it, as social theorists we have allowed ourselves to be ruled by a dominant ideology. And I think that this why certain problems have been such a puzzle to us: for instance, the problem of how an ideologically structured hegemonic 'common sense' can be sustained, and the form of an effective resistance to it; that is, the problem of how rulers dominate the ruled through the constitution of their subjectivities, and the opportunities available to the ruled legitimately to reply. For it is only within the informal, disorderly aspects of our lives, the aspects made 'invisible' to us by our disciplinary discourses, that the relevant influences here can be seen at work. It is only by moving into the zones between disciplines that we can create a space for the contrary, rhetorical, disorderly, and even playful (loose-jointed) nature of these activities, and begin to understand the formative influences they exert in the shaping of our social lives. And it is this that I want to discuss below.

Before proceeding any further, however, I have to say that owing, not simply to limitations of space, but to the sheer (continually contested) complexities of the topics involved, I cannot pretend to present below anything like a complete characterization of the concepts of citizenship and civil society. At best, I can only claim to present a set of considerations which I think are important in the long haul ahead of those of us who feel something of importance will have been lost if, as the new conservatives are now trying to achieve, the life of nations comes to consist only in the corporately organized activities of the State, the market, atomized individuals, and nuclear families.[2] For it is within the non-State, non-market realm of public life in civil society that, I think, material for the renewal of the vision of a genuine participatory democracy can be found. It is this contest, over the creation (or the destruction) of such multi-voiced 'spaces' in public life, that is at the moment central: it can be seen, for instance, in current philosophy (after the loss of confidence in 'foundational' philosophy), in the contest between professional analytic philosophy and those canvassing a more practical–public form of philosophy as an alternative (Sullivan, 1987; Toulmin, 1988).

Introduction: Personhood, order and chaos

The view of social life introduced above, of it as consisting not just in a set of orderly institutional structures, but as an *ecology* of self-sustaining orderly centres of activity, interactively embedded within a more disorderly flow of surrounding activity, has a number of implications: (1) for the nature of the individuals involved in it; (2) for the nature of the resources to which, as citizens, they have a right of access if they are to achieve personhood; and (3) for the nature of the freedoms available to them within the group to exercise those rights. Thus, before turning specifically to a discussion of the function of rhetoric and the nature of civil society, I would like to make some preliminary general remarks both about the nature of personhood in such circumstances, and about the relation between centres of social order and their more disorderly boundaries and surroundings.

Personhood: Identity and belonging

As what people say and do is always open to criticism and judgment by others, an essential part of them being free individuals in a modern society, is them being able to justify their actions to others when required to do so – they require a capacity to be able to articulate 'good reasons' for their conduct. For, in executing their own actions, in acting as free agents (and in qualifying for their status as such), people cannot just act as they please, when they please. They must also act with a certain kind of socially shared awareness, to do with making judgments about the *boundaries* in terms of which their surroundings should be organized perceptually, and within which their actions should be seen as making sense (Douglas, 1975): judgments, for instance, to do with what should be seen as obvious, as familiar, as similar or dissimilar, as ordinary, with what should be seen as extraordinary, as strange, as repugnant, awesome, enchanting, frightening, comic, as evocative of reverence or of unquestionable authority, as interesting or boring, with what can be used for one's own ends and what must be respected as an end in itself, and to do with which actions (as ends in themselves) must be taken seriously and responded to and which can be ignored and dismissed – and so on. And in respecting such boundaries in their actions, they of course continually reproduce them. Indeed, in relation to this last point, to qualify for the special, socially autonomous status of citizens, and to be allowed to move freely within all the 'spaces' in their society, human agents must be able to show in their actions, as a special aspect of their perceptual awareness of their surroundings, an awareness of how they are (currently) 'placed' or 'positioned' in relation to all the other agents around them. They must perceive themselves as being, not in an everywhere indifferently textured physical space, but as surrounded by a morally textured 'landscape' of 'opportunities for action' made differentially available to them according to their location amongst the other agents around them, and which they also may make available to them.

This is not, however, sufficient. For a person can only be said to be acting freely if they are not acting as a means, as a kind of puppet, through which others realize themselves. What is also required is a 'sense of belonging', a sense of 'being at home' in a reality that one's actions help both to reproduce and to develop. To live within a community which one senses as being one's own – as both 'mine' and 'yours', as 'ours' rather than 'theirs' – one must be more than just an accountable reproducer of it. One must in a real sense also play a part in its creative sustaining of itself as a 'living tradition'. One must feel able to fashion one's own 'position', within the 'argument' or 'arguments' to do with both constituting and reconstituting the tradition. One must be able to feel that one's formulations, whether ultimately accepted or not, will at least be at first welcomed and listened to seriously by the others around one. One must not feel that, in order to speak freely, one first has to prove to certain others, who already seem to possess a lifetime's unconditional membership of the community, that one is qualified. For, to live under terms set only by others is always to feel not just different, but inadequate in relation to them. Part of a sense of 'belonging', of a sense of being 'at home' in one's own community, is that one has an automatic right of initial access to the community simply by virtue of having contributed, in developing oneself, to the development of *its* ways of making sense. This does not mean that one will unthinkingly feel a sense of total harmony with those around one. Indeed, it means that one must live within a number of conflicting and competing 'forms of life' with their associated 'language games' (to use Wittgenstein's terms). But it does mean, not having a sense of being an intrusive alien, of having worth as who one is.

But inevitably, there is a scarcity of such opportunities to participate in this way, and their availability thus involves a *political economy*. This is because, for instance, other people can only realize themselves in the world as speakers if others are prepared to make themselves properly available to them as listeners. And to do that, they must treat what speakers say *seriously*; that is, listeners must treat their actions as having important consequences for them – which means them either giving up their own activities to become involved in those of the speaker, or giving speakers good reasons as to why they are not prepared to do so. Indeed, in general, any significant social identity entails in its realization the enactment of a certain set of rights and duties, a moral dependence upon others and a moral requirement to offer to them what I shall call *socio-ontological* resources – that is, the communicative opportunities we all require if we are we are to realize our own distinctive modes of being. We make these resources available to each other, not only when we act as primary caretakers (as parents to young children), or as teachers or instructors, or act explicitly to render help to others, but also when we act towards one another in merely routine ways, as listeners, as readers, as 'you's to their 'I's, as recipients of their actions in any way (Shotter, 1989b).

This is reflected in Aristotle's (1976) account of 'the Good' in *The Nicomachean Ethics*: it means that even when all alone and acting solely upon one's own account, if our actions are to be accounted by others as good actions, as directed (in his terms) towards some 'self-sufficient final end', then they must in some way take into account in their performance our relations to others. For by such an end, he says (Aristotle, 1976: 74),

> we mean not what is sufficient for oneself alone living a solitary life, but something that includes parents, wife and children, friends and fellow-citizens in general; for man is by nature a social being.

And indeed, to the extent that people's identities are a function of their social relations, if they want to sustain their identities, the ontological security of their social being, they must sustain – that is, morally respect – both the identities of those around them, and the social relations which sustain those identities. This is a task, the practicalities of which are as difficult to articulate as they are to execute. But I emphasize its nature as a task here, however, to make the point that we are not *naturally* endowed with this kind of freedom; it is an achievement of a puzzling and arduous kind. In order to possess it, we must continuously labour to create the social conditions which make it possible; and its burdensome nature becomes especially apparent in times of social crisis, when a breakdown of public life threatens, and people's relations to the others around them become particularly unclear. In such times, individuals want to be rid of such a bewildering responsibility;[3] they lose their confidence in their power to change the social circumstances of their lives through argumentation and co-ordinated deliberative action; and they return to a belief in the power of 'magical' or 'mythical' entities in Nature at large to solve their problems (Cassirer, 1946) – such as our current belief that the 'natural' power of 'the invisible hand' of 'the market' will most certainly produce what 'socialist' central planning failed to achieve.

Order and chaos

I want to claim, however, that little in human social affairs remains simply 'natural'; that human social orders, to put the matter in Vico's words, 'do not settle or endure out of their natural state' (Vico, 1968: para. 134); that human beings, in becoming 'rooted' in circumstances of their own making, induce in themselves a new or second 'nature', and in making 'virtues of their passions' (Vico, 1968: para. 136), become themselves responsible for much of their own nature. Their responsibility is expressed in the fact that to maintain their nature they must constantly reproduce in their actions the surroundings required to sustain it. And to do this, as we have seen above, one must be a free individual who, when challenged by the others in the group to which one belongs, can argue for the 'fit' between their actions, and the group's form of life. It is in this way, that socially constructed forms of life, by the continuous regulation of countless individual transactions *at their boundaries*, can maintain their integrity.

This would seem also to be the implication of a surprising discovery made in the natural sciences by Prigogine: that while *isolated* systems tend, according to the second law of thermodynamics, towards increasing disorder, the situation is different with regions of activity which exist *in continuous interaction with* their surroundings. Under certain special conditions, they can exhibit a sudden transformation in the opposite direction, from disorder and instability to an order and stability which, as long as the continuous interaction is maintained, is also maintained (Prigogine and Stengers, 1984). And indeed, not only is the nature of the activity within the region transformed in such circumstances, but so are its surroundings also; the activity creates in its environment the conditions (resources) necessary for its own maintenance, its own ecological 'niche', so to speak. Prigogine calls such structures 'dissipative structures' to emphasize the fact that the formative processes responsible, for both their initial creation and their maintenance in existence, consist in continuous energy exchanges between them and the chaos of activity surrounding them. Dissipative structures do not settle or endure out of their natural state; constant activity is required at their boundaries.

Thus, in arguing both for the importance of rhetoric and of civil society in the conduct of the everyday social affairs of a people, and in arguing for the importance in their social ecology of intermediate zones – somewhere between order and chaos – within which they can find the resources they require constantly to sustain, renew, and to transform their social orders as new contingencies arise, I shall be attempting to explore the consequences of Prigogine's concept of interactively created and maintained structures for social theory. And I shall claim that a social order which, in denying certain activities to its members, gradually isolates itself from the disorderly surroundings sustaining it, is not in Aristotle's sense of the term a *good* society: it lacks a *polis*.

These arguments are not new. Many social theorists in the past have suggested that the provenance of order is to be found in disorder, on the edge of chaos, in spontaneity and playfulness (Bahktin, 1965; Gadamer, 1975; Gramsci, 1971; Huizinga, 1949; Vi̇co, 1968; and Vygotsky, 1962); and they have already produced arguments similar to mine. However, as I have already mentioned, an exclusive concern with order in official academic writing about social theory, has rendered their discussions of disorder 'rationally-invisible'[4] to us. It is as if disorder, chaos, playfulness, and spontaneity have lacked a 'voice' in our discussions of social theory, and because of this we have ignored them. They are not taken seriously as free subjects of discussion and debate; our current forms of discourse have repressed them.

The turn to rhetoric

But now a movement is afoot, of which this book is a part, which may to a degree lift their repression and give them a 'voice': it is a shift away from what can be called the Cartesian method of doubt – the supposed logical derivation of truths from a first truth about which one can be certain, even in the middle of one's doubts about everything else; the idea of a self-justified starting point – back towards the ancient tradition of rhetoric. There is no point at this stage in attempting, historically, to give reasons for this shift, but it is worthwhile to explore its character, for it marks 'a break with the concept of reason and reasoning due to Descartes which has set its mark upon Western philosophy for the last three centuries' (Perelman and Olbrechts-Tyteca, 1969: 1), and bids fair to change our whole conception of what we take 'rationality' to be (MacIntyre, 1988).

If we characterize some of the main aspects of the Cartesian style of thought and mode of inquiry as follows – (1) that true knowledge begins in doubt and distrust; (2) that reality is studied as atomic matter in lawful mechanical motion; (3) that the world is treated as an 'external', physical world, devoid of any mental content; (4) that proper knowledge, that is scientifically respectable knowledge, consists in beliefs which have been methodically *proved* to be true; (5) that knowledge is a 'possession' and we are in an ownership relation to it; and that (6) as true knowledge is one, a unified system of propositions, disagreement must be a sign of error – then, what is happening now involves a reversal of all these characteristics. It is now beginning to be argued: (1) that science does not start in doubt but with assent to a story or narrative (Booth, 1974; Lyotard, 1984) possessing a degree of rhetorical force;[5] (2) that the social world is best seen as a continuous flux or flow of mental activity containing regions of self-reproducing order, reproduced at their boundaries, surrounded by 'chaos' (Giddens, 1984; Prigogine and Stengers, 1984); (3) that such activity can only be studied from a position of involvement 'within' it, instead of as an 'outsider', studying it as merely 'physical' activity (Bernstein, 1983; Giddens, 1984); (4) that primarily, knowledge is practical-moral knowledge, and as such does not depend upon justification or proof[6] for its practical efficacy (Bernstein, 1983: Rorty, 1980); (5) that we are not in an 'ownership' relation to such knowledge, but we embody it as a part of who and what we are, and to try to give it up would be like trying to give up our bodies, who we 'are' (Giddens, 1984) – for we are dealing just as much with matters of ontology as epistemology

(Bhaskar, 1986); and finally (6) that practical-moral knowledge is not a unified system, but constituted in large part *argumentatively* (Billig, 1987), that is, within traditions of argumentation structured in terms of commonplaces (or *topoi*), whose discursive formulations are 'essentially contested' (Gallie, 1955-56).

In other words, instead of *convincing* arguments – arguments which, if a first truth is admitted, will compel belief in their conclusions in all rational minds, generally and mechanically, that is by calculation – we are once again investigating the nature of *persuasion*, the different ways of achieving assent in different, particular audiences. In recent times, rhetoric has suffered at the hands of logic; in a debased form, it has been seen (from within a Cartesian perspective) as just having to do with the merely emotional side of argumentation. Classically, however, rhetoric was seen as a necessary recourse in those circumstances where it was (1) necessary to reach a decision, and (2) impossible to use methods of calculation aimed at absolute certainty. In such circumstances, because there are no agreed first truths, or universal methods of inquiry, all conclusions must be arrived at by the persuasion of others. And an argument is settled, not by the production of calculations, but by the giving of *good reasons* to one's audience, particular reasons as to why they should, in that situation, assent to one's claims – where good reasons are reasons which, at the time they are given, no one can think of a way of challenging or criticizing. In other words, with regard to a particular audience, they work as some kind of ultimate justification; they touch on something in the 'basic' vocabulary of that audience (Mills, 1940).

The current turn to rhetoric consists in quite a number of relatively independent strands; there is, for instance, the *New Rhetoric* first set out in Belgium by Perelman and Olbrechts-Tyteca in French in 1958 and translated into English in 1969 (Perelman and Olbrechts-Tyteca, 1969); there are in America all the writings of Kenneth Burke, and Wayne Booth (such as Booth, 1974; Burke, 1950), to do with rhetoric in literary matters; there is also the *Rhetoric of Inquiry* movement begun by McCloskey (1983), which resulted in the Iowa conference in 1984 on 'The Rhetoric of the Human Sciences', and which has now been followed up in many further publications (such as Nelson et al., 1987); while in England, there are the books of Billig (1987) and Billig et al. (1988), setting out a whole new 'argumentative' approach to the nature of common-sense knowledge and social psychology. There is not the space here to review all these different movements (and their undoubted relations to the many other movements in other areas of thought, in, for instance, philosophy, literary theory, mathematics, communications and psychology). But I think that it is relevant to say again, that they all share a disquiet with the ideal of reason as a process of calculation working to produce *certainty*, by the process I mentioned above: that of extending the self-evidence of certain foundational axioms to claim the certain truth of derived theorems – they all view that process as an unwarranted limitation upon our understanding of the nature of reasoning (and its fallibilities and failures).[7]

Interestingly, this 'loss of certainty' (Kline, 1980) has recently extended even into mathematics. For what mathematicians are now beginning to realize, so Kline, and Davis and Hersh (1983, 1986) maintain, is that there is *no formal definition of what an acceptable proof is*. Davis and Hersh (1986: 66) put the issue thus – they ask:

> What does it mean for a mathematician to have convinced himself that certain results are true? In other words, what constitutes a mathematical proof as recognized by a practising mathematician?

And they answer:

> Disturbing and shocking as it may be, the truth is that *no explicit answer can be given*. One can only point at what is actually done in each branch of mathematics. All proofs are incomplete from the point of view of formal logic.

Indeed, they go on to claim that neither 'computerizability' nor 'mechanizability' provides, as it was once thought they would, the hallmarks of a correct proof – for how can one be sure that at each stage in a long and complex process, the machine has functioned correctly? All that seems to guarantee mathematicians' claims as to the correctness of their proofs is them being able to account for and to justify their conduct to other mathematicians in the face of their criticisms – but there is no single way in which that can be done. Thus the way out of these difficulties, Davis and Hersh suggest, is to give up the needless and useless goal of complete rigour and formalization. And simply to recognize that like all other argumentation, mathematical argumentation is addressed to a human audience, which (if appropriately trained) possesses the knowledge of mathematical practices required to judge and evaluate the activities involved.

Indeed, much of the unease felt today had already been expressed by Vico (1982: 41–2) in his oration of 1708, 'On the study methods of our time'. There he expressed his worry that:

> in expending so much effort on the natural sciences, we neglect ethics, and in particular that part which deals with the nature of the human mind, its passions, and how they are related to civil life and eloquence.

It is the contrast – between the natural sciences and eloquence – that highlights for Vico the value of rhetoric and practical wisdom in civil life: the way in which they lead one to judge things, not in terms of how in theory they ought to be, ideally, but in terms of how *in practice* they are.[8] And in practice, many situations are vague and uncertain, incomplete and open to further specification, not just because of our ignorance, but because in fact they are *in reality* vague and ill-defined, and open to further change and development[9] (Giddens, 1984; Prigogine and Stengers, 1984; Shotter, 1983a).

The 'essentially contested' nature of social life

As we have already seen, the radical openness of many aspects of social life raises awkward problems with respect to their formal conceptualization. These have been discussed in relation to logic by Myhill (1952), and, in relation to the social conditions they engender by Gallie (1955–56). Let me discuss Myhill's[10] claims first: he discusses three kinds of logically distinct features or properties that things or situations might possess – effective, constructive, and prospective characteristics – and discusses whether there are specifiable procedures or techniques[11] in terms of which they might be identified. What he argues is that: (1) while there is a whole class of characters or characteristics, effective characteristics, for which a recognition technique can be specified; and (2) another whole class, constructive characteristics, for which a procedure can be specified for the production (given enough time) of every conceivable exemplar; there is (3) still a whole further class of characteristics, prospective characteristics, of which we can clearly possess a sense, but for which we can neither specify a recognition nor a constructive procedure. Such a sense is, for instance, our sense of beauty. What his argument means is:

> that not only can we not guarantee to recognize it when we encounter it, but also that there exists no formula or attitude, such as that in which the romantics believed, which can be counted upon, even in a hypothetical infinitely protracted lifetime, to create all the beauty that there is. (Myhill, 1952: 191)

In other words, there is no school of art which permits the production of all beauty and excludes all ugliness, nor is there any token (such as pleasure or the like) by which the beautiful can always be recognized – conclusions which, although they are expressed in a different idiom, are very much in line with Gallie's account of essentially contested concepts.

The special concepts that Gallie discusses are, he says, to do with organized or semi-organized human activities: with aesthetics, religion, politics, philosophy and history, and are to do with what are thought of in these areas as achievements, and with their evaluation. He calls them 'essentially contested concepts' because they give rise to disputes which,

> although not resolvable by argument of any kind, are nevertheless sustained by perfectly respectable arguments and evidence. This is what I mean by saying that there are concepts which are essentially contested, concepts the proper use of which inevitably involves endless disputes about their proper uses on the part of their users. (Gallie, 1955–56: 172).

This formulation has, it is worth pointing out, the same reflexive character to it as MacIntyre's description of a living tradition (see below, and in previous chapters), and is clearly connected with Billig's notions of two-sided topics (see Billig, 1987: 147).

While it is not necessary to repeat in detail here Gallie's account of the conditions which give rise to the irresolvable disputes involved in conceptualizing the nature of human achievements, the following features are worth mentioning: although their worth or significance must be attributed to them as a whole, they must be such that there is nothing absurd in describing their worth or significance in different ways. Indeed, while their character is persistently vague, it must be 'open' and 'prospective' in the sense that it could permit development along a number of different lines, with the best line being radically unclear, because *there is no general method* for deciding among the possibilities available. In such circumstances, there is a recognition by those who choose to follow one of the available lines that their choice is contested by those party to another; in fact, to use an essentially contested concept is to use it *against* other uses, both aggressively and defensively: as taking an individualistic, cognitivist position in psychology, implies taking a position against a more social, noncognitivist position. As Billig (1987: 91) claims, to understand the argumentative meaning of what someone claims:

> one should not examine merely the words within that discourse or the images in the speaker's mind at the moment of utterance. One should also consider the positions which are being criticized, or against which a justification is being mounted. Without knowing these counter-positions, the argumentative meaning will be lost. (1987: 91)

But the conditions Gallie states above are still inadequate, he argues, to distinguish between a concept about which there is disagreement, due simply to radical confusion, and essentially contested concepts – something about their nature must sustain and 'motivate' the dispute, the contestants must see themselves as in competition for the 'same' thing, and the competition for it worthwhile. Thus, he argues, two further conditions are required: (1) the derivation of the concept from an original exemplar whose authority is acknowledged by all the contestant users of the concept; and (2) the possibility that the continuous competition amongst the contestants, not only enables the original exemplar's achievements to be sustained or developed, but also prevents the ending of the contest, so that new developments and improvements may continuously take place. These conditions ensure that there is endless 'competition' between rivals, not only for the right to realize a distinctive own line of development, but between them for converts to it.

In giving examples Gallie, like Myhill, discusses matters of aesthetics as being essentially contested, but (what is more important for us) he also discusses political concepts and in particular, democracy. Does it satisfy his list of defining and justifying conditions? Well, it is certainly vague, but 'Its vagueness reflects its actual inchoate condition of growth' (1955–56: 181), he believes; and if we want effectively to develop it, then the first step is to recognize its essentially contested nature. It is certainly an appraisive concept; indeed, during the last one hundred years many would argue that it has established itself as *the* appraisive political concept *par excellence*. It is also internally complex and admits of a variety of descriptions in which its different aspects can be graded in order of importance.[12] In discussing it, people try to make their meaning clear by use of exemplars – the French Revolution, for instance – for its use seems to consist in 'a number of mutually contesting and contested uses' (Gallie, 1955–56: 182). But can we add that the continual competition for acknowledgement between rival uses of the concept will/can lead to improvements in its uses?

In raising that question we must be careful about the nature of the clarification and improvements through competition in question here; for, as Gallie points out, it is competition of a quite different kind to that supposed in science. In science, because (we at least think that) there is a principled way of settling rival claims, certain lines of development can reach a definitive end, rivals eliminated, and the sciences in question 'finished', for example optics and electromagnetism (Hanson, 1958) – giving rise theoretically to an applied mathematics and practically to a technology. But in social life, there can be no end to such contests because, given the 'prospective' or 'essentially contested' nature of the issues involved, there are no general methods or principles for deciding between rivals. Indeed, we can go further, and point out that while rival scientific hypotheses may be developed by individuals or groups *in isolation* from others, the very nature of the rivalry here is such that each group's claim to have a better line than its rivals, only makes sense *in relation* to the claims of their rivals, and is developed as a counter to them.

And this is the point of Gallie's concern with shared exemplars mentioned above. For such developments, provoked by an 'otherness' from outside one's own group, have a different character to those provoked within it: instead of further articulations and refinements in one's own line (systematic developments), they provoke its metamorphosis, developments of a transformational (nonsystematic) kind.

For occasionally, in reaction to one's own moves, 'others' develop an alternative way of doing things which, to the extent that it wins converts, is seen as being *better*. One's own group must then attempt to develop a counter to it, and so on. Thus what is at issue in the 'competition' involved here is not its ending, the Neo-Darwinian elimination of one's rivals, but one's continued participation in it *with them* in a tradition of argumentation; and they, in constituting the new surroundings to which one's group must now adapt, also constitute resources (enabling new modes of development) unavailable to one within one's group.[13] In this respect, democracy would seem to be a kind of politically ultimate concept, to the extent that it reflexively includes within itself an account of the conditions required for its own effective implementation and continued development: clarificatory arguments about its nature must allow a voice to all the citizens; that is, must be democratically structured. As MacIntyre (1981: 207) put it, a living tradition is 'an historically extended, socially embodied argument, and an argument precisely in part about the goods which constitute that tradition'. This is only possible if the basis upon which argumentation and debate about its nature, i.e., about what democracy 'is' for us today, can be arranged in such a way as to admit the expression of the mutually contested and contesting, lines of further development currently in existence in our society – hence the project under discussion here, the recovery of civil society, and the attempt to specify the social conditions within which such a multi-voiced conversation becomes a possibility. And how within it, people can make available to each other the *socio-ontological* resources required to explore amongst themselves the development of different modes of being.[14]

In such argumentative contexts, however, there is a very understandable human tendency to ignore the developmental resources and the possibilities made available to one by others – particularly by those others from outside one's own group – and to think that one could demonstrate the correctness of one's own line of approach, if only the resistances preventing its full and proper implementation could be removed. Thus there is always a tendency for a group of people to constitute themselves as rulers and to claim the right to arrange the social conditions under which those others, the ruled, should live – with the aim of eliminating all (wrong) opposition. Indeed, we now have almost world-wide, governments so intent upon instituting a 'market order' and 'corporate relations' in their societies at large, that they are confining their claimed 'minimalist'[15] interventions to the enforcement of the social conditions thought to be required to ensure the 'natural' working of such 'markets'. Indeed, they see 'the free market' as both a necessary and a sufficient condition for a just society, and see themselves as morally justified in coercing their subjects to live in ways designed to sustain it in existence. Thus, on the basis of arguments very like those above – to do with establishing the conditions for public 'spaces' and a civil society – they argue for the importance of competition, and that interference by governments in the economies of their societies conflicts with 'one of the strongest and most creative forces known to man – the attempt by millions of individuals to promote their own interests, to live their lives by their own values' (Friedman, 1962: 200).

But if the analysis of 'competition' outlined above is correct, then even the control of the social conditions theoretically required for the 'natural' functioning of a market is an undemocratic intervention in the social processes required to pursue democracy: it is the false or counterfeit imposition of one form of 'contest' in the name of another; that is, it substitutes for the ontological opportunities at stake in the truly political sphere of a civil society, the commodities 'competitively' available in a market-place, as if buying a 'life-style' can make up for one's exclusion from the political process – a process now conducted by 'experts'. In a true democracy, people do not need a special caste of self-licensed experts to run their affairs for them, for even ordinary people have the ability (and the right) to play a part in *the shaping* of their lives with others, and to have what they say or do taken seriously. And the true nature of the competition or contest required in maintaining such a state of affairs as this, is of another kind altogether from that constituted by a free market, populated by supposedly rational, self-interested individuals. It involves the use of language in a non-State, non-market realm of public life, in which it is used, not for the communication of information provided by experts, nor for the doing of financial transactions between individuals, but with its traditional rhetorical function: to do with groups giving a shape to their lives together.

Concluding comments: Civil society and its resources

As Billig (1987) makes very clear, a major consequence of the suppression of the tradition of rhetoric has been the disenfranchisement and disembodiment of the common-sense background to social life, the taking for granted of the view that a people's *sensus communis* is either a harmonious repository of more or less shared, noncontroversial, but outdated (merely propositional) beliefs; or something that is useless and confused – which in either case, it is the purpose of the social sciences, of course, to replace in the interests of a better (expert's) order. In this view, what one person knows (and feels) is taken to be, more or less, the same as another. But on further examination, it is clear that common sense is far from unitary (and far from lacking in passion too). In fact, as we have seen, in the tradition of rhetoric it was thought to be a source of the 'seeds' from which arguments strong enough to move people in some way could be developed. But these 'seeds' or 'commonplaces' are such that, by their very nature, it is perfectly possible for every *logos* – that is, every persuasive formulation – to be confronted by an *anti-logos* (to use Billig's terms), formed from the same commonplace or topic. The two-sided or contrary nature of common sense in this respect is so pervasive that Billig marks it by citing what he calls 'Protagoras's Maxim': 'that in every question there are two sides to the argument exactly opposite to one another'.[16] In other words, the contrary nature of common sense is such that while certain matters are taken for granted in the community, and an appeal to them will close off arguments (cf. Mills, 1940), others, which are just as much a real part of people's common sense as the first, will unavoidably open them up again. In other words, what has been ignored, is that our traditions are traditions of argumentation.

Thus, in this view, common sense is a great repository of culturally developed, two-sided resources, not a 'market-place' of possibilities put forward by already ontologically well-developed individuals in competition with one another for personal profit, but a great 'carnival' (Bahktin, 1965) of different ways of socially constituted *being* in which everyone can have a 'voice' – in which they can play a part in the shaping and reshaping of their lives. It is these forces, operating in civil society, not the forces of the market, which are 'the strongest and most creative forces known to man', for they provide the resources from out of which other cultural products, including the market, are shaped. But, as already mentioned above, a political economy is at work here, involving a scarcity of opportunities for being, a political-ethics in which we are in contest with others around us for the very nature of our being, for the kind of person we feel we would like to be. And this is what I think is *still* at stake in our activities as citizens in the hurly-burly of everyday life in civil society, and this is why its recovery, and the tradition of rhetoric (and arts of 'civility') with which it is associated, is such an important project for us in these somewhat uneasy and troubled times – in which, on the one hand, we are beginning to understand a great deal about how in making the conditions of our own lives, we can make ourselves; and in which, on the other hand, this knowledge is being put to use in false and counterfeit ways: ways which, in the short term, will advantage the few, but which, in the long term, will debase the very coinage we must all use in those exchanges which contribute historically to the maintenance and further cultural development of our society.

Notes

1. My concept of civil society – as the set of *zones* of activity in which socio-historical processes develop neither by chance nor by necessity, but *providentially*, i.e., by providing in the 'organized settings' produced by social activity in the past, resources for use in current activities – is drawn more from Vico than elsewhere (see Shotter, 1986).

2. No one on the left will forget Margaret Thatcher's claim that: 'There is no such thing as Society. There are individual men and women and there are families' (*Observer* (London), 1st Nov. 1987).

3. 'To a German grocer, not unwilling to explain things to an American visitor', relates Stephen Raushenbush, 'I spoke of our feeling that something invaluable had been given up when freedom was surrendered. He replied: "But you don't understand at all. Before this we had to worry about elections, and parties, and voting. We had responsibilities. But now we don't have any of that. Now we are free." ' Quoted in Cassirer, 1946: 288.

4. Here I am appropriating the inverse of one of Garfinkel's (1967: vii) terms, when he speaks of our everyday activities as containing within themselves devices for rendering what we do and say as 'visibly-rational-and-reportable-for-all-practical-purposes, i.e., "accountable", as organizations of commonplace everyday activities'. For what is also of importance here, is how such devices work as well to render certain other aspects of our activities *rationally-invisible*, i.e., 'unaccountable' in commonplace terms. As Bahktin (1965: 421) makes clear: 'All peoples . . . have enormous spheres of speech that have not been made public and are nonexistent from the point of view of literary, written language.' These are the chaotically available resources people can make available to one another in times of carnival.

5. Indeed, it now becomes clear that Descartes uses rhetoric to deny rhetoric, to persuade us, as he says, 'to demolish everything completely and start again right from the foundations'. But as Bernard Williams (in Descartes, 1986: xiv) points out in his introduction to a new edition of the *Meditations*, it is a contrived work of fiction: 'It is at the beginning', he says, 'that all the seeds are sown of the philosophical system which has come to life by the end of the *Meditations*.' Descartes affects the investigation of a great mystery by his method of doubt, and one is persuaded that it is by that method that all the results he presents have been obtained, but the fact is otherwise.

6. '. . . proofs are what Littlewood and I call *gas*, rhetorical flourishes designed to affect psychology, pictures on the board in lectures, devices to stimulate the imagination of pupils' (the mathematician G.H. Hardy, quoted in Kline, 1980). Long before they ever find proofs, great mathematicians know certain theorems to be true – Fermat in his vast and classic work on the theory of numbers and Newton in his work on third-degree curves gave neither proofs nor even indications of proofs (Kline, 1980). Proofs are *post hoc*; indeed, there is no clear agreement among mathematicians as to what a rigorous proof is (Davis and Hersh, 1983; Kline, 1980).

7. This unease is expressed by Wittgenstein (1980, I: no. 38) as follows:

> The basic evil of Russell's logic, as also of mine in the *Tractatus*, is that what a proposition is is illustrated by a few commonplace examples, and then pre-supposed as understood in full generality.

8. 'Para. 131. Philosophy considers man as he should be and so can be of service to very few, those who wish to live in the Republic of Plato and not fall back into the dregs of Romulus.

Para. 132. Legislation considers man as he is in order to turn him to good uses in human society. Out of ferocity, avarice, and ambition, the three vices which run throughout the human race, it creates the military, merchant, and governing classes, and thus the strength, riches, and wisdom of the commonwealths. Out of these three great vices, which would certainly destroy all mankind on the face of the earth, it makes civil happiness' (Vico, 1968).

9. Time and again Wittgenstein warned against the unwarranted completion (in theory) of circumstances which in practice were still open and incomplete, and the necessity to accurately describe the character of their indefiniteness (e.g., Wittgenstein, 1980, I: no. 257).

10. What is remarkable about Myhill's general line of argument in this paper is its anticipation of those now being motivated by the rhetoric of inquiry movement (e.g., Davis and Hersh, 1981). He is concerned with how doubts about the legitimacy of an alleged application of a rule might be dispelled. For a real proof, he says, 'consists not merely in what is published as a proof, but also in the testimony adduced in support of the statement that [an] axiom *was* correctly applied' (Myhill, 1952: 175). And the discussion of procedures and techniques he presents in his paper, is to do with the 'forms of testimony' which would persuade us of the correct application of an axiom.

11. The paper is in fact an exploration of the implications of both Gödel's and Church's theorems to do, respectively, with 'undecidable' and 'unsolvable' classes of problems in symbolic logic.

12. Gallie mentions a number of exemplary accounts: '(a) Democracy means primarily the power of the majority of citizens to chose (and remove) governments . . . ; (b) Democracy means primarily equality of all citizens, irrespective of race, creed, sex, etc., to attain to positions of leadership and responsibility; (c) Democracy means primarily the continuous active participation of all citizens in political life . . .' (1955–56: 191).

13. The aim here is to resonate with Prigogine's claims mentioned earlier.

14. As a project, the recovery of 'civil society' may seem at first glance to share many features with Habermas's (1979, 1984) study of *communicative action* and the *ideal speech situation*, within which undistorted communication is said to be possible – whether an account of that situation is arrived at by the kind of transcendental arguments he offered in his earlier work, or by what he now calls 'reconstructive analysis'. The project is, however, one of a quite different kind. For instead of the assumption that, given the appropriate background consensus, mutual understanding is normally obtained with ease and *discourse* about validity claims is only necessary during the breakdown of consensus, the assumption here (obviously) is that understanding is always only partial and dispute about validity claims is an endemic part of everyday life activity. Furthermore, what is treated as a 'consensus' is always, I shall argue, an 'argumentative consensus' (Billig, 1987), i.e., a consensus revolving around a set of generally accepted paradigms, exemplars, or commonplaces, which does not in fact bear close examination – else it dissolves in differences. Without the openness of such commonplaces to differently formulated claims, communicants in Habermas's ideal speech situation would have little to say to one another about their different 'positions' concerning such matters. In other words, while Habermas (1979: 3) is concerned with people achieving 'agreements which terminate in the mutuality of intersubjective understanding', the problem here is a quite different one: it is to do with the social conditions required to maintain a set of precariously interlinked identities, when no agreements terminating in the mutuality of intersubjective understandings are possible.

15. Adam Smith's (1976: 687–8) view of the roles of government are often cited by the new right as justification for a supposed 'minimalist state'. 'According to the system of natural liberty', he said, 'the sovereign has only three duties to attend to', they are: (1) to protect the society from violence by others outside it; (2) to protect individuals from

violence from other individuals within it; and (3) to erect and maintain certain public works and institutions which, although 'the profit could never repay the expense to any individual or small number of individuals, . . . it may frequently do much more than repay it to a great society'. The nature of the 'profits' involved here are, of course, essentially contested.

16. It is, of course, the obverse of Descartes's claim that the proper method in philosophizing is to proceed upon one's own, starting with clear and distinct ideas, rationally to construct the single, correct order which will account for observed events. And as Billig quite rightly points out, with Protagoras's Maxim, 'the practice of rhetoric [is] elaborated into an innovative philosophy' (Billig, 1987: 41) – for it is a philosophy which, amongst other things, not only denies the existence of Absolute Truth, but positively asserts that both sides to an argument can both be right.

Epilogue: Rhetorical–Responsive Social Constructionism in Summary Form

> The notion of theory as a toolkit means: (i) The theory to be constructed is not a system but an instrument, a *logic* of the specificity of power relations and the struggles around them; (ii) That this investigation can only be carried out step by step on the basis of reflection (which will necessarily be historical in some of its aspects) on given situations.
>
> Foucault, 1980: 145

> The task consists of not – or no longer – treating discourses as groups of signs (signifying elements referring to contents or representations) but as practices that systematically form the objects of which they speak.
>
> Foucault, 1972, 49

In our reflective thought, upon the nature of ourselves and the world in which we live, we can either take what is invariant as its primary subject matter and treat change as problematic, or, activity and flux as primary and treat the achievement of stability as problematic. While almost all previous approaches to psychology and the other social sciences have taken the first of these stances, social constructionism takes the second. Thus, in this view, centres of stable social practice have to be sustained in existence by the efforts of those involved in them to 'regulate' and 'repair' them; they 'do not settle or endure out of their natural state' (Vico, 1968: para. 134). And it is only 'from within' such stabilized practices that we usually make our claims to knowledge. Social constructionists, however, are interested, not so much in what can be done from within such centres once in existence, as in the process of their construction in the first place. Hence their claim that, in general, our conversations do *not* take place in an already well-ordered reality, but in a pluralistic, only fragmentarily known, and only partially shared world (Rommetveit, 1985: 183)[1] – in other words, they take a view from a position much more on the margins, or in the boundary zones, between the more settled, orderly institutional centres of social life, for it is here in these boundary regions that new constructions first emerge. This is the nature of joint action. Because of this, because our task is that of attempting to understand how, *practically*, we can promote this move from disorder to order from within that disorder itself, I have argued that no orderly, systematic theories as such are possible. But what can be of help is, I have claimed, a rich 'tool-bag' of useful 'conceptual prosthetics', through which, perhaps, to see some of the processes in the movement from chaos to order at work. In such a context as this, it will be useful to end this book by gathering together in one place the doctrines and claims, a set of 'instructive statements', constituting the rhetorical–responsive version of social constructionism explored in it.

Social constructionism in general:

1 Common to all versions of social constructionism is the central assumption that – instead of the inner dynamics of the individual psyche (romanticism and subjectivism), or the already determined characteristics of the external world (modernism and objectivism) (Gergen, 1991; Taylor, 1989) – it is the contingent, really vague (that is, lacking any completely determinate character) flow of continuous communicative activity between human beings that we must study. Thus, the assumption of an already stable and well-formed reality 'behind appearances', full of 'things' identifiable independently of language, must be replaced by that of a vague, only partially specified, unstable world, open to further specification as a result of human, communicative activity.

2 Concern in the past with one or the other of the two polarities above – as well as an Enlightenment urge to produce single, unified, monologic[2], *systems* of knowledge – gave rise to an ambition to locate a world beyond the social and historical[3] and to attempt to discover this world, in the depths either of the organic or the psyche, or, perhaps, in abstract principles or systems. As a result, this third sphere of activity has usually been left in the background.

3 It is *from within* this not wholly orderly flow of relational, background activities and practices (that is, with its historically already-specified-further-specifiability), constructionists maintain, that all our other socially significant dimensions of interaction – with each other and with our 'reality' – originate and are constructed in 'joint action' (see Chapter 1 and Shotter, 1980, for the properties of joint action).

The rhetorical–responsive version of social constructionism

Words, utterances, genres

4 Words as such lack any specific meanings in themselves; they are 'interindividual' (Bakhtin, 1986: 121); as a *means* – for making

differences within the developing developed context of a dialogue – they work to *specify* meanings only within that dialogue.

5(a) As an intrinsic unit of dialogue, an utterance is always produced *in response to* previous utterances, and bounded by a change in speaking subjects; (b) further, utterances are not understood referentially, but also *responsively*, that is, not by listeners coming to possess the same ideas as speakers, but in terms of an answering response such as affirmation, disagreement, puzzlement, elaboration, application, etc. – common understandings (that is, truly shared representations or references), in this view, are difficult to achieve.

6 Such responsive meanings are always first 'sensed' or 'felt' from within a conversation, that is, they are embodied as vague, unformulated 'intralinguistic tendencies', and as such, are always amenable to yet further responsive (sensible) 'development' or specification with the dialogue.

7 Utterances have their meaning within a *genre*, that is, within a *way* of speaking associated with a form of social life with a 'history'[4] to it, such that certain words produce a 're-sensing', or 're-feeling' of past, authoritative usages; in Billig et al.'s (1988) terms, this is a 'living ideology': a way of speaking, thinking, perceiving, acting, and *evaluating* constitutive of a form of social relations, privileging some in the group over others.

Ideologies

8 It is in 'words in their speaking', in their tone and in other aspects of their 'temporal shaping', that utterances realize these ideological influences; thus, within the context of speaking, we are only interested in 'patterns or forms of already spoken words' (*formative forms*) to the extent that they provide the (enabling and constraining) *resources* constituting a genre – it is the activity of speaking that is of primary interest to us, not what has been or was said.

9 Our 'official' ways of being, our 'selves', are produced in our 'official' ways of interrelating ourselves to each other – these are the terms in which we are socially accountable in our society (Shotter, 1984) – and these 'traditional' or 'basic' (dominant) ways of talking are productive of our 'traditional' or 'basic' psychological and social ontologies.

10 What we have in common with others in our society's traditions is not a set of agreements about meanings, beliefs or values, but a set of intrinsically two (or more) sided 'topics' [Gr. *topoi* = 'places'] or commonplaces, from out of which we may draw the two or more sides of an argument (Billig, 1987) – plus (a political

economy of) access to the resources of various genres, for use in the formulation of a 'position' in a dialogue (with a genre to it).

11 Often, dialogues take the form of arguments, and utterances the form of criticisms and justifications; living social traditions have this form (MacIntyre, 1981).

Descriptions and their grounds

12 Although *vague* and amenable to an indefinite number of descriptions, the only partially specified events in the social constructionist's open, unstable world, cannot allow or afford just *any* description; many are arguably false. They are not 'afforded' either by the events themselves, or by the background circumstances of our lives.

13 While a fictional narrative may be described as functioning to 'create' a structure, to articulate a wholly mental world, the structure 'given' to vague events by a claimed factual account must be *grounded* in the background circumstances; that is, logically, the events as seen from within the framework of the account, can be seen as corroborating or refuting it; and historically, the framework can be seen as having emerged from the background circumstances.

14 Such descriptions function to 'give' or to 'lend' a determinate *structure* to such open events which they do not in fact have, to *formulate* them definitely as being of this or that kind[5].

15 In talk of such events, it is useful to introduce the concept of the imaginary, for we need to distinguish between whether our claims are based upon merely fictional possibilities, or upon genuine empirical possibilities, existing in the social background at the moment of our talk.

Rhetoric and talk of 'psychological states'

16 The way in which events are 'lent' their structure by the words in which they are described, brings to the fore the intrinsically *formative* or *shaping* function of language, its figures of speech (metaphors, metonyms, synecdoches and ironies, etc.); tropes are not something which can be added to or subtracted from a language as necessary, but are an intrinsic part of its nature (De Man, 1979).

17 Thus there is no way one can stand outside of our conversational forms of communication with others, or use another specialist (formal) language to criticize them; the same everyday linguistic resources, that afford the formulation of various claims, also afford their questioning, their doubting, their negation and their

warranting – there is no such thing as a metalanguage that can replace our ordinary conversational forms of communication.

18 Neither are there any *extralinguistic* entities whose significance is linguistically clear prior to talk 'about' them; there are no extralinguistic 'somethings' in the world merely awaiting precise or accurate description (Rorty, 1980).

19 Thus psychological talk – supposedly 'about' our 'perceptions', 'memories', 'motives', 'judgments', etc. – does not refer to any already existing, inner reality of mental representations. It consists in formulations, in claimed versions of psychological states constructed on the basis of vague (but not wholly non-specific 'feelings'), to serve rhetorical purposes in *accounting* for ourselves and others in response to challenges from those around us. Instead of 'about' our mental states, we should talk 'of' them.

20 The 'grounds', or the 'standards', in terms of which to judge whether such claimed versions should be taken seriously or not, within the argumentative or responsive context in which they are offered, are to be found (at the time of the requisite judgment) within the argumentative context itself, not outside it – as an outsider to the intralinguistic reality of another, however, one can make revealing comparisons between it and one's own.

21 But there is no last word, whether inside or outside the time–space of dialogue, to bring dialogue to an end.

22 Given the practical, socio-relational nature of language, what matters in a tradition of argumentation, is the terms within which the arguments within it are conducted: to argue in relational rather than individualistic terms, is to attempt to interrelate ourselves to each other in a relational rather than an individualistic fashion, to begin to 'socially construct' a relational society.

23 The change from arguing about psychology in behaviourist terms to arguing about it in cognitive ones, has not brought argument in psychology to an end – but it has changed the whole style of what people now think it important to research into. The aim of social constructionist argumentation, is to bring about yet another change in psychology's research agenda.

The 'basis' and 'function' of social constructionist analyses

24 What 'social analysts' have available to them as a 'basis' for their analyses, is a 'sensibility' of what is involved in 'boundary crossings', that is, in taking a marginal stance, they can 'sense' the changed intentionality[6] involved in 'moving' from 'membership' (inclusion within a social group) to 'exclusion' (outside it) with respect to a group's tradition of argumentation. All their claims,

their formulations, must be such as to be 'permitted' or 'afforded' by such a 'sense'. See Wittgenstein's method of comparisons (Chapter 3).

25 Central to a rhetorical–responsive approach is 'the fundamental plurality of unmerged consciousnesses' (Bakhtin, 1984: 9); the fact that every way of speaking embodies a different evaluative stance, a different way of being or position in the world. It is this that keeps everyone in permanent dialogue with everyone else. It thus precludes the attempt to capture the nature of communicative activity ever in a unified, systematic theory.

26 But what it does allow us to do, is to display in our empirical investigations the dilemmatic character of the dialogues (Billig et al., 1988), and through the analytic unit of the utterance, to study the different ways in which different people, at different times, in different contexts, resolve the dilemmas they face *in practice* – with the result that, among the many other interesting features of what we can then claim their practices to be, we can construct reasons for our claims as to their ideological character.

What social constructionist analyses do not do

27 Provide accurate representations of an underlying reality.

28 Treat knowledge as consisting in static systems of forms, cognitive structures, or frameworks, and as defined in terms of their ordered contents.

29 Assume that social life consists in already pre-determined social structures.

30 Assume that psychological processes consist in already pre-determined cognitive processes in individuals.

31 Assume that language consists in a pre-determined code for linking inner psychological events to outer events in social life.

32 Separate, in this way, our talk from the conversational contexts in which it occurs and has its influence: upon our lives; upon who we are and become (our psychological make-up); and upon our social actions and thus upon the nature of our society and its culture.

33 Finally, in not claiming the provision of the one true view, it does not claim a privileged voice in the conversation of humankind; while it expects to be taken seriously, it expects only a voice in a critical dialogue with others.

Indeed, it is a part of the very notion of a rhetorical–responsive social constructionism, that all the claimed 'instructive statements' or 'tools' offered above may be contested. For it is a major part of the approach being canvassed here, as I have argued before, to suggest that an important aspect of such contests lies, not so much in their specific outcomes, as in the vocabulary, in the forms of talk, in which they are conducted. The very terms which render some aspects of our lives rationally-visible to us, render other aspects rationally-invisible. And indeed, that has been the claim explored in this book: that a special form of practical-moral knowledge, embodied in the conversational background to our lives, has been rendered invisible to us, ironically, by the very 'visual' vocabulary in terms of which we currently conduct our investigations into our own nature. To grasp its nature, a more practical, historically or temporally oriented lexicon of nonvisual, speech communicational terms is required. And it is towards the fashioning of such a vocabulary that this book has been aimed.

Notes

1. Thus 'vagueness, ambiguity, and incompleteness – but hence also versatility, flexibility, and negotiability – must for that reason be dealt with as inherent and theoretically essential characteristics or ordinary language' (Rommetveit, 1985: 183).
2. The isolated, finished, monologic utterance, standing divorced from its verbal and actual context, is open only to a passive understanding which excludes an active response (Volosinov, 1973: 73). But in Bakhtin's (1984: 110) view, 'truth is not to be found inside the head of an individual person, it is born *between people* collectively searching for truth, in the process of their dialogic interaction'.
3. A 'sui generis fear of history, an ambition to locate a world beyond the social and the historical' is, as Volosinov (1976: 14) sees it, a basic motif in 'contemporary bourgeois philosophy'. As Rorty (1989: 189) says, what 'I have been urging in this book is that we try *not* to want something that stands beyond history and institutions'.
4. What that 'history' is, is of course always contested.
5. See in this connection, the '*ex post facto* fact fallacy' (Chapter 5).
6. From within, we adopt various ways of looking, talking, evaluating, etc., unquestioningly; from the outside, however, we see that there are clear alternatives to these ways – and we ask, why aren't they adopted instead? The answer to that question is given in ideological terms.

Afterword

Roy Bhaskar

In this Afterword, I want to describe what I think are John Shotter's main achievements in this book; to take up some of the specific criticisms he makes of my developing position; and to indicate what I think are the crucial weaknesses within his own.

In this perpetually stimulating, intellectually vibrant piece of work, Shotter has done two main things. First, drawing on a staggering range of sources, he has provided us with a whole tool-box or set of 'analytic devices or resources' for doing research: knowing 'from within' as a third kind of knowing; mind and identity as boundary phenomena or imaginary entities, and as the product of joint activity; the 'rational-invisibility' of disorder; the open, unfinished and negotiated character of social phenomena; structures as formative activity; making and inventing vs. finding and discovering; responsive as opposed to referential understanding; prostheses and indicators; 'ethical logistics'; etcetera, etcetera. Second, he has furnished us with a novel revindication of the Vichian hermeneutical tradition. This is, on Shotter's account, as old as Aristotle's phronesis or practical-moral knowledge (Bernstein). But its immediate provenance lies in Vico's *fantasia*; and it is contrasted both with Aristotle's theoretical and productive knowledge and with Ryle's 'knowledge that' and (instrumental) 'knowledge how'. It has the 'from–to' structure that Polanyi analysed in the tacit; and it is rhetorical and subject to negotiation. It is of course what the hermeneutical tradition, initiated by Schleiermacher, through Dilthey and Weber to Gadamer and Winch, has called '*Verstehen*' (interpretive understanding, as distinct from *Erklären*, casual explanation). All this is a considerable achievement, and this book deserves to be widely read for it.

I turn now to Shotter's criticisms of me (in Chapter 4). Accepting that social activity consists in the transformation of, or work on, given materials, he takes my 'crucial and wrong step' to be the claim that:

> If such work constitutes the *analogue* of natural events, then we need an *analogue* for the mechanisms that generate them' (JS's emphases),

remarking that if, as I go on to say, social structures must be social products themselves:

> Precisely! But if they are social products, why not treat them as such? Why treat them in terms of a mechanistic analogue? (see above, p. 74).

Now I think this is partially based on a misunderstanding. In *A Realist Theory of Science* (second edition, Harvester Press, 1978 (Harvester-Wheatsheaf, 1989)), I argued that not only was the concept of a generative mechanism not to be understood mechanistically, but that even mechanics could not be understood mechanistically! But this does not get to the heart of our differences here, which are I think rooted in two 'tendencies of feeling' Shotter has: (1) he wants to treat social psychology as a humanity or humane study, rather than as a science; and (2) he wants to look at the transactions that people conduct between themselves rather than the structures which I argue underpin (and enable) them.

Now in *The Possibility of Naturalism* (first edition, Brighton 1979; second edition, Harvester-Wheatsheaf, 1989) I made clear that I was not concerned to argue that the social sciences were sciences in the same way as the natural sciences, but rather to elaborate the generic similarities and specific differences between studies in the natural and the social domain. Although I called my position a 'critical naturalism', I could equally have described it as a 'critical anti-naturalism'. Secondly, in *Scientific Realism and Human Emancipation* (Verso, London, 1986), I stressed that I saw social structures as ontologically rooted in the everyday transactions between agents and their material transactions with nature (see p. 130 and *passim*).

Shotter continually opposes realism and social constructionism. But I want to ask: are they indeed incompatible? Shotter affirms that there is a dialectical interdependency between making and finding. Insofar as society affords us only *some* possibilities there is an intransitive dimension, in my terms, to social life (as well as the transitive one we theorists construct). Shotter seems to think that I am committed to a things ontology, but in *The Possibility of Naturalism* (chapter 3, section 6 and chapter 4, section 4) I stress that people are social products. (Social products can have causal powers.) Moreover, given what he says about *joint action* (pp. 38–40), Shotter is very close to accepting the transformational model of social activity. Indeed, elsewhere, he says that the 'historical process of self-transformation . . . involved is just as Marx described it – that we do indeed make our own history, but not under conditions of our own choosing' (Shotter, 1990c: 11). Furthermore I am opposed, as my critique of Winch in *The Possibility of Naturalism*, chapter 4 shows, to any 'actualist' interpretation of rules. Again, I argue that hermeneutics must be the starting point of any social inquiry; and that the hermeneutical paradigm, even in its Winchian form, is consistent with a realist account of science. So I think Shotter and I are closer than he allows.

But important differences – of emphasis – remain. There is a tendential dualism in Shotter's position. It seems clear that he wants to prioritize making over finding, discourse over material embodiment. This is the Achilles' heel of hermeneutical accounts: what we cannot make we can have no privileged understanding of (see *Reclaiming Reality* (Verso, 1989) p. 97). But one can accept that conceptuality is (uniquely) distinctive of social life, without supposing that it is exhaustive of it. 'Being imprisoned' involves more than the negotiation of meanings; it means being physically excluded from certain spaces for a certain time. Connected to this is Shotter's emphasis on formative activity as distinct from (relatively) enduring structure. But *if* there are real socio-economic–political structures causing people in these 'new times' to be out of work, to feel isolated and/or to lose their sense of citizenship, then not to acknowledge this is to fall prey to the very 'rational-invisibility' of disorder to which the 'new (political) realism' succumbs. An emancipatory politics (or therapy) depends upon, though it is not reducible to, a depth science of society insofar as there *really* are deep structures at work. Moreover it is difficult to see how radical social change can occur – or this book have any effect – unless agents' reasons for acting really can be causes of changes in the social world, which is also an emergent property of, as it is embedded in, manifest in and continually reacts back on, the natural world.

I think that Shotter is wanting to bend the stick in social psychology for wholly commendable reasons. But as he says, quoting Billig (citing Diogenes Laertius on Protagoras), 'in every question there are two sides to the argument exactly opposite to one another' (see above, p. 174). What we require is to capture this balance exactly. I think John Shotter has bent it too far – in favour of a purely humane study (against naturalism) and in favour of conversationality (as distinct from material determinations), tilting his account in the direction of voluntaristic agency rather than transformative praxis. But I can only close this Afterword by repeating my praise for this book as an invaluable resource not just for social psychologists and social scientists generally, but potentially for all citizens and would-be citizens in what we both agree is a still-to-be-made, open world.

References

Anderson, B. (1991) *Imagined Communities: Reflections on the Origins and Spread of Nationalism*, 2nd ed. London: Verso.

Anderson, H. and Goolishan, H. (1988) Human systems as linguistic systems: evolving ideas about the implications for theory and practice. *Family Process*, 27, 371–93.

Anderson, H. and Goolishan, H. (1990) Beyond cybernetics: comments on Atkinson and Heath's 'Further thoughts on second-order family therapy'. *Family Process*, 29: 157–63.

Anderson, H. and Goolishan, H. (1992) The client is the expert: A not-knowing approach to therapy. In K.J. Gergen and S. McNamee (eds), *The Social Construction of the Psychotherapeutic Process*. London: Sage.

Aristotle (1976) *Nicomachean Ethics*, trans. J.A.K. Thompson. Harmondsworth: Penguin Books.

Austin, J. (1962) *How to do Things with Words*. London: Oxford.

Bachelard, G. (1927) *Essai sur la connaissance approchée*. Paris: J. Urin.

Bachelard, G. (1934) *La Formation de l'esprit scientifique*. Paris: J. Urin.

Bakhtin, M. (1965) *Rabelais and His World*, trans. Helen Iswolsky. Cambridge, MA: MIT Press.

Bakhtin, M.M. (1981) *The Dialogical Imagination*, edited by M. Holquist and trans. by C. Emerson. Minneapolis: University of Minnesota Press.

Bakhtin, M.M. (1984) *Problems of Dostoevsky's Poetics*, edited and trans. by Caryl Emerson. Minneapolis: University of Minnesota Press.

Bakhtin, M.M. (1986) *Speech Genres and Other Late Essays*, trans. by Vern W. McGee. Austin, TX: University of Texas Press.

Barnes, B. (1982) *T.S. Kuhn and Social Science*. London: Macmillan.

Baron, R.A. and Bryne, D. (1984) *Social Psychology: Understanding Human Interaction*. Boston: Allyn and Bacon.

Barthes, R. (1983) *A Lover's Discourse*. New York: Hill and Wang.

Bartlett, Sir F.C. (1932) *Remembering: A Study in Experimental Psychology*. London: Cambridge University Press.

Beckett, S. (1956) *Waiting for Godot*. London: Faber.

Beckett, S. (1986) *Samuel Beckett: The Complete Dramatic Works*. London: Faber and Faber.

Bellah, R.N., Madsen, R., Sullivan, W.M., Swidler, A. and Tipton, S.M. (1985) *Habits of the Heart: Individualism and Commitment in American Life*. Berkeley: University of California Press.

Benveniste, E. (1971) *Problems in General Linguistics*. Florida: University of Miami Press.

Berger, P. and Luckman, T. (1966) *The Social Construction of Reality*. New York: Doubleday and Co.

Berlin, I. (1976) *Vico and Herder*. London: The Hogarth Press.

Bernstein, R.J. (1983) *Beyond Objectivism and Relativism*. Oxford: Basil Blackwell.

Bhaskar, R. (1975) *A Realist Theory of Science*. Leeds: Leeds Books.

Bhaskar, R. (1979) *The Possibility of Naturalism*. Sussex: Harvester Press.
Bhaskar, R. (1986) *Scientific Realism and Human Emancipation*. London: Verso.
Bhaskar, R. (1989) *Reclaiming Reality: A Critical Introduction to Contemporary Philosophy*. London: Verso.
Bhaskar, R. (ed.) (1990) *Harré and his Critics: Essays in Honour of Rom Harré with his Commentary on them*. Oxford: Basil Blackwell.
Bhaskar, R. (1991) *Philosphy and the Idea of Freedom*. Oxford: Basil Blackwell.
Billig, M. (1987) *Arguing and Thinking: A Rhetorical Approach to Social Psychology*. Cambridge: Cambridge University Press.
Billig, M. (1991) *Ideology, Rhetoric and Opinions*. London: Sage.
Billig, M., Condor, S., Edwards, D., Gane, M., Middleton, D. and Radley, R. (1988) *Ideological Dilemmas*. London: Sage Publications.
Blum, A. (1971) Theorizing. In J.D. Douglas (ed.), *Understanding Everyday Life*. London: Routledge and Kegan Paul.
Bocock, R. (1986) *Hegemony*. London: Tavistock.
Bohm, D. (1965) *The Special Theory of Relativity*. New York: Benjamin.
Bohm, D. (1980) *Wholeness and the Implicate Order*. London: Routledge and Kegan Paul.
Bohm, D. (1985) *Unfolding Meaning: A Weekend of Dialogue with David Bohm*. London and New York: Ark Paperbacks.
Booth, W.C. (1974) *Modern Dogma and the Rhetoric of Assent*. Chicago: University of Chicago Press.
Broadbent, D.E. (1970) In defence of empirical psychology. *Bull. Brit. Psychol. Soc.*, 23: 87–96.
Burke, K. (1950) *A Rhetoric of Motives*. New York: George Braziller.
Buss, A.R. (1978) Causes and reasons in attribution theory: A conceptual critique. *J. of Pers. and Soc. Psychol.*, 36, 1311–21.
Cassirer, E. (1946) *The Myth of State*. New Haven: Yale University Press.
Cassirer, E. (1951) *The Philosophy of the Enlightenment*, trans by Fritz C.A. Koelln and James P. Pettegrove. Princeton, NJ: Princeton University Press.
Castoriadis C. (1987) *The Imaginary Institution of Society*. Cambridge, MA: MIT Press.
Cavell, S. (1969) *Must We Mean What We Say?* London: Cambridge University Press.
Chalmers, A. (1988) Is Bhaskar's realism realistic? *Radical Philosophy*, 49: 18–23.
Chomsky, N. (1957) *Syntactic Structures*. The Hague: Mouton.
Code, L. (1987) *Epistemic Responsibility*. Hanover and London: University Press of New England.
Coulter, J. (1979) *The Social Construction of Mind*. London and Basingstoke: Macmillan.
Coulter, J. (1983) *Rethinking Cognitive Psychology*. London and Basingstoke: Macmillan.
Coulter, J. (1989) *Mind in Action*. London and Basingstoke: Macmillan.
Crites, S. (1986) Storytime: Recollecting the past and projecting the future. In T.R. Sarbin (ed.), *Narrative Psychology: The Storied Nature of Human Conduct*. New York: Praeger.
Danziger, K. (1990) *Constructing the Subject: Historical Origins of Psychological Research*. Cambridge: Cambridge University Press.
Davis, P.J. and Hersh, R. (1983) *The Mathematical Experience*. Harmondsworth: Penguin Books.
Davis, P.J. and Hersh, R. (1986) *Descartes's Dream: The World According to Mathematics*. Sussex: Harvester Press.

De Man, P. (1979) *Allegories of Reading: Figural Language in Rousseau, Nietzsche, Rilke and Proust*. New Haven: Yale University Press.

Derrida, J. (1976) *Of Grammatology*, trans. Gayatri Spivak. Baltimore: Johns Hopkins University Press.

Descartes, R. (1986) *Meditation on First Philosophy*, trans. J. Cottingham, intro. by B. Williams. London: Cambridge University Press.

Douglas, M. (1966) *Purity and Danger*. Harmondsworth: Penguin Books.

Douglas, M. (1975) *Implicit Meanings*. London: Routledge and Kegan Paul.

Dreyfus, H.L. and Rabinow, P. (1982) *Michel Foucault: Beyond Structuralism and Hermeneutics*. Sussex: Harvester Press.

Eagleton, T. (1991) *Ideology: An Introduction*. London: Verso Press.

Eco, U. (1979) *The Role of the Reader: Explorations in the Semiotics of Texts*. London: Hutchinson.

Eco, U. (1984) *The Name of the Rose*. New York: Harcourt Brace.

Edwards, D. and Potter, J. (1992) *Discursive Psychology*. London: Sage.

Edwards, J.C. (1982) *Ethics without Philosophy*. Tampa, FL: University of South Florida Press.

Evans-Pritchard, E.E. (1976) *Witchcraft, Oracles and Magic among the Azande*. London: Oxford University Press.

Fleck, L. (1979) *The Genesis and Development of a Scientific Fact*. Chicago: Chicago University Press.

Foucault, M. (1970) *The Order of Things: An Archaeology of the Human Sciences*. London: Tavistock Publications.

Foucault, M. (1972) *The Archaeology of Knowledge*, trans. A.M. Sheridan. London: Tavistock.

Foucault, M. (1980) Power and strategies. In *Power/Knowledge: Selected Interviews and other Writings 1972–1977*, ed. by C. Gordon. New York: Pantheon Books.

Fraser, N. (1989) *Unruly Practices: Power, Discourse and Gender in Contemporary Social Theory*. Cambridge: Polity Press.

Fraser, R. (1984) *In Search of the Past: The Manor House, Amnersfield, 1933–1945*. London: Verso Editions.

Freud, S. (1953–74) J. Strachey (ed.) *The Standard Edition of the Complete Psychological Works of Sigmund Freud*, 24 vols. London: Hogarth Press and Institute for Psychoanalysis.

Freud, S. (1961) *Civilization and its Discontents*. New York: W.W. Norton and Co.

Freud, S. (1973) *Introductory Lectures on Psychoanalysis*. Harmondsworth: Penguin.

Friedman, M. (1962) *Capitalism and Freedom*. Chicago: University of Chicago Press.

Gadamer, H.-G. (1975) *Truth and Method*. London: Sheed and Ward.

Gallie, W.B. (1955–56) Essentially contested concepts. *Proc. of the Aristotelian Soc.*, 56: 167–98.

Garfinkel, H. (1967) *Studies in Ethnomethodology*. New York: Prentice-Hall.

Gauld, A. and Shotter, J. (1977) *Human Action and its Psychological Investigation*. London: Routledge and Kegan Paul.

Gavin, W.J. (1976) William James and the importance of 'the vague'. *Cultural Hermeneutics*, 3: 245–65.

Geertz, C. (1975) On the nature of anthropological understanding. *American Scientist*, 63: 47–53.

Geertz, C. (1983) *Local Knowledge: Further Essays in Interpretative Anthropology*. New York: Basic Books.

Gergen, K.J. (1982) *Toward Transformation in Social Knowledge*. New York: Springer.

Gergen, K.J. (1985) The social constructionist movement in modern psychology. *American Psychologist*, 40: 266–75.

Gergen, K.J. (1989) Warranting voice and the elaboration of self. In J. Shotter and K.J. Gergen (eds), *Texts of Identity*. London: Sage.

Gergen, K.J. (1990) Organizational theory in the postmodern era. In M. Reed and M. Hughes (eds), *Rethinking Organization*. London: Sage Publications.

Gergen, K.J. (1991) *The Saturated Self: Dilemmas of Identity in Contemporary Life*. New York: Basic Books.

Gibson, J.J. (1966) *The Senses Considered as Perceptual Systems*. Boston: Houghton Mifflin.

Gibson, J.J. (1979) *The Ecological Approach to Visual Perception*. London: Houghton Mifflin.

Giddens, A. (1976) *New Rules of Sociological Method*. London: Heinemann.

Giddens, A. (1979) *Central Problems in Social Theory: Action, Structure and Contradiction in Social Analysis*. London: Macmillan.

Giddens, A. (1984) *The Constitution of Society*. Cambridge: Polity Press.

Gleick, J. (1987) *Chaos: the Making of a New Science*. London: Cardinal.

Goffman, E. (1959) *The Presentation of Self in Everyday Life*. New York: Doubleday.

Goodman, N. (1972) The way the world is. *Problems and Projects*: New York: Bobbs-Merrill.

Gramsci, A. (1971) *Selections from the Prison Notebooks*. London: Lawrence and Wishart.

Grassi, E. (1980) *Rhetoric as Philosophy*. University Park and London: Pennsylvania State University Press.

Greenfield, P.M. (1987) Video games as tools of cognitive socialization. *Proceedings of Computers, Cognition and Epistemology: An International Symposium*. Sandbjerg Slot, Denmark, April 1987.

Greenwood, J. (1989) *Explanation and Experiment in Social Psychological Science*. New York: Springer.

Greenwood, J. (1992) Realism, empiricism, and social constructionism: psychological theory and the social dimensions of mind and action. *Theory and Psychology*, 2: 131–51.

Habermas, J. (1979) *Communication and the Evolution of Society*. Boston: Beacon Press.

Habermas, J. (1984) *The Theory of Communicative Action, I: Reason and Rationalization of Society*. Boston: Beacon Press.

Hanson, N.R. (1958) *Patterns of Discovery*. London: Cambridge University Press.

Haraway, D.J. (1991) Situated knowledges: The science question in feminism and the privilege of partial perspective. In *Simians, Cyborgs, and Women: The Reinvention of Nature*. New York: Routledge.

Harré, R. (1970a) *Principles of Scientific Thinking*. London: Macmillan.

Harré, R. (1970b) Powers. *Brit. J. Philos. of Sci.*, 21: 81–101.

Harré, R. (1979) *Social Being: A Theory for Social Psychology*. Oxford: Basil Blackwell.

Harré, R. (1983) *Personal Being: A Theory for Individual Psychology*. Oxford: Basil Blackwell .

Harré, R. (1986) An outline of the social constructionist viewpoint. In R. Harré (ed.), *The Social Construction of Emotions*. Oxford: Basil Blackwell.

Harré, R. (1990) Exploring the human *Umwelt*. In R. Bhaskar (ed.), *Harré and his Critics: Essays in Honour of Rom Harré with his Commentary on them*. Oxford: Basil Blackwell.

Harré, R. (1992a) The second cognitive revolution. *American Behavioral Scientist*, 36: 3–7.

Harré, R. (1992b) What is real in psychology: A plea for persons. *Theory and Psychology*, 2: 153–8.

Harris, R. (1980) *Language-Makers*. London: Duckworth.

Harris, R. (1981) *The Language Myth*. London: Duckworth.

Heidegger, M. (1967) *Being and Time*. Oxford: Basil Blackwell.

Heider, F. (1958) *The Psychology of Interpersonal Relations*. New York: Wiley.

Heider, F. and Simmel, M. (1944) An experimental study of apparent behaviour. *Amer. J. Psychol.*, 57: 243–59.

Hirschkop, K. and Shepard, D. (eds) (1989) *Bakhtin and Cultural Theory*. Manchester and New York: Manchester University Press.

Hirschman, A.O. (1977) *The Passions and the Interests: Political Arguments for Capitalism before its Triumph*. Princeton, NJ: Princeton University Press.

Huizinga, J. (1949) *Homo Ludens*. London: Routledge and Kegan Paul.

Jahoda, M. (1977) *Freud and the Dilemmas of Psychology*. London: Hogarth.

Jakobson, R. (1956) *Fundamentals of Language*. The Hague: Mouton.

James, W. (1890) *Principles of Psychology*, vols 1 and 2. London: Macmillan.

Kline, M. (1980) *Mathematics: The Loss of Certainty*. Oxford: Oxford University Press.

Kuhn, T.S. (1962) *The Structure of Scientific Revolutions*. Chicago: University of Chicago Press.

Lakatos, I. (1971) History of science and its rational reconstructions. In R.C. Buck and R.S. Cohen (eds), *Boston Studies in the Philosophy of Science*, vol. 8. Dordrecht: Reidel.

Lakoff, G. and Johnson, M. (1980) *Metaphors We Live By*. Chicago: University of Chicago Press.

Lewis, C.S. (1939) Bluspels and flalansferes. In *Rehabilitations and Other Essays*. London: Oxford University Press.

Lienhardt, G. (1961) *Divinity and Experience: The Religion of the Dinka*. New York and Oxford: Oxford University Press.

Lyotard, J.-F. (1984) *The Postmodern Condition: A Report on Knowledge*. Minneapolis: University of Minnesota Press.

MacIntyre, A. (1981) *After Virtue*. London: Duckworth.

MacIntyre, A. (1988) *Whose Justice? Which Rationality?* London: Duckworth.

McCloskey, D.M. (1983) The rhetoric of economics. *Journal of Economic Literature*, 21: 481–516.

Mair, J.M.M. (1988) Psychology as storytelling. *International Journal of Personal Construct Psychology*, 1: 125–37.

Manicas, P.T. and Secord, P.F. (1983) Implications for psychology of the new philosophy of science. *American Psychologist*, 38: 399–413.

Marquand, D. (1988) *The Unprincipled Society: New Demands and Old Politics*. London: Jonathan Cape.

Marx, K. and Engels, F. (1977) *The German Ideology*. London: Lawrence and Wishart.

Masson, J. (1984) *The Assault on Truth*. London: Faber and Faber.

Maturana, H. and Varela, F. (1980) *Autopoiesis and Cognition: The Realization of the Living*. London: Reidel.

Mead, G.H. (1934) *Mind, Self and Society*. Chicago: University of Chicago Press.

Merleau-Ponty, M. (1962) *Phenomenology of Perception*, trans. C. Smith. London: Routledge and Kegan Paul.

Merleau-Ponty, M. (1964) *Signs*. Evanston: Northwestern University Press.

Mills, C.W. (1940) Situated actions and vocabularies of motive. *American Sociological Review*, 5: 904–13.

Mink, L.O. (1978) Narrative form as a cognitive instrument. In R.H. Canary and H. Kozicki (eds), *The Writing of History: Literary Form and Historical Understanding*. Wisconsin: University of Wisconsin Press.

Mooney, M. (1985) *Vico and the Tradition of Rhetoric*. Princeton: Princeton University Press.

Morgan, G. (1986) *Images of Organization*. London: Sage Publications.

Myhill, J. (1952) Some philosophical implications of mathematical logic. *Review of Metaphysics*, 6: 165–98.

Nelson, J.S. and Megill, A. (1986) Rhetoric of Inquiry: Projects and Problems. *Quarterly J. of Speech*, 72: 20–37.

Nelson, J.S., Megill, A. and McCloskey, D.M. (eds) (1987) *The Rhetoric of the Human Sciences*. Wisconsin: University of Wisconsin Press.

Norris, C. (1990) *What's Wrong with Postmodernism: Critical Theory and the Ends of Philosophy*. Baltimore: Johns Hopkins Press.

Ossorio, P. G. (1981) *Ex post facto*: The source of intractable origin problems and their resolution. Boulder, Colorado: Linguistic Research Institute Report no. 28.

Parker, I. (1992) *Discourse Dynamics: Critical Analysis for Social and Individual Psychology*. London: Routledge.

Peat, F.D. (1990) *Einstein's Moon: Bell's Theorem and the Curious Quest for Quantum Reality*. Chicago: Contemporary Books.

Pepper, S.C. (1942) *World Hypotheses: A Study in Evidence*. Berkeley: University of California Press.

Perelman, C. and Olbrechts-Tyteca, L. (1969) *The New Rhetoric: A Treatise on Argumentation*, trans. by J. Wilkinson and P. Weaver. Notre Dame: University of Notre Dame Press, 1958.

Polanyi, M. (1958) *Personal Knowledge: Towards a Post-Critical Philosophy*. London: Routledge and Kegan Paul; also New York: Harper and Row Torchbook, 1962.

Pompa, L. (1982) *Vico: Selected Writings*, edited and trans. by Leon Pompa. London: Cambridge University Press.

Popper, Sir K. (1963) *Conjectures and Refutations*. London: Routledge.

Prigogine, I. and Stengers, I. (1984) *Order Out of Chaos: Man's New Dialogue with Nature*. New York: Bantam Books.

Reddy, M. (1979) The conduit metaphor. In A. Ortony (ed.), *Metaphor and Thought*. London: Cambridge University Press.

Rommetveit, R. (1985) Language acquisition as increasing linguistic structuring of experience and symbolic behaviour control. In J.V. Wetsch (ed.), *Culture, Communication and Cognition: Vygotskian Perspectives*. London: Cambridge University Press.

Rorty, R. (1980) *Philosophy and the Mirror of Nature*. Oxford: Basil Blackwell.

Rorty, R. (1989) *Contingency, Irony and Solidarity*. Cambridge, UK: Cambridge University Press.

Rosnow, R. and Georgoudi, M. (1986) *Contextualism and Understanding in Behavioral Science*. New York: Praeger.

Ryle, G. (1949) *The Concept of Mind*. London: Methuen.

Sacks, O. (1986) *The Man Who Mistook his Wife for a Hat*. London: Duckworth.

Sampson, E.E. (1985) The decentralization of identity: toward a revised concept of personal and social order. *American Psychologist*, 40: 1203–11.

Sampson, E.E. (1988) The debate on individualism: indigenous psychologies of the individual and their role in personal and societal functioning. *American Psychologist*, 43: 1203–11.

Schaeffer, J.D. (1990) *Sensus Communis: Vico, Rhetoric, and the Limits of Relativism.* Durham, NC: Duke University Press.

Schafer, R. (1980) Narration in psychoanalytic dialogue. *Critical Inquiry*, 7: 29–53.

Schon, D. (1983) *The Reflective Practitioner: How Professionals Think in Action.* London: Maurice Temple Smith.

Searle, J. (1981) *Intentionality: An Essay in the Philosophy of Mind.* Cambridge: Cambridge University Press.

Shotter, J. (1970) Men, the man-makers: George Kelly and the psychology of personal constructs. In D. Bannister (ed.) *Perspectives in Personal Construct Theory.* London and New York: Academic Press.

Shotter, J. (1975) *Images of Man in Psychological Research.* London: Methuen.

Shotter, J. (1980) Action, joint action, and intentionality. In M. Brenner (ed.), *The Structure of Action.* Oxford: Basil Blackwell.

Shotter, J. (1983a) 'Duality of structure' and 'Intentionality' in an ecological psychology. *J. for the Theory of Social Behaviour*, 13: 19–43.

Shotter, J. (1983b) A sense of place: Vico and the social production of social identities. *Brit. J. of Soc. Psychol.*, 25: 199–211.

Shotter, J. (1984) *Social Accountability and Selfhood.* Oxford: Basil Blackwell.

Shotter, J. (1985) Speaking practically: A contextualist account of psychology's context. In R. Rosnow and M. Georgoudi (eds), *Contextualism and Understanding in the Behavioral Sciences.* New York: Praeger.

Shotter, J. (1986) A sense of place: Vico and the social production of social identities. *British Journal of Social Psychology*, 25: 199–211.

Shotter, J. (1989a) Rhetoric and the recovery of civil society. *Economy and Society*, 18: 149–66.

Shotter, J. (1989b) Social accountability and the social construction of 'you'. In J. Shotter and K.J. Gergen (eds), *Texts of Identity.* London: Sage.

Shotter, J. (1990a) Underlabourers for science, or toolmakers for society. Review essay on R. Bhaskar, *Reclaiming Reality: A Critical Introduction to Contemporary Philosophy*, 1989. *History of the Human Sciences*, 3: 443–57.

Shotter, J. (1990b) Social individuality vs. possessive individualism: The sounds of silence. In Ian Parker and John Shotter (eds), *Deconstructing Social Psychology.* London: Routledge.

Shotter, J. (1990c) *Knowing of the Third Kind: Selected Writings on Psychology, Rhetoric, and the Culture of Everyday Social Life.* Utrecht: ISOR.

Shotter, J. (1990d) Rom Harré: realism and the turn to social constructionism. In R. Bhaskar and R. Harré (eds), *Realism and Human Being.* Oxford: Basil,Blackwell.

Shotter, J. (1991a) Wittgenstein and psychology: On our 'hook up' to reality. In A. Phillips-Griffiths (ed.), *Wittgenstein Centenary Lectures.* Cambridge: Cambridge University Press.

Shotter, J. (1991b) Rhetoric and the social construction of cognitivism. *Theory and Psychology*, 1: 495–513.

Shotter, J. (1991c) A poetics of relational forms: the sociality of everyday social life. *Cultural Dynamics*, 4: 379–96.

Shotter, J. (1993a) Vygotsky: The social negotiation of semiotic mediation. *New Ideas in Psychology*, 11: 61–75.

Shotter, J. (1993b) *Cultural Politics of Everyday Life: Social Constructionism, Rhetoric, and Knowing of the Third Kind.* Milton Keynes: Open University Press.

Shotter, J. and Gergen, K.J. (eds) (1989) *Texts of Identity.* London: Sage.

Smail, D. (1984) *Illusion and Reality: The Meaning of Anxiety.* London: Dent.

Smedslund, J. (1988) *Psycho-Logic.* Berlin: Springer-Verlag.

Smith, A. (1976) *An Inquiry into the Nature and Causes of the Wealth of Nations*, edited with an introduction by E. Cannan. Chicago: University of Chicago Press.
Smith, D. (1978) 'K is mentally ill': The anatomy of a factual account. *Sociology*, 12: 23–53.
Spence, D.P. (1986) Narrative smoothing and clinical wisdom. In T.R. Sarbin (ed.), *Narrative Psychology: The Storied Nature of Human Conduct*. New York: Praeger.
Stapp, H.P. (1972) The Copenhagen interpretation. *American Journal of Physics*, 40: 1098–116.
Still, A. and Costall, A. (eds), (1991) *Against Cognitivism: Alternative Foundations for Cognitive Psychology*. Hemel Hempstead: Harvester Press.
Stolzenberg, G. (1978) Can an inquiry into the foundations of mathematics tell us anything interesting about mind? In G.A. Miller and E. Lenneberg (eds), *Psychology and Biology of Language and Thought: Essays in Honour of Eric Lenneberg*. New York: Academic Press.
Sudnow, D. (1983) *Pilgrim in a Microworld*. New York: Warner.
Sullivan, W.M. (1987) After foundationalism: The return of practical philosophy. In E. Simpson (ed.), *Anti-Foundationalism and Practical Reasoning: Conversations between Hermeneutics and Analysis*. Edmonton, Alberta: Academic Printing and Publishing.
Taylor, C. (1987) Overcoming epistemology. In K. Baynes, J. Bohman and T. McCarthy (eds), *After Philosophy: End or Transformation?* Cambridge, MA: MIT Press.
Taylor, C. (1989) *Sources of the Self: The Making of the Modern Identity*. Cambridge, MA: Harvard University Press.
Tharp, R.G. and Gallimore, R. (1988) *Rousing Minds to Life: Teaching, Learning, and Schooling in Social Contexts*. New York: Cambridge University Press.
Toulmin, S. (1979) The inwardness of mental life. *Critical Inquiry*, 6: 1–16.
Toulmin, S. (1982a) The genealogy of 'consciousness'. In P.F. Secord (ed.), *Explaining Human Behavior: Consciousness, Human Action, and Social Structure*. Beverly Hills: Sage.
Toulmin, S. (1982b) The construal of reality: Criticism in modern and postmodern science. *Critical Inquiry*, 9: 93–111.
Toulmin, S. (1988) The recovery of practical philosophy. *American Scholar*, 57: 337–52.
Uexküll, J. von (1957) A stroll through the world of animals and men. In C.H. Schiller (ed.), *Instinctive Behavior*. London: Methuen.
Verene, D.P. (1981) *Vico's Science of the Imagination*. Ithaca and London: Cornell University Press.
Vico, G. (1965) *On the Study Methods of Our Time*, trans. by Elio Gianturco. New York: Bobbs-Merrill.
Vico, G. (1968) *The New Science of Giambattista Vico*, edited and trans. by T.G. Bergin and M.H. Fisch. Ithaca, NY: Cornell University Press.
Vico, G. (1982) The order of our inquiry. In *Selected Writings*, edited and trans. by L. Pompa. London: Cambridge University Press.
Vico, G. (1988) *On the Most Ancient Wisdom of the Italians*, trans. by Lucina Palmer. Ithaca: Cornell University Press.
Volosinov, V.N. (1973) *Marxism and the Philosophy of Language*, trans. by L. Matejka and I.R. Titunik. Cambridge, MA: Harvard University Press.
Volosinov, V.N. (1976) *Freudianism: A Critical Sketch*. Bloomington and Indianapolis: Indiana University Press.
Vygotsky, L.S. (1962) *Thought and Language*, edited and trans. E. Hanfmann and G. Vakar. Cambridge, MA: MIT Press.
Vygotsky, L.S. (1966) Development of the higher mental functions. In A.N. Leont'ev, A.R. Luria and A. Smirnov (eds), *Psychological Research in the USSR*. Moscow: Progress Publishers.

Vygotsky, L.S. (1978) *Mind in society: The development of higher psychological processes*, edited by M. Cole, V. John-Steiner, S. Scribner, and E. Souberman. Cambridge, MA: Harvard University Press.

Vygotsky, L.S. (1986) *Thought and Language*. Translation newly revised by Alex Kozulin. Cambridge, MA: MIT Press..

Wertsch, J.V. (1991) *Voices of the Mind: A Socio-Cultural Approach*. Hemel Hempstead: Harvester Press.

Whorf, B.L. (1956) *Language, Thought and Reality: Selected Writings of Benjamin Lee Whorf*, edited by J.B. Carroll. Cambridge, MA: MIT Press.

Williams, B. (1986) Introduction to René Descartes, *Meditations on First Philosophy*. Cambridge: Cambridge University Press.

Williams, R. (1977) *Marxism and Literature*. Oxford: Oxford University Press.

Winograd, T. and Flores, F. (1986) *Understanding Computers and Cognition: A New Foundation for Design*. New York: Ablex.

Wittgenstein, L. (1953) *Philosophical Investigations*. Oxford: Basil Blackwell.

Wittgenstein, L. (1961[1922]) *Tractatus Logico-Philosophicus*. London: Routledge and Kegan Paul.

Wittgenstein, L. (1965) *The Blue and Brown Books*. New York: Harper Torchbooks.

Wittgenstein, L. (1969) *On Certainty*. Oxford: Basil Blackwell.

Wittgenstein, L. (1980) *Remarks on the Philosophy of Psychology*, vols I and II. Oxford: Basil Blackwell.

Wittgenstein, L. (1981) *Zettel*. Oxford: Basil Blackwell.

Index

Printed in the United Kingdom
by Lightning Source UK Ltd.
101288UKS00002B/1-72